The Gospel of FATHER JOE

Revolutions and Revelations
in the Slums of Bangkok

Greg Barrett

Foreword
A Kindred World
The Most Reverend Desmond M. Tutu,
Archbishop Emeritus

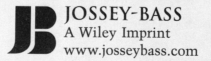

JOSSEY-BASS
A Wiley Imprint
www.josseybass.com

Published by Jossey-Bass
A Wiley Imprint
989 Market Street, San Francisco, CA 94103-1741—www.josseybass.com

Jossey-Bass books and products are available through most bookstores. To contact Jossey-Bass directly call our Customer Care Department within the U.S. at 800-956-7739, outside the U.S. at 317-572-3986, or fax 317-572-4002.

Jossey-Bass also publishes its books in a variety of electronic formats. Some content that appears in print may not be available in electronic books.

Permission to quote Bono's speech to members of the United States Congress and President George W. Bush during a national prayer breakfast, February 2, 2006, granted by DATA (Debt, AIDS, Trade, Africa), www.data.org.

Library of Congress Cataloging-in-Publication Data

Cataloging-in-publication data has been applied for.
ISBN 13: 978-0-4702-5863-7

Printed in the United States of America
FIRST EDITION
HB Printing   10 9 8 7 6 5 4 3 2 1

CONTENTS

PART III: THE LIGHT

A Kindred World

The Most Reverend Desmond M. Tutu,

Archbishop Emeritus

Roused by compassion, we awake to life as God created it, as Jesus expressed it, as the Buddha and the Prophet Muhammad taught it. We see the holiness imbued in all humanity. It doesn't matter if you're African, Asian, Arab, European; Christian, Buddhist, Muslim, Jewish, or something else. It doesn't matter the denomination you pledge or if you pledge. We are God-shaped and God-filled. Affluent, poor, American, Iranian, Somali, Ethiopian, Israeli, Palestinian. The Divine is our common bloodline and birthright. It's our bond in Goodness. We're kin in that way, but we often miss that part. We don't always view our shared space and shared responsibilities from the Divine's perspective.

We lose focus; attention wanes. Or we *forget,* as the Rev. Dr. Joe Maier reminds us in these pages, which draw attention to a perpetual blind spot. I suspect that some of us would prefer to keep this book closed, continue to feign ignorance, go on with our comfortable lives, and forget the uneducated, neglected children in our charge. They are difficult to see if you choose to never look.

Read on, however. Open your eyes; stare at reality. You will see possibilities realized and feel delightfully inspired by the power of

Goodness in a world pregnant with change. You may even be moved to join in.

The story of Father Joe and the Bangkok squatter land he calls holy is a critical chapter in the modern-day memoirs of humankind. His Mercy Centre is more than a refuge and grassroots education system for children caught in the bramble of our new prosperity; it's the vivid expression of God's will for how we are to treat family. In effect, it's the Bible for how best to lift families from the poverty that kills millions of children every year: you plow the ground with textbooks and local muscle.

I know of no aid dropped from a helicopter or dictated from afar that has ever taken root. Whenever Jesus entered the slums, he came on the back of a donkey and in a cloud of dust, face to face with poverty. Biblical scripture attempts to focus our attention on the poor and the downtrodden more than two thousand times. We're told explicitly how to treat them. No wiggle room is left for moral interpretations or federal treasuries stretched by war. In the Gospel of Matthew, Jesus tells us, "As you have done it unto the least of these my brethren, you have done it unto me."

How, then, can we *forget?*

In 1990, near the onset of the West's unprecedented economic growth, wealthy nations pledged that all poor children by the year 2000 would have access to at least a basic education. At the United Nations World Summit for Children in New York City, seventy-three governments signed a declaration that made the goal a global imperative. The Cold War had ended, and a new world order was looking toward greater cooperation and an abundant sharing of resources across international borders and economic lines. On the summit's final day in the General Assembly Hall, U.S. president George H. W. Bush told his fellow world leaders, "All children must be given the chance to lead happy, healthy, and productive lives."

He acted outraged that "education is a mystery for one hundred million children" in the poorest parts of the world.

"Saving one child is a miracle," he concluded. "As world leaders, we can realize such miracles, and then we can count them in the millions."

One hundred million children fell through the cracks of that broken pledge. The reasons and excuses are complicated. So in 2000, the pledge was renewed as one of the eight Millennium Development Goals. All UN member states signed a pledge declaring that by the year 2015, "children everywhere, boys and girls alike, will be able to complete a full course of primary schooling."

When Father Joe agreed to collaborate on this book in 2005, there were still one hundred million children with no access to a basic primary education. The UN had begun sounding alarms, calling the year a crossroads for the state of human development. Slight improvements have occurred in the years since, though not nearly enough.

The vast majority of our uneducated and neglected reside in the shacks of sub-Saharan Africa and South Asia, children like those in Father Joe's slums who miss school for lack of shoes and milk money. Because even as cheap airfare and broadband Internet erase borders and distance, our mightiest barrier is being reinforced. The ever-widening economic divide defines us as strangers.

But I maintain great confidence in humanity. I see the Divine in its grand swells of compassion. I bear witness to its manifestation after aberrant hurricanes and tsunamis rip life and limb from the U.S. Gulf Coast to South Asia. I am encouraged by the grassroots activism that today draws millions of volunteers to the cause of global poverty. And I am delightfully inspired by the kindred spirits that endure the rubble of squatter land that Father Joe knows to be holy.

If you look, you will see what he sees: shared responsibility. Family.

Political bodies may be hampered by self-interest and wear blinders of bias, indebted as they are to districts, constituents, and lobbies. But what politicians cannot or will not achieve, I have faith that individuals can and will. God-shaped and God-filled.

PROLOGUE

Facing Poverty

. . . for those spirit/truth seeking friends
who long ago stopped trusting anything from a pulpit
—FATHER JOE MAIER'S PERSONAL DAILY JOURNAL

Father Joe's catwalk slum wasn't the first place I'd come face to face with what World Bank economists call "extreme poverty," a definition pegged in 1990 to the ambiguous threshold of "income equivalent to one U.S. dollar or less per day." I'd seen its face before, and I've seen it since, both as a reporter and as a spectator.

On the bumpy ninety-minute ride from the airport in Montego Bay, Jamaica, to my honeymoon suite in Ocho Rios in 1992, I stared at it like everyone else: from a Sandals Resort bus with an iced bottle of Red Stripe in my hand. If the reggae of Bobby McFerrin hadn't played nonstop in our air-conditioned tour bus, an otherwise perfect honeymoon might've felt like something less. "Don't Worry, Be Happy" became our lilting mantra.

On assignment in Egypt following 9/11, I saw it in the unfinished cinderblock apartment complex en route to the childhood home of American Airlines hijacker Mohamed Atta. Veering off the road leading into Giza, I discovered that the abandoned construction site was government housing, though some windows, doors, and plasterboard were missing. Children emerged from the slabs of concrete looking like they'd walked straight off the pages of

Dickens: little faces smudged dirty, grimy ankle-length abayas and thobes, and Western-styled shirts and jeans looking like hand-me-downs that had been handed down a great many times.

In Iraq, as war approached in February 2003, I saw it in a Baghdad garage where an Iraqi widow had fashioned a tidy two-room home for herself and her eight children. They shared an out-house, a couch, and a single mattress on the floor. It wasn't a problem normally, the mother insisted, but as the Pentagon's threat of "Operation Shock and Awe" neared, one of her eleven-year-old twins had begun wetting the bed every night. A few days later in Basra, I watched school-age Iraqis play on a mountainous landfill reeking of raw sewage. Climbing down, I saw that their hands were flecked with a brown goo that someone told me later was the exact thing I had suspected. The same stuff I'd seen on the broken streets of Basra's al-Jummhurriya neighborhood, where children dashed in sandals through gullies and potholes filled with urine-yellow puddles—and knuckle-sized human feces. Crap floated in such overwhelming abundance that parents had apparently given up. Mothers sat calmly on cement stoops and watched the young play.

Father Joe's Bangkok was not much different. Different continent, different peoples, but the same culture of poverty.

"No one *chooses* to live in a slum," Father Joe told me in 2000, the first time I saw his shack in a Bangkok shantytown. Its catwalk was planted in a canal that looked like a Basra landfill and smelled like an al-Jummhurriya street. "You're never there by choice."

But he'd been living on that catwalk for three decades. *By choice.*

A squeaky-clean room in an air-conditioned Redemptorist monastery was his for the asking a few miles away on a shaded street across from a 7-Eleven. He never asked.

Leaving his slum in 2000, I couldn't decide if *choosing* to live in muck and sewage with the poorest of the poor made Father Joe a madman or just madly devoted. But in the long run, perhaps it didn't matter—masochist, saint, or masochistic saint—because in a void notorious for starving one's spirit, he was feeding it. And in the act of feeding, he'd been fed. That much was obvious, because beyond the palm trees, rain trees, and indoor plumbing that made his Mercy Centre schools, hospice, and orphanages a shaded utopia in the middle of desperate poverty, there was something else. A palpable, powerful something else ran through the small campus, breathed a sense of joy into children dying. Although I couldn't fully capture and define it, I felt it. That ineffable *it*.

Returning five years later to investigate what it was that I couldn't put into words, I narrowed my inquiry to one or two questions. Each, of course, came layered with more.

Why didn't the children in my affluent Washington, D.C., area cul-de-sac or in my own comfortable home hop and skip at the same excited clip as the sick, dying, orphaned, abandoned, abused, neglected, or otherwise broken children of the Mercy Centre? What in God's name did Father Joe know that I didn't?

In my quest to know what he knew (as much as one could without living it), I visited the Mercy Centre with his blessings three times between 2005 and 2007. For a total of four weeks, I shadowed Father Joe, occasionally ate with him, consumed pots of coffee while sitting across from him, and just hung around his odd slice of heaven until I'd made a nuisance of myself. Our most fruitful discussions, however, occurred away from Mercy and the distractions that pull Father Joe this way or that way, often in midsentence.

In Bangkok's blazing sunrises, we walked broad loops on weekday mornings in the city's finest park. We talked God and politics, wealth and poverty, and matters of the East and matters of the West in my plodding effort to understand the magnanimous *it*—whatever it was that crackled through Mercy—and Father Joe's effort to bridge our world of differences and similarities—economic and cultural, secular and religious.

All told, I would record nineteen hours of interviews with him in Bangkok's Lumpini Park, a few dozen more outside it, and many more with just pen, paper, or Microsoft Word. These were bolstered by thirty-one hours of phone calls from my home to his in Bangkok and 641 e-mails (at last count) sent or forwarded from Father Joe to me. I met with his relatives twice in their blue-collar Washington State hometown and interviewed his former Bangkok Holy Redeemer Parish rector, who had retired to Seattle. When Father Joe's mother passed away in the fall of 2006, I attended the funeral in her conservative hometown parish and went to the family party afterward; Kentucky Fried Chicken, cold beer, wine coolers, and lots of family history and laughter were shared. The morning following the burial of Helen Mary Maier in Longview, Washington, Father Joe and I met for our usual walk—this time in his hometown's finest city park.

Our last face-to-face meeting for this book took place in Vancouver, British Columbia, one day after we'd flown to Vancouver Island to visit a Mercy child who is set to graduate in 2008 from Lester B. Pearson United World College of the Pacific.

We reviewed draft chapters in various states of repair on the afternoon of November 1, 2007. Father Joe had just returned to his hotel energized by a speech given hours earlier by former president Bill Clinton at Vancouver's Pacific Economic Forum. Clinton had spoken of the "godsend" of business opportunity available in the work that will be required to curb greenhouse gas emissions. He'd also warned of the dangers inherent in allowing our status quo to continue unchecked. If current trends in economic inequality and depletion of natural resources continue until 2060, when the world's population is expected to hit nine billion people, there could be hell to pay. Terrorism, AIDS, Iraq, Iran, all the front-page worry that consumes federal budgets today, would be white noise compared to the Darwinian struggle that could ensue. Echoing world leaders secular and religious, Clinton stressed to a sold-out crowd of eighteen hundred that it was high time for nations, cultures, political parties, churches, temples, mosques—the whole of civilization—to start working *together* to safeguard our children's futures.

"A herd of elephants is in the yard, and we're sitting on the stoop counting ants," Father Joe said, summarizing the message.

There was an urgency in Father Joe that afternoon as he paced in his hotel room listening to me read from a book that would bear his name. He seldom interrupted, and when he did, it was only to correct Thai translations or add details to anecdotes. A couple of times, I quit reading to ask if he would like to save himself unnecessary trouble, maybe soften some of the sharpest criticism he'd leveled at the pope or the Vatican or some other authority with an element of control over him. He's an Old Testament Amos in his rebuke of the heresy he sees in greed and pious self-righteousness or in any religion that dares to invoke Christ while placing service of its own cause above serving the poor. He'd never asked me to go "off the record," a request commonly made and granted on Washington's Capitol Hill.

The last thing I wanted was to stir up trouble for a revolutionary Catholic who has no problem stirring up his own.

C'mon, I offered, let me redact some of the record.

He looked at me like I was a Washington bureaucrat or a Vatican robe.

"No," he growled. "Print it."

To the name on my tattoo,

baby, oh baby,

there should be a book written about you.

The Gospel of
FATHER JOE

WHATEVER *thoughts you have about God, who He is or if He exists, most will agree that if there is a God, He has a special place for the poor. In fact, the poor are where God lives.*

Check Judaism. Check Islam. Check pretty much anyone. . . . God may well be with us in our mansions on the hill. I hope so. . . . But the one thing we can all agree on, all faiths and ideologies, is that God is with the vulnerable and poor. God is in the slums, in the cardboard boxes where the poor play house. God is in the silence of a mother who has infected her child with a virus that will end both their lives. God is in the cries heard under the rubble of war. God is in the debris of wasted opportunity and lives, and God is with us if we are with them.

—U2's Bono speaking to members of the United States
Congress and President George W. Bush
during a national prayer breakfast,
February 2, 2006, in Washington, D.C.

Bangkok preschool students en route to class on the main campus of the Mercy Centre

PART I
The
Crucible

The Human Development Foundation/Mercy Centre graduates several
hundred slum children every year from its three-year preschool program.

ONE
Mustard Seeds

*The only thing necessary for the triumph of
evil is for good men to do nothing.*

—Father Joe's daily journal,
quoting a saying attributed to the
British statesman Edmund Burke

The story begins like the parable it's become, in a no-man's-land with the seed of dreams strewn in the most foolish of places: slum rubbish. This was the 1970s when few people believed anything good could grow from the backwater of the undeveloped world. There were no official addresses or property deeds in the cordoned-off corners of Bangkok, nothing much for the municipal books, just putrid ground so primal and bleak that land was free for the staking. It's where squatters pretended to own real houses and children made do with make-believe.

But these seeds were sown by an angry young Catholic chased from finer society. A priest, stubborn and cursing. The local Buddhists, Muslims, and Christians nurtured that seed, and in time the people and the priest, the abbot and the imam, worked together, as though the Buddha, Muhammad, and Jesus Christ were brothers and best friends. No doctrine, dogma, or creed was lorded. No growth tethered chapter to verse. The only belief that mattered was the one they shared. In the children. That was common, sacred ground.

Nourished like this, the seeds exploded with growth. There was a harvest, then another and another. The seeds grow still today, more than three decades later, a genus of hope thriving in the muck, as if it had been indigenous to the slums all along.

Tales of it grow too, spreading from those roots in Thailand to the media of North America and Europe, and in the retelling, it can begin to sound legendary. How in Gideon's name does something grow from nothing and multiply like New Testament fishes and loaves? But nothing about it is myth. Every tale is true.

You can see for yourself when a new crop is gathered each year just before the yearly monsoons. For two, three, and often four days, a cordoned-off corner of the world blossoms in a brilliant hue of graduation gowns.

So it was on the sunstruck first week of March 2007—thirty-three years after the first seeds were planted.

The Mercy Centre preschool graduation was standing-room-only; moms, dads, aunties, uncles, siblings, cousins, the neighbor next door and next door to that one. Seven commencements stretched half the week and through a half dozen slums in celebration of seven hundred graduates from thirty-two schools built "officially illegally," as the priest says, on the Thai government's squatter land. Children six and seven years old accustomed to flip-flops and hand-me-downs strutted around in black mortarboard caps and matching silk gowns trimmed in a shade of blue my folk back home call Carolina. And while girls and their mothers and aunts fussed with lipstick and rouge, the boys did what boys do: swirl their heads until the tassels on their caps whir like the blades of a helicopter. Dizzy, they fall to the ground.

The priest was there, of course, more bald with each and every harvest. He conferred the diplomas and delivered the commencement address wearing the black and burgundy of Thailand's revered Thammasat University. Draped across his left shoulder was a velvet sash with white stripes of cotton, thick enough to brush and braid: three stripes in front, three in front, three in back representing the honorary rank of a Thammasat Ph.D. If you were new to the slums or to their graduation rituals, a sash like that in a place like that might stop you. It might even if you weren't.

Arriving at each school, the American known by tens of thousands of Thai as simply Khun Phaw Joe ("Mister Father Joe") would park down a ways and out of sight. He'd pull on the gown, fix the sash just so, and then begin "the Walk"—a purposeful stride intended to put education on parade. Each route was different but familiar: past walls of plywood, lopsided floors, rusty tin roofs, and bare-bottomed babies; through humidity flavored by garbage and a subsistence watched over by sun-wrinkled village matriarchs who smiled even as they spit pinpoint tobacco-brown streams of betel nut juice. Heads turned to watch. Motorbikes slowed in deference. Cars stopped to let him pass. Old and young joined in, falling in behind or alongside, knowing full well where he was headed, knowing it was time.

In a backwater where nothing good was supposed to grow, graduation today is a rite of passage.

Some of the hardiest seed will scatter and continue maturing. There are graduates thriving now in the high school and college classrooms of North America with majors in economics, business, biology, computer science, and neuroscience. It's why Khun Phaw Joe gave the Class of '07 the same speech he has given every class since the Class of '95, the same he will give the Class of '08. Something about it seems to work.

As the Walk approached the first podium, the room fell silent. Pigeons gurgled their Rs, a mobile phone tweeted, somewhere a baby shrieked. Khun Phaw Joe waited. A small, heavy statue of the Virgin Mary sat in a May altar (on cloth surrounded by flowers) next to a Buddhist shrine of joss sticks and a portrait of the Thai monarch, Massachusetts native King Bhumibol Adulyadej, framed in gold leaf.

Fitted for kid-sized attention spans but fired like buckshot, the commencement address was aimed at everyone crowded into the ceremony.

Khun Phaw cleared his throat.

"If you don't have anything to eat in the morning," he began, speaking Thai and scanning his attentive audience of children, "then go to school!"

Most of the students sat erect or leaned slightly forward on the edge of their benches or chairs.

"If you don't have any shoes to wear . . . ," he continued, pausing for effect, "go to school!"

"If Mommy or Daddy says you can stay home . . . go to school!

"If your friends want you to sell drugs . . . go to school!

"If Mommy gambles and Daddy's a drunk . . . go to school!

"If all the money is gone and you can't buy lunch . . . go to school!

"If your house burns down and you don't have anything or anywhere to sleep . . . go to school!

"Go to school! Go to school! Go to school!"

Children joined in, louder and louder, chanting what sounded to me like "Tong by wrong rain high die!"

Go to school! *Dhong bai rong rien hai dai! Dhong bai rong rien hai dai! Dhong bai rong rien hai dai!*

Moms, dads, aunts, uncles, cousins, brothers, sisters, and the neighbor next door joined in. Khun Phaw Joe directed the burgeoning chorus, his Thammasat gown waving until the bell sleeves billowed.

Dhong bai rong rien hai dai! Dhong bai rong rien hai dai! Dhong bai rong rien hai dai!

And that's the sprint from beginning to now, three decades of harvests. But in the journey, as in the parable, lie the lessons and wisdom of a social revolutionary who bucks convention, the law, and what the rest of us might consider common sense or self preservation.

The Reverend Joseph H. Maier, the eldest child of a philandering Lutheran father and pious Catholic mother, survived his own poverty and dysfunction to become a throwback of sorts: the durable, American-made export. It should be no surprise, then, that he settled on the wrong side of our economic divide and discovered a comfortable fit. The neglected children of Klong Toey (three hard syllables sounding like a curse but meaning "canal of the pandanus," a plant growing near the water and cultivated for its flavorful leaves) would put a nice sheen of perspective on his own welfare beginnings.

Today, whenever Khun Phaw Joe feels a pang of self-pity, and often when he sees it rising in others, he quashes it with self-mockery and echoes of an earlier time: "Yeah, yeah, everybody hates me, nobody loves me, all I'm ever fed is worms. That's my life story. Blah, blah, blah. . . . Well, guess what? The sun is rising, the rooster is calling, and another day is here. I guess ol' Joe better get his ass out of bed and get going."

"Go to school!" Khun Phaw Joe keeps the commencement address simple and direct.

TWO

The Joe in the Know

Need to whisper to ourselves this system stinks and public life was not meant to be this way. . . . If we continue saying it, the ideas behind the words will come alive and grow wings.

—Father Joe's daily journal

Find a guy named Father Joe, I was told.

It was spring 2000, and I was a U.S. reporter assigned to a topic that burns still today, from time to time, depending on competing news and the day's political wind: trafficking in humans, the billions of dollars a year trade of prostitutes—adults and children, willing and unwilling. Lawmakers were working themselves into an election-year lather to assure the electorate that "sex slavery" would not be tolerated. The offense was bipartisanly reprehensible, and Washington would eventually declare war on it, just as it had declared on poverty in the '60s, cancer in the '70s, illicit drugs in the '80s, just as it would declare on terrorism in 2001 and on Iraq in 2003.

So on a rainy April day, the news media, the general public, and Ivy League nongovernment types were invited to a hearing on sex trafficking held in Washington's most storied caucus room, the cavernous home to congressional hearings on Watergate, Iran-Contra, and the Vietnam War, a Corinthian-columned chamber first famous for the 1912 investigation into the sinking of the *Titanic*.

This was that important. It was seven months before the Bush-Gore election.

Senator Sam Brownback, a folksy Kansas Republican who'd just returned from meeting with trafficked and AIDS-infected girls in Kathmandu, Nepal, rapped his gavel, and the crowd in the Russell Senate building fell quiet. He began, "I hope these proceedings will help pry open a door of freedom just a little further for those who are presently trapped and in despair."

❖

That year, the United Nations would adopt a convention and two new protocols to combat sex trafficking, and as usual with these stories, the narrative led to families living on the margins and charities dealing in consequences—which, it seems, always pool at the feet of Father or Sister Somebody.

Father Joe just happened to be standing where I looked.

"Could you please help me . . ." began my first e-mail to him, an introduction that in retrospect sounds like an absurd intrusion on his time.

Six weeks later, I would mangle Father Joe's directions with my tourist-book Thai while trying to find his Human Development Foundation and Mercy Centre charities. From the backseat of a taxi, Bangkok's shantytown streets all looked cut and pasted from the annual UN Human Development Report. "In the developing world 1.2 billion people are income poor, about 1 billion adults illiterate, 1 billion without safe water and more than 2.4 billion without basic sanitation. . . . Serious human deprivations remain," the report from 2000 would read, similar to the reports from 1999 and 1998 and so many other years.

The deeper the cab went into Father Joe's slums, the more eager I became to meet the gritty priest with the reputation of a saint. Colleagues, Google, and the foreign media had all led me to the Reverend Joe Maier with the same sort of reference.

"Like Mother Teresa—but with a twist," Bangkok journalist Laurena Cahill had told me, confirming stories I'd read in papers from Canada to China. The fact that the path to him was well beaten by competing media didn't particularly bother me. It meant only that I was on the right track, if not the correct road.

"Soi See-Sip," I told the cabbie, repeating the street's name for probably the fifth time.

He stared ahead, nodding as if to say, *Yeah, yeah shut up.* His dashboard shrine with a pretzel-legged Buddha in a snow globe didn't have a GPS that I could see, and with each turn, the houses became shacks became hovels became worse. Roads morphed similarly until we crawled into alleys with no stoplights, stop signs, or thoroughfares in sight. That I could become a fleshy lump of robbed American roadkill seemed entirely plausible.

"Mercy Centre. *Mercy. Centre,*" I offered again, calmly, I hoped. "Khun Phaw Joe."

I wiped my palms on my khakis. "*Coooon. Poooow. Jooooe.*"

Already I sounded like a dead man talking.

Mister Father Joe was the story's go-to guy, a unique character and holy man worth the eighteen thousand–mile round-trip. That's what people said. Fluent in the language and ways of the slum street, he was an expatriate who lived and worked in the middle of "it," as defined by the U.S. Department of State. And in the presidential election year of 2000, *it* was defined as "sex slavery" and promptly assigned by American bureaucrats and politicians to someplace else, anywhere but home. This guilt wasn't ours. Human trafficking was an abomination of others. Its hubs were Mumbai (Bombay), Kolkata (Calcutta), and Bangkok. Importers and exporters. Pick one. They were (are) equally prolific.

My cab turned for the last time, raced ahead, and then braked suddenly, sending me into the clutches of my seat belt. Dashboard Buddha faded to white. "*Coooon. Poooow. Jooooe,*" the driver said, staring at me from the rearview mirror.

His tone sounded mocking. I suspect he'd known the way all along, probably from my first Southern-accented "Mir-see Sin-ter on Soi See-Sip." He pointed out the window toward a large wall of buildings. "Soi See-Sip," he said. "Mir-see Sin-ter."

He craned his neck to look into the backseat and smiled like the joke was on me.

"One hundred," he said in crisp English, speaking fluent Inflated Fare. I craned my neck for a better view of a meter that had been turned off. I returned his smile, feeling half-sorry that the joke was actually on him, because the five twenty-baht bills adorned with King Bhumibol's stern, slender face equaled only $2.50 U.S. I added a twenty-baht tip.

⚜

Father Joe had told me to meet him at the largest of four orphanages run by his Mercy Centre and Human Development Foundation, a home for street kids called Soi (Alley) See-Sip (Forty), named for its address. Its three stories stood on a crumbled curb, and on each side, there appeared to be two shophouses identical to the orphanage in the middle: pale blue siding, gray concrete, storefront windows on the ground floor, sliding doors gated and locked. On the upper floors, rooms appeared to be spread three or four across, judging from the windows I counted curbside.

But Soi (rhymes with *boy*) Forty was actually a seamless twenty thousand square feet cut from five double-wide shophouses, including those to the left and right. It teemed with some of the poorest residents of Klong Toey: children sick, dying, orphaned, abandoned, abused, neglected, or otherwise broken. Standing in the alley, I could hear a gust of them. The clamor streamed from open windows and jalousies sounding like a school hallway between bells, but more fun, like recess.

I took a couple of steps toward the sliding doors when something louder echoed up the alley. A motorbike roared to a dead stop beside me.

"Khun Phaw Joe, Khun Phaw Joe," shouted a guy in a dark helmet. He held out a pale yellow helmet and waved it as though I should take it. The engine revved. I looked around and saw that my cabbie was gone.

"Khun Phaw Joe." Louder this time. He patted the seat behind him.

Seconds later, I was squeezing the motorbike seat with my knees and my satchel with my arms, zigzagging through another warren of slums en route to meet this guy Father Joe but unaware that I was headed to a Mercy Centre AIDS hospice whose need that day for Khun Phaw Joe was far greater than mine.

The Mercy Centre houses, feeds, clothes, educates, and attempts to successfully raise 250 kids in its orphanages and safe houses. It instructs, feeds, and conducts health screenings on 4,500 more in its thirty-some three-year preschool programs built in the city's worst slums. It had helped build or rebuild some 10,000 slum houses, and its new fifty-bed hospice, still under construction in 2000, was Thailand's first and largest free AIDS hospice. Without land title or explicit and official permission, Mercy had had to ply workers and bureaucrats with bribes of whiskey and money and then raise blue tarps curbside like stage curtains. This concealed the most egregious construction from the direct view of the land's owner, the Port Authority of Thailand.

The motorbike braked in front of a two-story ramshackle building. White paint on wood and concrete was faded to the color of dirty rice, and burglar bars on the ground-floor windows were chipped and rusty. To me, it looked like a journeyman's boxing gym—Muay Thai, they call it in Thailand. With a nod of his helmet, the motorbike guy pointed toward a darkened breezeway that seemed more like a subway tunnel than an entrance to a hospice. One wall was painted dull pink, the color of Pepto-Bismol. The other was a canvas for a cityscape, an artistic row of brownstones beneath a blue sky full of white cottony clouds. A white breezeway sign with blue foot-tall Thai and English letters read "Human Development Foundation" and, in smaller letters underneath, "Mercy Centre & Community Human Development Centre."

So this is where human trafficking stories lead: to a suspect street fronting a narrow alley abutting an unpaved road that feeds into more suspect streets and narrow alleys that abut unpaved roads. If two decades of reporting had taught me nothing else, it was this: faces and names, heroes and villains may change, but victims' narratives all typically cross to this side of the tracks.

I climbed off the motorbike, handed the helmet back, combed my fingers through my flattened buzz cut, and took a second look around. The dusky street was broad and congested, not so much with cars as with motorbikes, pushcarts, and people coming and going. Standing six-foot-one with blondish hair and a ruddy complexion, I felt like a prom-night pimple screaming from the forehead. But no one seemed to notice the *farang* (foreigner) standing in their path. When I turned to ask the motorbike driver how much I owed, he yelled "Khun Phaw Joe" over the roar of his engine, nodding toward the large white sign above the Pepto-Bismol wall. He zoomed away before I could pay. I never saw his face.

On both ends of that breezeway—packed in and around the pockmarked facade or drawn up in blueprints or rising that very minute in a racket of drills, hammers, and saws—were the Mercy medical clinic, the Mercy legal aid clinic, the Mercy soccer fields, the Mercy loan program for slum mothers, a new preschool, a new orphanage, a special-needs school for illiterate street kids too old for preschool, an HIV/AIDS educational outreach and home care program headed by an HIV-infected employee, and a series of expansions that would include art, music, dance, computer, and language labs. Mercy's staff was also growing, expanding from about 200 to 280. Teachers, nurses, counselors, janitors, social workers, office administrators, cooks, drivers, housemothers, guards, accountants, and more volunteers—Buddhist, Muslim, Catholic, Jewish, Protestant, agnostic, and probably a few atheists—than Mercy could accept or process. More volunteers were being turned away than accepted.

⚜

"Talk."

That's how Father Joe was answering his cell phone that morning. A Mercy staff member asked me to wait for Khun Phaw Joe in the children's AIDS hospice. It was clean and well lit and smelled like the just-scrubbed floors of my childhood YMCA. A three-foot-tall plastic Christmas tree blinked from a corner table (a springtime request from the HIV children), and a half dozen Big Wheels and tricycles were neatly parked alongside it. Single beds arranged in straight rows filled two wards: one for children and another for parents, in which thin sheets of plywood allowed grown-ups a slice of privacy and a sense of residence. Calendars, flowers, and framed photos of His Royal Highness King Bhumibol decorated cubicles no larger than a half bath. A humongous aquarium held a school of large goldfish.

The hospice children had all been infected with HIV in utero, so dying in a Bangkok slum had become something of a mother-child affair. In 2000, antiretroviral drugs in Thailand were not freely or cheaply available. The medications given to Mercy's AIDS patients by the government were generally prolonging life but rarely sparing it. Mercy's adjoining hospice wards allowed the sickest kids and their mothers (and sometimes a father) time together near the end of one life, the other, or both.

Three fans taller than preschoolers circulated dry heat in a hollow roar in the children's ward and muffled most of the construction noise. Lying sweaty and deflated in the artificial breezes were a half dozen kids, but when I walked in, you'd have thought a puppy had padded across the linoleum. Five children gathered around me, smiling but not sure of what to say to the *farang*. Soon a small boy named Nuth extended a greeting. With his palms pressed in front of his face, he bowed his head once. I reciprocated the *wai,* the traditional Thai greeting: I bowed, smiled, and nodded, then smiled, nodded, and bowed again. The children then smiled and nodded, and we all bowed again, laughing. Walking backward bowing, laughing, and waving awkwardly, I retreated a few steps to a cast-off recliner that had stuffing blooming from its arm like buds of cotton, figuring I'd sit and wait for the great Khun Phaw.

Nuth, five years old and dressed for the heat in gray cotton shorts and a sleeveless T-shirt embroidered with lions and rabbits, crawled immediately onto my lap, as if it were the sole reason I sat. He stared at the wallet-sized notebook open in my hand, looked up at me, and then stared again at the notebook. He expected me to read, I thought, so for what my cryptic notes were worth, I did.

"Alley Forty. Loud voices. Open windows, chatter, laughter, can hear it all the way to the road. Kids, lots and lots of kids," I said, reading almost verbatim from those few seconds outside Soi See-Sip.

"Good stuff, heh?" I said, nodding yes-yes, trying to prod a positive review.

Nuth was two years older than my firstborn son but identical in size. His trimmed brownish hair also resembled my son's, and I thought I caught whiffs of the familiar and child-friendly, tearless Johnson & Johnson shampoo. Nuth kept staring at the notebook, like he was waiting for more, so this time I embellished in an effort to entertain.

"Its street was narrow and busy but quiet. The windows were opened wide, and the sliding front doors looked like they belonged to a shop, not a house. Maybe that's because the house wasn't a *house . . .*"

A girl smaller than Nuth sidled up alongside, smiling but looking perplexed by her roommate's sudden grasp of my gibberish. She leaned on the recliner with her arms crisscrossed, planted her chin in the crook, and stared at my notebook. I felt pressured to finish with a flourish.

"The house was a *laaarge* building with *maaany* kids. It was like a schoolhouse. I heard something approach with a *roarrrr.* Again, *roarrrr.* I looked around and there was a . . . motorbike!"

With my exclamation they looked up, staring at me. "A man in a helmet shouted, 'Khun Phaw Joe! Khun Phaw Joe!'"

They looked around the room expectantly.

I exhaled.

"The end."

In the room's only double-sized bed was the dorm elder, Boi, twelve years old and silent. Her blue jean shorts and frumpy white T-shirt looked far too large on arms and legs three sizes smaller than normal for her age and mottled with bruises the size of quarters. As I'd been reading, she was lying on her back with her eyes closed, her head moving from side to side to the beat of whatever was playing through her radio headphones. From the recliner, I'd sneak glances at her and jot notes, like a sketch artist drawing with adjectives instead of talent.

"The batteries are dead," Father Joe said, walking in and catching me by surprise. "The others don't know it. She pretends. If she's listening to music, the little ones leave her alone. She can race away that way. Go into her own world."

He thought about that for a second.

"That could be rather nice, I suspect. To race away."

The great Khun Phaw didn't tower over me like I'd imagined he would. There was no swagger in his step, no baritone to his voice, nothing to compel me to kneel, weep, confess, atone. He was dressed simply: black slacks cuffed at the top of black loafers worn sockless, like they'd been slipped on in a mad dash out the door. His cotton casual button-down was untucked and splotched with sweat. I saw no Saint Christopher medal, clerical collar, or priestly garb of any kind. Nothing about him shouted God. As a boy reared in the Baptist South, I had cowered in the presence of preachers. The practiced pitch of their Sunday rebuke and the omniscient way they could stare from the pulpit had made my wooden pew feel as hard as concrete.

This guy seemed different. He mopped his forehead with the back of his hand, slung the sweat to one side, and then crossed thick forearms across a Buddha belly.

"I'm Father Joe. How do you want to do this?"

Pretty cool, I thought.

I asked for the children's stories. I needed to flesh out the consequences of abject poverty, the conditions fueling sex trafficking and tempting mothers to sell themselves or their children and fathers to sell wives and children. Desperation and neglect, AIDS and death—I needed details.

I didn't dare say it exactly like that, but I knew I was fishing in a stocked pond.

He began with a consequence he called typical, a morning not long before when a five-year-old AIDS girl named Nong Bla had wandered the hospice delivering this news: "My mother just died. My mother just died. My mother just died. . . ."

No one had told her, she just knew. Something stirring in her gut had convinced her of it, he said, nodding as though he was sure I understood such intuition. Nong Bla's mother had been moved three days earlier to a government hospital where she had died of AIDS and tuberculosis. Barely one hour after her passing, Nong Bla had begun her dispatch. She'd kept it succinct and on a loop, announcing it dryly and to everyone. No one could recall her screaming or crying. She was matter-of-fact.

"My mother just died. . . ."

"She just needed to tell us," Father Joe said. "She needed to know that *we* knew."

I was surprised when he pointed her out. She was the girl who had sidled up to that old recliner. She had dark hair and a pageboy haircut like Boi, and when she smiled, her cheeks pinched into dimples—it was the brightest smile in a small village of curious, bright smiles.

For a child born into biological civil war, this made no sense to me. HIV/AIDS had invaded before she had a newborn's fighting chance. It was the same with every child in this little Village of Six: HIV had advanced father to mother to womb. Nong Bla had never experienced an entirely healthy day, only degrees of better and worse. Maybe there was some comfort in that. She lacked a normal frame of reference.

So like Nuth, who'd listened to my reporter's notes like they were verses from Dr. Seuss, she cheerfully attended a Mercy school as often as her health permitted, and she lived the relatively normal life of a Mercy orphan. She was learning to read and write and play well with others, and she apparently did all of it while flashing the occasional dimpled smile.

"As long as they're alive, they need to *live*," Father Joe said. "If they survive past age three, they'll be with us for the next seven, eight, nine, ten years. That's how long they live typically. We don't talk about it, but we don't *not* talk about it. They have AIDS and they go to school and they live the rest of their lives with us. It is what it is. We walk through it with them, and you look for the joy in life. You try to laugh with them. That's very important. Laughter. That's where God is, of course, in the laughter."

He nodded toward Boi, who rocked her head like the slowest pace of a metronome.

"It's rare for any of them to survive past age twelve," he said softly, as if he didn't want to interrupt her music. "Boi. That's the word for the fuzzy stuff at the top of the forehead, that little bit of nappy hair. You know, the softest of the soft part right there at the front. Anyhow . . . that's this little girl's name. *Boi.*"

It sounded like *boy.* He kneeled beside her, rested an arm on her Mickey Mouse bedsheets, and caressed her forehead with two fingers combed through the softest of the soft part. She opened her eyes, smiled, and continued rocking back and forth to the imaginary music.

"She is truly and entirely and completely innocent," he said, louder now. "She has never harmed anyone. Jesus was the Lamb of God—the innocent one. Lambs don't harm anyone. They can be dumb and do dumb things, like us, just like us, but they don't hurt anyone. They do no harm. Like Boi."

Nuth and Nong Bla carried an abacus onto the recliner where they fiddled with it like it was a strand of prayer beads. The rest of the children picked quietly through boxes of toys or returned to bed. On the dorm's pale blue walls were dozens of photos of Mercy mothers and children arranged into corkboard collages. It made a hospice that smelled like the Y feel more like home.

Father Joe kept his gaze on Boi, and she maintained her radio charade.

"You know the difference between men and women? If we get AIDS, the wife and daughters take care of us. If the wife or daughter gets AIDS, the man will visit a few times and then we don't ever see him again."

Boi's mother and father had died years earlier, the latter for the better, I would soon gather.

"A real *asshole,* that one," Father Joe said.

Boi had never really known her dad, he said. She was six months old when he threw her and her mother out. Said they weren't much fun sick. A local barfly, he met Boi's mother when she was a teenager serving up beer and more in a karaoke bar a dozen drunken steps from the dirty sheets of a short-time hotel. By age seventeen, she was an AIDS-infected mom of twins and pregnant with a third child. Boi came by her bad blood honestly—a poor girl's inheritance.

The father gave the twin boys to his sister and sent Boi and her mother to a slum shack. Boi became the primary caregiver, massaging her mom's pain away every evening after school. She was eight the day Mom asked for rope but settled for plastic twine instead. The next afternoon, Boi came home to find her hanging from a plastic noose.

Tuberculosis had settled in her brain. "That's a headache you don't massage away," Father Joe said.

Aunties and neighborhood women initially took Boi in as their own, but just one week later, Boi was turned over to Mercy. "No one wants an AIDS kid around, especially if it's not yours," Father Joe explained.

I rolled my eyes and shook my head. I felt beat up just hearing the story. How does a child find laughter after living through that?

"You do the best you can; that's all you can do. Your best. You tell them I will be here for you. I will be your mommy and I will be your daddy; I will be here in the morning and I will be here at night."

He touched his cheek to hers, then stood and walked over to an office that was about the size and temperature of a sauna. I followed, picking up along the way a stack of photos of the Mercy children that I'd noticed earlier on a bookshelf. I sat down across from his desk and handed him the pile of Polaroids—a collection of happy-go-lucky children with lively eyes and smiles. Many of the kids appeared to be bubbling with laughter or on the verge of it. There was one shot of Boi, back in the day when her face was full and her legs were limbs, not twigs.

I had come to Klong Toey with a different image in mind. Little chins would quiver. I expected to see long faces, tears, some anger, and stereotypical sick, skinny children. Not exactly the starving kids of Sally Struthers' commercials, but something like that. Pain and suffering would be obvious in their facial expressions. Yet here at Mercy, I could see the illness but not the rest, not exactly. I couldn't make much sense of what I was seeing, and even as I was telling Father Joe this, I could hear Nong Bla laughing.

I leaned across the desk to pick out a couple of favorites in that two-inch stack of Polaroids. "Like this kid"—it was of a boy who resembled Nuth, light skin with hints of European blood; he was grinning and hugging a soccer ball—"what's this guy's story? How did he end up here?" I asked innocently. "Why is he so *happy*?"

Father Joe didn't respond. He shuffled through the deck silently. He glanced up, stared at a spot behind me in a way that suggested I should leave stray Polaroids alone, and then looked back down. As I watched his jaw muscles tighten, so did my stomach. Seconds passed like minutes before he spoke. His voice was stern and slightly hoarse.

"Where did you get these? These are old. He's dead. She's dead. She's dead. . . ." He dealt those photos toward me like playing cards, then pushed the rest of the stack across the desk.

The Village of Six at the Mercy Centre hospice in May 2000. Boi is at the far left with radio headphones. Nuth is third from the left, mimicking the photographer. Nong Bla is on the far right, standing on the castoff recliner.

THREE

Undeveloped, Unpaved Parallels

Do not depend on the hope of results. When you're doing the work you have taken on, you may have to face that your work will be apparently worthless. . . . As you get used to this idea you will start more and more to concentrate not on results but on the value, the rightness, the truth of the work itself.

—Father Joe's daily journal, paraphrasing the Catholic mystic Thomas Merton

At five foot nine and two hundred or so pounds, Father Joe is squat like a bulldog and moves with similar bowlegged resolve. The runner's physique that carried him to Klong Toey in 1971 is a comfortable sixty-something today, but the anger driving him still burns.

I'd seen it on that very first day. In the office and over those Polaroids, his freckled Irish cheeks flared red-hot. I'd heard the anger too. It had a hint of brogue.

"It's a fookin' shame! A fookin', *fookin'* waste!" he snapped as we were leaving Mercy's headquarters to drive to the Soi Forty house.

I didn't know if he was cursing the wasted lives in our wake or the wasteland that lay ahead. It didn't matter; they both looked tragic to me.

We'd taken a shortcut from Mercy to Soi Forty, a hard right turn intended to jar more than my spine. He wanted to knock the glib out of me, I suspected. For the irreverent waving of the Polaroids. So leaving the hospice in his four-year-old Toyota Corolla—a gift from the Mother Church—he took a route I would've never figured as an option. We dipped into a gully and slogged onward, plowing through mud and brush to enter an undeveloped stretch of the developing world. Lock Six, he called it, a squatter's slum that sounded to me like a cell block from nearby Bang-Kwang prison, nicknamed "Big Tiger" for the lives it chewed up. On the ruttiest patches, the Corolla's speedometer only hiccupped, and every hundred meters or so, a mother, sister, or auntie flagged us down, hailing the car like a cab. Father Joe would climb out, fold his arms on the shelf of that belly, and listen, really listen, the sort of ear lent only by priests, therapists, and first dates. If the nasally Thai words came at him fast and furious, he didn't shift, yawn, or inch backward. He leaned closer into them, squinting as if reading fine print.

My water is cut off, my baby is sick, my boyfriend hit me, my girl can't go to school (no shoes), my mother was arrested, my husband didn't come home, my son is selling drugs, my sister is missing, my uncle lost our money gambling, my daughter is pregnant again, my motorbike was stolen, my auntie has the Virus.

The Virus, that's what they called it in 2000, as if the acronyms were more threatening. HIV/AIDS could get you summarily evicted from a Bangkok slum, and Lock Six was a last resort unless you slept in the damp stench beneath Three Soldiers Bridge. The "slum bridge," as it was known, is a twenty-minute walk from the first Catholic preschool opened in 1973 by Father Joe and a Macau-born nun, Sister Maria Chantavarodom, downstream even from downstream. Pretty much rock bottom.

Nong Bla of the hospice village—she of the ready dimples and dead mother—had been chased two years earlier from a slum near the Don Muang Airport. Neighbors thought that the Virus that had traveled from father to mother to daughter was contagious, like the flu. In a tone far more damning than pardoning, Father Joe had recalled for me the lesson in that eviction. We were in the hospice office, and looking out, you could see Nuth and Nong Bla picking at the cotton protruding from the old recliner's arm.

"I guess all the smart, pretty ones come to us and die," he said softly, speaking of slum children in general. Then, adopting a biting tone, he expressed what he thought of the adults who chase sick kids and their parents away: "The *dumb* ones get to keep living— out by the airport."

Later, as he walked around, arbitrating Lock Six crises and phoning Mercy to arrange handouts of clothes, shoes, milk, rice, water, whatever, the smart and pretty congregated. They formed curtains around him. With his cell phone in one hand, the free hand would fish into his trouser pockets to execute a sleight of hand so subtle I missed it the first few times.

Where I grew up, grandmoms and grocers baited themselves with sticks of Juicy Fruit gum or hard candies, to reel kids closer for goodness' sake or to curry customer favor. Father Joe was feeding the smart and pretty with one-baht coins the size of communion wafers, discretely distributing them, thumb to forefinger, into tiny waiting hands. Emerging on the far side of the slum, there was not a single jingle left in his bowlegged stride.

"My tithe," he said.

I looked at him cockeyed and smiled in a way that suggested that slum priests shouldn't need to tithe money. Sweat and tear equity covers the debt.

"But that's the way it should be, isn't it?" he asked, shrugging, returning my smile for the first time since we'd met. "A slum priest should empty his pockets for the smallest and the poorest. Most of these kids' mommies have absolutely nothing—nothing!—to give them. If a slum kid has a little something to buy candy with? Wow! Hey man, that's a holiday!"

He looked back toward the spot where his last coin had disappeared. Children had scattered to wherever children with newfound wealth scatter.

"A little bit is a big deal around here," he said. "You see?"

I couldn't miss it. For in that unpaved stretch of nothingness, I'd seen grown-ups and kids living together in the crawl spaces of homes too small to accommodate man, wife, children, cousins, aunts, whomever. They slept on blankets tied like hammocks to posts or beams, but crawl spaces being what they are, the hammocks didn't really hang; they puddled to the ground. And the homes weren't really houses; they were sheds, shanties, huts, hovels, tents, and lean-tos cobbled from scrap on land designated as waste. Beneath Klong Toey's overpasses and the merciful canopy of the Buddha's revered fig, the unemployed and unemployable were huddled quietly in the shade, like they'd been anchored to the gnarly roots of the bodhi tree. Their distant stares didn't reflect any sort of acute pain, just dull resignation. If you smiled, they smiled back. Always. Same with the *wai*. No bow ever went unanswered.

And if this were all I'd seen, I might've thought it peaceful, all things considered. But that wouldn't have explained the things urgent and miraculous that I sensed in Mercy's poignant name. That a charity could begin in a shed of corrugated tin beneath a slum bridge and expand into a train of slashes—preschools/hospices/orphanages/safe houses/medical clinics/sports leagues/vocational schools/et cetera—was just a hint of its universal truth. So it seemed to me. Because on the far side of Lock Six stood the light of an orphanage housing fifty or so happy kids who'd been beaten, molested, infected, orphaned, or put up for sale.

"From the slums . . . and *worse*" is how Father Joe described the children living and playing and apparently celebrating the day in that Soi Forty mansion—the source of that gust of joy that had sounded like recess earlier in the day.

As we stepped inside, Father Joe pointed to the abused kids of Klong Toey. There they were, in carefree piles, watching dubbed Disney flicks. And there, he pointed, lying on patched beanbags and couches, giggling and gossiping and writing and drawing. And there, lying splay-legged on the cool tile with gangly limbs entwined like chains of origami, comfortable with one another and smiling for the most part.

These are the orphaned, abandoned, abused, neglected, or otherwise broken?

Yes, he assured me, pointing to the entire downstairs; they were right there.

❦

Upstairs, where I'd heard the loudest swell of children that morning, Father Joe showed off long rows of single metal-frame beds spaced close together, each with clean sheets tucked military-tight and stuffed animals sprinkled on frilly bedspreads, like hotel chocolates on uptown pillows. White lace curtains tied apart with baby blue slivers of ribbon, bookshelves without a speck of dust, shards of fluorescent light bouncing off the floor's polished tile, and children's drawings tacked to the walls. I stared at my distorted reflection in a floor that seemed to stretch as long as a football field. In the hollow of it all, the hum of a dozen or so ceiling fans lulled us into a long silence. A minute or two passed while I looked around and around, breathing it in and nodding in admiration.

Father Joe's chest swelled.

"It's a big barn, isn't it?" he said, smiling again, his voice resonating from the middle of a 2,000-square-foot bedroom. It was larger than my entire childhood home, a brick split-level in rural Virginia. Soi Forty felt like home: mom and dad, brothers and sisters, secure in your family and routine of schoolwork, homework, playtime, dinnertime, and lights out.

"So you can feel it?" he asked.

Feel it?

"The energy. This room has a strong energy field, good, positive energy. . . . Same with your house, I'm sure. I think I know enough about you—good parents, good wife, good kids, good job; you're trying to do something to help. Your home would have this same energy. God's energy, of course. This isn't about you *personally.* It's about prayers and good actions and the love that's accepted and given. It's about you trying to make a dollar to feed your kids and about leading a good life, creating some happiness along the way. . . . That generates good energy, the good stuff that keeps the bad stuff out. You build on that."

He took another look around at what Mercy had built. Five double-wide shophouses converted into a giant 20,000-square-foot home.

"We've tried to get some good momentum going, some good energy, and to keep building on it. That's the essence, the foundation of this place, this room. Of Mercy."

He took a deep breath, as if he wanted to fill up on good energy. The whoosh of the ceiling fans washed over us, a few degrees cooler than outdoors but still hot. Scents from outside wafted indoors through the jalousies and mixed with the hearty fragrances of the kitchen downstairs. It could've been a warm evening in any urban area where the aroma of neighborhood dinners travels from house to house in the shared humidity.

Voices and a clatter of pans carried upstairs from the Soi Forty kitchen, along with screams, laughter, and the sounds of a Disney flick.

"You're standing in the middle of *it,*" Father Joe said, looking through me to the frilly covers and children's drawings. "A field of good energy."

Like a parent boasting, his chest swelled again as he began talking about a Soi Forty girl named Sai (pronounced like *sigh*). She'd arrived late one evening about two years earlier after neighbors discovered her and her brother living alone after both parents had been arrested on a drug offense. When she awoke the next morning in the Soi Forty dormitory, every bed was empty and neatly made up, exactly as they were now. Her Soi Forty roommates had left for school. But on a day when no one would've blamed her if she'd remained sleeping in her new bed, Sai got up, got dressed, and got busy.

Father Joe shook his head in awe at what Sai did next. I smiled and nodded and waited for the schmaltzy silver-lining-in-every-cloud lesson, but he spoke instead of a theft. Determined to find fortune in her misfortune, Sai had climbed out of bed to seize the day . . . and more. She gathered up all the stuffed animals her tiny arms could cradle and tiptoed out of Soi Forty. Later that morning, the Mercy staff found her on a street corner hawking Raggedy Ann dolls and teddy bears. This was the first time I'd hear Father Joe's laugh, a high pitch and a roll with an infectious rat-a-tat-tat.

"That's a Klong Toey street kid for you!" he said. "When your mommy and your daddy are locked up and you've got no parachute, nothing, not a thing, not a pot to piss in, what do you do? . . . Street kids, man. They're quick learners. They're smart."

⚛

That evening's table would be set by children who moved with the speed of three-card monte. The same kids, aged four to teens, would serve plates heaping with pasta, meat and tomato sauce, and dense bread ideal for sopping up excess. Waste not, want not, Father Joe said.

Dirty dishes would be hand-washed, hand-dried, and put away without complaint, grumble, or gripe, and personalized pewter mugs would hang alphabetized on hooks attached to the wall. It was the same with toothbrushes and book bags—the everyday accessories of life neatly sorted and ordered for easy focus and flow. With so many kids and so much emotional baggage, little things can provide traction.

"Yes, I know you were molested; that's terrible. But where are you *now*? Where are you *today*? At this very moment, are you safe? Are you being molested? Abused? Beaten? Sold? . . . No? OK, then, let's use the moment we're in to move beyond the past. It's the only guarantee we have, the instant, this very instant we're in. We might as well use it, just in case we're lucky enough to get another."

Father Joe will sometimes give versions of that one-minute sermon to kids who are feeling anchored to their heaviest baggage. "You keep building instant by instant, minute by minute, day by day, and you just pray for momentum, for something good to catch fire," he tells me. "If you open a door for a child just a little bit, they *will* motivate themselves."

We're relaxing in an after-dinner crush of children who could be any of the happy-go-lucky faces from the Polaroids I'd seen back at the AIDS hospice. Father Joe's standing with hands on hips like a den mother, assessing the house and its brood, a crowded home that doesn't feel crowded. A Buddhist shrine is on the shelf near a statue of the Virgin Mary, donated couches and beanbags are duct-taped and sagging from the weight of kids, and in a far corner of the downstairs, a trio of teenage girls rehearses a dance routine that sounds like something from *Saturday Night Fever.*

"Ohhhh," Father Joe moans, hearing the monotonous disco beat over and over again. He winces, but when he surveys the room, he drinks it all in slowly. This time, his cheeks are colored by something other than angst, anger, or annoyance with reporters waving old Polaroids.

"The kids we have in this house, the kids running around right now, these are the strong. Why did Jesus deal with the ones left over? In all of his teachings, he went to them. The kids who make it to Mercy, they're survivors. They're not *poor.* On the streets, they may not have had much to eat; it gets pretty bad on the streets. But these kids were never poor in the real sense of poor."

He wasn't referring to the puddles of hammocks I'd seen in Lock Six or one-baht coins or paper currency bearing images of dead presidents.

"The poorest of the poor you can never touch—you can never really help them. The truly poor are not just without a job and without money. They are physically poor, they are emotionally poor, and they are intellectually poor. You meet them now and then."

Under the bodhi tree? In Lock Six?

"It's not a popular thing to say, but yes, some of them are beyond help."

There was a clamor in the kitchen—cups, plates, forks, spoons, a dish dropping and breaking—but otherwise the dishwashing line moved with trained efficiency.

"These children here have had some poor luck, some poor parents; and some really lousy adults have done some really lousy things to them. But these kids got through it; they survived. They're stronger for it, not poor. These kids *pray* for the poor."

In that orphanage named for an alley, children from the slums (and worse) were hosting spaghetti night and movie night and disco night. They cooked and cleaned and reveled each night in the unrivaled camaraderie of the slumber party. Each morning, they helped one another get up and get moving. Together they'd found traction. Some were on their way to making the Mercy Travel Team—slum kids who had moved from shacks to Soi Forty to high schools and colleges abroad, leaving Klong Toey fluent in English and with full scholarships.

Several years earlier, Father Joe had paid a brothel owner the equivalent of $800 for one of the children. She was twelve at the time. She'd go on to major in international business at an American university. The Mercy Travel Team might have a half dozen to a dozen members in any given year. Children beaten, molested, infected, abandoned, orphaned, or put up for sale were not just enduring; they thrived.

To a native Southern Baptist reared in the majestic valleys of the Appalachians, the story was downright water to wine. That's what I had told Father Joe when we were standing in that barrack he called a barn. I had chicken skin. I had come to the cordoned-off corner to find pimps, pedophiles, and their prey, but I'd stumbled across something else entirely: a joyful oasis of suffering, a contradiction, it seemed—in the middle of "it."

The Mercy Centre was a testament to human resilience and the redemptive power of community or spirit or love or laughter. I wasn't exactly sure which.

"Of goodness," Father Joe offered. "We all have that in common. Religions may be different. People aren't."

He paused two beats.

"Inherently," he added. "We're all *inherently* good."

Ageless advice handed down by parents everywhere, secular and devout, East and West: Water that seed. Treat others as you would like to be treated. That's the universal Golden Rule. All the big tents teach it or preach it.

The law of karma is the lifeblood of Buddhism and Hinduism: What goes around comes around. Muhammad in his final pilgrimage to Mecca told followers: "Hurt no one so that no one may hurt you." In Buddhist scripture, Siddhārtha Gautama, the first Buddha and founder of Buddhism, said, "Consider others as yourself." The supreme philosopher of ancient China, Master Kung (Confucius), said, "What you do not wish upon yourself, extend not to others."

The great Jewish scholar Rabbi Hillel, a sage and spiritual leader in the time of Jesus and King Herod, was once asked to sum up all the lessons of the Torah (the first five books of the Hebrew and Christian Bibles, written by Moses and accepted by Islam). Hillel was asked to deliver his answer while standing on one foot. Succinctly, in other words. He replied, "What is hateful to you, do not do to your fellow man: this is the whole law; the rest is just commentary."

My parents preferred the gospels of the New Testament, pulling from Jesus' own words as quoted in the book of Luke: "Do unto others as you would have them do unto you."

I've repeated it countless times to my own sons, adjusting it to fit the situation. If you don't want his hands in your food, keep yours out of his. If you don't want him to tease you, then don't tease him. If you want him to share his Pokémon cards with you, then share yours with him.

The Golden Rule should be elementary to follow, I told Father Joe.

"It is," he said. "In theory."

⚜

That day and the following few, Father Joe would show me the various slums of Klong Toey, where 122,000 of the city's poorest were crowded into thirteen square kilometers (about five square miles) south of downtown. On flood-prone land beneath overpasses, pushed against the cement pillars of highways and the railway, families lived on the polluted tributaries that ferry Thailand's economy to and from the Chao Phraya River. Long ago, you could fish in slum canals, Father Joe said; you might even spot a sea turtle that had lost its way from the river to the sea. Kids could wade ankle or knee deep into the canals without pause. Now the water choked on so much garbage, sewage, and the effluvia of butchered pigs, cows, and water buffalo that if kids went in at all, they wore "slum boots"—plastic trash bags pulled up over their feet and calves. They tiptoed, careful not to splash for fear of infection and disease. Everyday kid scrapes could turn into life-threatening infections.

From the windows of my business-expensed suite at the Banyan Tree Bangkok, I'd been looking out over these slums without knowing it. The panoramic view included the U.S. embassy and the jewel of downtown, Lumpini Park, and could extend all the way to Mercy's cordoned-off corner, maybe a half-dozen kilometers, less than four miles. But framed by windows stretching from ceiling to floor and fifty-one stories high, the murky Chao

Phraya looked almost inviting. Shantytowns were just indiscernible specks in the distance.

From the street, even, the view deceives. Klong Toey's four-star hotels, modern health clubs, nightclubs, cigar bars, and gourmet restaurants mask the squatter camps backed up to the canal and spilling from beneath the Chalerm Mahanakhon Expressway. Homes constructed from pirated shipping crates sit on mud the color of tar just a few kilometers from spas selling aromatherapy mud wraps at 2,800 baht, about $70—three times the monthly income that defines Thailand's poverty line (886 baht, or $22.15).

Such gaps in the economy are best measured by cause and effect, not distance. Nevertheless, if you hopped a motorbike taxi today outside the Klong Toey Starbucks, directly across from a Boston-based Au Bon Pain franchise (free Wi-Fi hot spot), cut through the McDonald's parking lot next to the new BMW dealership, and then merged with six lanes of congestion crawling toward the roads and alleyways that feed into Klong Toey Port, you could pretty much traverse the global economy. Depending on rush hour and the derring-do of your motorbike driver, it takes six to ten minutes to go from the terraced rooftop pool of the boutique Davis Hotel to Father Joe's crook in the road.

Like all ambitious metropolises, Third World or First, Thailand's capital city dresses for visitors in a stylish array of international brand hotels, broad public parks, convention center, Jack Nicklaus golf courses, and stylish shopping malls bulging with discounted American brands manufactured in nearby China. Foreigners whisked along the airport toll road to the Bangkok Banyan, Millennium Hilton, Westin Grande, or Oriental will get only a passing glance at the urban underbelly.

Father Joe grants no such pass.

"C'mon," he'd say at the end of one interview or another, and I'd follow, never knowing for sure where we were headed.

Father Joe being greeted respectfully and with
wai in a slum alley of Klong Toey

© Stefan Irvine

FOUR

Rise of the Underground

*What you see and what you don't see: The
poor are hungry. Bars and restaurants are
full.*

—Father Joe's daily journal, two years after the
onset of the Asian financial crisis in 1997

Through migrant slums nicknamed for butcheries (Slaughterhouse, or *Rong Mu*), shards of trash (Crushed Bottle, or *Tap Gaew*), makeshift homes (Build It Yourself, or *Ban Chua Gan*), and others that sound bureaucrat-branded—Lock Six, Zone Eight, Flat Twelve, et cetera—we burrowed into Bangkok's home-grown economy.

In any given year, the majority of Thailand's labor pool is found in its "informal sector," according to Kasikorn Research Centre, the economic analyst for Bangkok's large Kasikorn Bank Group. That's roughly twenty-two million people (about two-thirds of the country's adult workforce) employed in the black market, without the retirement plans, labor unions, health insurance, and other social security benefits typically attached to "formal sector" jobs such as doctor, lawyer, banker, bellhop, bartender, waitress, and McDonald's cashier.

"Casual laborers," as Kasikorn refers to the underground workforce, includes sex industry workers, curbside food vendors, garland makers and sellers, fortune-tellers, touts for strip shows, cashew orchard pickers, and the like. It does not include children (nearly 2.5 million in 2000) listed by the Office of the National Education Commission as not attending school, representing about 70 percent of the eleven-to-fourteen age group thought by the International Labor Organization to be earning its keep in 2000 somewhere, somehow, in Thailand's "underground."

"Underground" is a misnomer, though. The underground is aboveground and in your face. Klong Toey's alleyways and catwalks are packed with far more than shacks, hovels, shanties, and lean-tos made of plywood, cardboard, and giveaway blankets. Along its crooked paths are soda stands, gambling dens, mom-and-pop candy makers, backroom distilleries, the occasional noodle shop tucking sales of speed or heroin in with orders of rice soup, and in large rattan cages set out like decorative planters, the poor man's ticket out—fighting cocks. Thousands of baht can be won (or lost) gambling around shallow pits where men scream themselves hoarse while their prize fowl duel. Gambling may be illegal in Thailand, but so is prostitution.

Coexisting in those tight spots (literally and figuratively) are garbage collectors pushing two-wheeled carts rented for 20 baht a day; loan sharks charging 2-baht interest on every 100 baht loaned (compounded daily); motorbike taxi drivers too high on drugs to trust with a fare after nightfall; go-go dancers; karaoke singers; massage parlor girls, boys, and women; and in the Slaughterhouse slum, the few dozen butchers who'd remained after most of the chop shops fled the district in the mid-1990s. As in large cities East and West, Bangkok's urban core is a jumble of all this, a cultural hotchpotch of people sharing the fate of having no other option. It is also a mix of Buddhists, Muslims, and Catholics, a mélange of Thai, Hmong, Cambodian, Korean, Malaysian, Burmese, Chinese, and Vietnamese. Crushed together beneath overpasses and backed up to the city's polluted canals are the unemployed, unemployable, and self-employed; card players and crap shooters next door to gambling bosses; dope addicts next to dope pushers; prostitutes next to pimps next to kindly schoolteachers, grandmothers, and wizened village elders—everyone living close enough that they could pass a beer window to window.

"But somehow," Father Joe said, smiling in the middle of a thick stench in the Slaughterhouse, "it works."

Or *worked*. Past tense.

When the Thai baht collapsed in July 1997, initially losing half its value against the U.S. dollar at the start of the so-called Asian financial crisis, 75 percent of Thailand's "formal sector" had no more than a primary school education, according to reports later published by the World Bank and the National Statistical Office of Thailand. The decade-long economic boom that had drawn immigrants from poorer countries to Thailand and to other areas of East Asia had left them especially vulnerable. Lacking jobs, legal citizenship, and access to social welfare programs, migrant laborers became "a convenient cushion to absorb the worst effects [of the crisis,] . . . shielding native citizens," the UN Development Program reported in 1999. "In Thailand, the impact on recent migrants was extremely severe."

During the first year of the crisis—traceable in large part to reckless (some allege criminal) borrowing, lending, and cronyism between Thailand's elite banking sector and international financial markets—unemployment tripled. In effect, uptown had played high-stakes poker with Thailand's national reserve and lost. All $40 billion of it. A year later, Thailand would still be bleeding jobs, at the rate of two thousand per day, according to the International Labor Organization. Predictably, the least educated and least skilled workers were the first to be purged from formal sector payrolls.

When I arrived in the spring of 2000, hundreds of thousands of low-wage, uneducated workers were still officially missing from formal sector jobs, according to the World Bank. But Thailand, hoping to attract new investors, could present its labor pool to the outside world as something more sophisticated and educated than before the crisis. Only 66 percent of its workforce of thirty-six million had only a primary school education or less.

An improvement on paper, but a catastrophe in slums, where the black market absorbed the unemployed.

Between 1998 and 1999, two million additional residents of Thailand fell below the country's unusually low poverty line, defined by the Royal Thai Government in 1999 as personal income amounting to no more than 75 cents per day. It equaled less than one-fourth the nation's minimum daily wage and three-quarters of the $1-per-person-per-day criterion commonly used by economists to define extreme poverty internationally.

In Father Joe's slums, the economic crash had been a collision of crises. All but one of the Slaughterhouse butcheries, which had employed hundreds of slum Catholics because Buddhists are told not to kill anything and Islam forbids the touching of swine, had closed in the mid-'90s, the last and largest in 1996. It had employed five hundred. The slaughterhouses were moved from the river port area of Klong Toey to city districts northwest (Bang Khae and Taling Chan) and northeast (Min Buri) of downtown and apparently to other unknown locations, according to a *Bangkok Post* investigation in March 1999. Some five thousand pigs (roughly half the city's daily consumption) were now being killed and dressed without government oversight.

"In the Slaughterhouse part of the Klong Toey slum the bloom is off the rose," Father Joe wrote in a *Bangkok Post* column soon after the baht's collapse in the summer of '97. "Our slum eco system is in trouble . . . all up and down the food chain. We used to slaughter over 2,000 pigs [daily]. Now it's 300 maximum."

For reasons having to do with city congestion, food sanitation, pollution of the Chao Phraya River, and, as Father Joe says, "kickbacks, paybacks, and favors" owed to bureaucrats and gangsters, the butcheries were paved over to make room for a vibrant new slum capitalism. "Eco gangsterism," Father Joe called it. It was a merciless black market that laced methamphetamines with heroin to hook users quicker—but didn't stop there. As drug and gambling debts soared from their daily compounded interest rates, old-timer slum shanties and even slum children were used as collateral. Slum kids too young even for Little League baseball were given away as bonds to the family debt, then taught by the crime bosses to work as beggars, prostitutes, and drug runners.

"What frightens me the most is the morality leakage. Like you had a pot full of ethics and the pot somehow cracked. . . . All the morality seeps away, and all you have left is a cracked, dry pot.

That's the essence of this Economic Slaughterhouse Crunch,"
Father Joe wrote in a *Bangkok Post* column about Klong Toey,
which the city's largest English-language paper began publishing a
few times each year soon after the financial crisis began.

"The predators appear and there's no space left to run," he said.
"There's always been greed in the Slaughterhouse, but now we are
faced with our own greed and everyone else's greed."

Predator and prey were often distinguishable by satellite TV
dishes that popped up on tin slum roofs and the occasional upscale
car parked on unpaved dirt roads. During the economic recession
turned full-blown depression, a sort of caste system had developed
in the squatter neighborhoods. Some catwalks now had homes that
were two stories, brick, and air-conditioned. There was even a
decided air of haughtiness, the way squatters made it a point to say
exactly what *soi* in Klong Toey they lived on. Meaning, Father Joe
said, if you dealt in drugs and children, at least you were no longer,
as they say in Dublin, "Shanty Irish. You had lace curtains."

"Drug dealers," he added grimly, "like to stay close to the customer base."

In August 1999, the *Post* had reported that eight hundred to a
thousand homesteaders in Klong Toey had lost their homes during
the economic crisis because of debts and the stranglehold of the
slums' daily compounded interest rates. The same news story
quoted a community survey that estimated that 250 to 300 children just from Klong Toey's slums, some as young as seven, had
been roped into crime syndicates because of family debts. "Klong
Toey slum children are being forced by their parents to deliver
drugs to customers of influential narcotics dealers as the daily interest on gambling loans," the story began.

Yet during the recession, the Thai government cut to the nub
its program budgets for "poverty alleviation" and "job creation,"
reduced, respectively, from 560 million baht (about $15 million)

to less than 1 million baht ($27,000) and from 130 million baht ($3.5 million) to zero, according to its National Statistics Office. Housing assistance and development programs were cut similarly, but a jobs stimulus program in 1998 offered the unemployed poor a bailout. Public works projects, like roads repair and construction, gave temporary jobs to 3.5 million workers.

On average, this resulted in eighteen days of employment for each worker.

As the crisis continued and gambling dens and drug houses spread in Klong Toey, Father Joe warned city officials and *Bangkok Post* readers that the well-being of the Slaughterhouse was a barometer for the metropolitan whole.

"Tell me what's happening in the Rong Mu [Slaughterhouse], and I'll give you a 'tea leaf' reading of the city, accurate enough to choose a lottery ticket," he wrote in a Sunday column as the financial crisis was entering its second year. "Less work. Hungry kids. Less honest ways to earn food money. That makes my job as a priest a bit more difficult. It's easy to be virtuous when you've got a secure job. But hungry, a wink or a nod is all the same to a blind pig."

By then, hundreds of thousands of Thai children had quit school to help their families or because they could no longer afford Thailand's compulsory education. If a child couldn't pay school fees of approximately 4,500 baht (about $120) per semester for textbooks, lunch, and uniform, Thailand's "free education," as described by the ministry of education, wasn't compulsory—or even allowed. Tens of thousands of first graders had quit school in the depression's immediate aftermath, according to a *New York Times* story. It was estimated that primary school dropouts nationwide had perhaps tripled.

Thailand's free education was like its free medical clinics. "Free" meant only "not uptown expensive," Father Joe explained. Medical clinics intended for the poor charged 50 baht for emergency visits,

250 baht for an X-ray, 100 baht for an IV, and 250 baht for blood tests. Families toeing poverty's line couldn't afford the "free" health care. A visit to the clinic could require pawning the icebox, if you were fortunate enough to have one, or a visit to the loan shark, Father Joe said. At that point, you've been pulled into the cycle of ecogangsterism that was metastasizing and chewing through Klong Toey and much of the rest of Thailand like a cancer.

With the house and kids leveraged and no more credit extended, grown-ups and children were turning to sniffing glue for relief. A yellowish concoction called "505" was the latest craze for the poorest of the poor. Easy to make with paint thinner and standard everyday glue, people breathed it from pint-sized plastic bags pressed to their faces like oxygen masks. When you're broke and on the run from reality, Father Joe said, you might as well just go ahead and rot your brain. "Reality can't find you that way," he said.

So it was no surprise for Father Joe when a young mother approached him one afternoon at the peak of the economic crisis. With shoulders slumped and head down, she spoke as if she were at a confessional, and he listened as though she were. She was the sole support for a child and an ailing mother, and in the past, Mercy had helped her find work. She'd lost that job, but she'd found another—this one in the black market.

Father Joe nodded and didn't interrupt. He knew what was coming; it had been a slum refrain since July 1997.

A few weeks earlier, in March 1999, U.S. Secretary of State Madeleine Albright had carried Washington's procapitalist, antidrug, antiprostitution message from rural northern Thailand to Bangkok and also teased the possibility of the United States' selling Thailand some used F-16 fighter jets in place of the F-18 jets it could no longer afford. All the Royal Thai Government had to do, she said, was adopt a series of financial and banking reforms that mirrored those of the West. It was a bribe of fighter jets. Speaking to women in Chiang Mai who'd left the sex industry with the help of a U.S.-backed charity, Albright had sounded parental and scolding of Thai culture, insisting that it was in need of greater influence from the West.

"I think we are learning that if there are going to be improvements in democracy, in economic transformation for the people, that women have to be very much a part of it," the Associated Press quoted her telling the former prostitutes. "A society that can't use its women that way has lost at least half its resources or half its population."

The mother slumping in front of Father Joe rambled on for a few minutes before she finally delivered her confession. Her eyes filled with tears, she stammered, "I'm prostituting myself."

The noted twentieth-century psychologist Abraham Maslow explained in his "hierarchy of needs" that raw desperation trumps all other motivations. Ambition, character, self-esteem, the concept of right and wrong are ideas best contemplated on a full stomach. A mother with no income or job prospects living at Thailand's absurdly low poverty line is almost at the bottom of Maslow's pyramid of human development. Sustainable access to air, food, and water are at its foundation; security and income are close seconds.

Father Joe took a deep breath and thought to himself, "Father, forgive me." He then offered the woman the best advice he could think of at that moment and in that economy: "Charge as much as you can," he said. "Work only in the high-class places."

Retelling this story to me years later, he sounded defensive. Stones are thrown from the moral perches of affluence, even occasionally by a U.S. secretary of state. A reporter with an expense account and a Banyan Tree suite was not likely to understand.

"Would she have done it if I had said 'No, no, don't do *thaaat*'?" he said, beating me to the question. "She was going to do it no matter what I said. At least this way, in the high-class places, you *hope* she will be safe."

⚜

We were walking near Mercy in a row of cinderblock and rusted-tin shacks where electric cords and bare bulbs dangled from rafters and windows were mostly cut from plastic—middle-class in an Irish shanty way. As Father Joe moved down the dark, narrow alleyway, he poked his head into a doorway and motioned for me to stick my head in too.

Sleeping on the bare wood of a nearly naked room was a boy of about seven, dressed as children dress when every night is 90 degrees and you have no way to cool the air: barefoot, shorts, sleeveless T-shirt, strands of beaded sweat. Hanging above him was a portrait of his mother, framed and centered. Striking raven hair flowed from the camera's view, and a pretty, slender face was inlaid with large almond-colored eyes and a smile, forced like a pageant contestant's.

"*Sā wāt dee ka, sā wāt dee ka,*" Father Joe said, shouting, "Hello, hello, good evening."

The boy's grandmother shuffled from a second room, and seeing Father Joe, her pace quickened. She began speaking as though they were picking up in the middle of a conversation. It was early in the monsoon season, and the weather had been fickle, teasing sprinkles and breezes threatening to become more. Now it stormed sideways. With a two-step, Father Joe met Grandmom halfway inside, where they raised their voices above the percussion of rain on corrugated tin.

Like the earlier Lock Six talks, this one would be one-sided, with Father Joe nodding *yes-yes-yes, I understand,* his omnipresent Nokia phone in hand. Moments later, Grandmom paused, caught her breath, and forced a smile. She placed a hand on Father Joe's wrist, steadying herself for questions, him to her, followed by frowns both ways. Father Joe turned to leave and offered me nothing in the way of translation.

The alleyway was about six feet wide, covered more or less in old tarps and the splintered wood of shipping crates ripped apart. Two women squatted over fresh puddles in the partial shelter; one wore shorts and a bra to wash clothes in a plastic bowl while the other gutted several fish in rainwater. Stepping around them, I saw another woman approaching with a manic stare fixed on me. I shuffled sideways, but we nearly collided anyhow. She glared back at me, mumbling in Thai. I looked to Father Joe, for help or at least the English.

"Not important," he said. "*Yaba.*"

Swallowed, smoked, snorted, or injected, yaba ("crazy medicine") could keep the slums manic way past midnight. Synthetic speed slow-cooked in beakers and on hot plates uptown and down and imported from Myanmar, yaba was (still is) the biggest drug craze in Thailand. Whether mixed with heroin or on its own, it hooks users. At 40 baht (about $1 U.S.) a pill in 2000, profits were in quantity, not quality.

The new Slaughterhouse parking lots that replaced the butcheries brought yaba into the slums in quantities that truckers carry. And with this supply and its supplier, there'd come a demand. The new ecogangsterism that Father Joe spoke of injected the slums with more than inexpensive drugs. The sex trade picked up a steady new stream of customers. It proved to be a shot of relief for the overall black market, but before long, prostitutes were hooked on yaba and trading favors for amphetamines.

Worse, a younger generation of prostitutes grew from the cross-pollinating, drug-addicted girls who had to pay their daily compounded loan one way or another. Before yaba came by the truckload, "Klong Toey girls were *not* prostitutes," Father Joe said. Mostly it was the women—the mothers—older and trying to take care of their families, send money back home to the villages, pay the bills, whatever. . . . But it was not normal for Klong Toey *girls* to work as prostitutes."

But in 2000, they worked throughout the night and inside or between ten- and eighteen-wheelers parked a few feet apart, twenty to a lot. The underground economy hummed day and night.

This triggered a different spike. Mercy began seeing more AIDS cases, children and parents, despite a government-sponsored AIDS prevention program giving away millions of free condoms to brothels and massage parlors and a catchy half-minute radio ditty (set to the tune of "Jingle Bells") discouraging unsafe sex.

It seemed to me that uptown was making an effort to help downtown.

Father Joe looked sideways at me and grimaced. "Jingles and condoms are for tourists and massage parlors," he said, meaning uptown, not the Slaughterhouse. "In the slums, if the money says, 'No condom and I will pay you more,' then it's no condom. Simple math."

To show me, he drove us to a Slaughterhouse parking lot. Instead of pigs, cattle, and water buffalo screaming through the night six nights a week, there were now big rigs and milling people mixing with air brakes and piercing loud horns. The noise, the traffic, the deals being negotiated were constant, almost 24/7, he said.

"When you're coming off the *horse*"—slum slang for yaba—"you've got to have more of it. If all you have to do is peddle your bottom to get some money . . ."

He stopped talking and pressed both hands to his temples, resting his elbows on the Toyota's steering wheel.

"It's just that the money rarely ever—*ever!*—goes toward beans and rice."

And if it did, would the prostitution be OK then? I asked.

"No," he said. "It kills people. It ruins lives. But I could maybe look the other way for a little longer."

Like the mother you told to work only in high-class places?

"That's one case where the money *will* go to buy rice—I *think*."

I asked about the boy sleeping on the floor beneath a portrait of his mother. I wanted to know how prostitution, drugs, and the financial recession might have affected them. And what had the boy's grandmother been so eager to talk about? But before I could clear my throat and get the questions out, he interrupted.

"He's got AIDS," he grunted. "She died of a drug overdose."

The boy? The mother?

"He's got AIDS," he repeated. "She's *dead*. From a drug overdose."

We sat silently listening to the new sounds of the Slaughter-house: screaming air brakes and humming air conditioners. The latter kept the truck cabs cool and engines running through the night. It also explained the dense smell of diesel fuel.

"C'mon," he said suddenly, getting out and slamming the driver's side door.

I grabbed my satchel, camera, pen, notebook, then rushed to catch up. He looked at me like I was one of the dumb ones allowed to live out by the airport.

"Put the camera away," he sighed. "And don't stare—*never* stare."

Scrap-wood and corrugated-tin homes in the Slaughterhouse slum
© Bill Haggerty

FIVE

Smitten

*To be an outcast in a society where it's
acceptable to be an outcast and an alien—
so I came to Thailand.*

—Father Joe's daily journal

Beyond the parking lot's suffocating smell of diesel and as far as I could see was a slum held aloft on crisscrossing catwalks. Stilts of wood stuck into the muck of a dung-brown canal colored by nature, life, and a city sewage pump. Hundreds of family homes, each smaller than my two-room Banyan Tree suite, sat four feet or so above a soupy mix, give or take twelve inches, depending on the tide of the Chao Phraya River and the day's emissions from a Bangkok Municipal Authority pumping station.

A few of the more feeble homes leaned into neighbors, like buddies staggering home from a tavern, and at every curve of the catwalks, dense pockets of odor waited, some vaguely different but all sour. At one point, the stench was so strong that we stopped in our tracks, walked to the edge of the catwalk, and stared down.

I jerked reflexively, pulled my shirt over my nose, then lowered it just as quickly. I hoped he hadn't seen. Evidently he had. "Yeah," Father Joe said. "That's a battle I've lost."

Standing on the water was a pile of rubbish as high as raked leaves. Cans, bottles, wrappers, dirty diapers, spoiled food, and various other things I couldn't identify or see clearly in the murky water and evening's shadows. But in the boil of that evening, I could taste them. I wanted to spit.

As we watched, a milky oblong bubble of methane, as large as a head of cauliflower, gurgled to the surface along the edge of one pile. It jiggled like gelatin, then popped.

Daaamn! I couldn't help it; the curse slipped out.

This was Father Joe's neighborhood. His home was two hard turns away and on the left. Had I known, I would've shown more restraint.

Damn, I thought but didn't let slip again two minutes later, when he stood outside a door and fiddled with a lock and key.

Yours?

He waved me in. From where I stood two feet inside, it looked tidier and sturdier than the others, but it was still a wood-and-tin shack. It had two rooms and a floor made lopsided from the uneven settling of catwalk stilts. He had a single bed, a small TV, and in a corner of the first room, one of those Abdominizer sit-up gadgets.

The "house," as he called it, was proof of evolution. It was several rungs up from other Slaughterhouse shacks where he'd lived. "Top of the food chain," he said with a straight face. I couldn't tell if he was joking.

His first Slaughterhouse accommodations had consisted of an army cot, mosquito netting, and a fresh-swept spot in a second room, granted by a kindly Catholic parishioner who butchered pigs through the night. Father Joe slept in that spot in the middle of the room, away from the walls that cockroaches climbed and rats the size of cats tried to squeeze under. The catwalks back then were crowded with shacks built mostly from the remains of old pig stalls, walls of six-ply wood nailed six inches apart, far enough to let in the evening's breeze. Cooking, eating, and most living was done outdoors. "You don't actually *live* in a slum shack," Father Joe explained. "You only sleep there."

His current home was an exception. There was a solid wood door padlocked and varnished, gypsum-board walls, an electrical outlet tapped into city voltage, and enough permanence that he had decorated nicely. Framed on one wall was Jeff Widener's famous Associated Press photo of the Unknown Rebel at the 1989 Tiananmen Square massacre: a lone protester standing toe to tread to block an advancing column of huge tanks.

"Inspiration," Father Joe said, seeing me study it. "For when you're all beat up."

On another wall was the church's blessed red vestments, framed and hung like a van Gogh.

"Sometimes I need reminding," he said, "that I *am* a priest."
He elaborated. "A *slum* priest."

⚜

The Slaughterhouse wasn't exactly what he'd envisioned for
himself after twelve years of seminary training, beginning with six
years of high school seminary at the Holy Redeemer School in
Oakland, California, novitiate in Wisconsin, an internship at a predominantly black church in Saint Louis, and two years of culture
and language training in the war-torn hills of northeastern Thailand and Laos.

"No one *plans* to live in a slum," he told me on the catwalk. "It's
something that just happens."

At the beginning of major seminary training in 1961, he'd
imagined himself working in Mexico or in the migrant-poor, Span-
ish-speaking areas of California. He admired the Marxist struggles
of social revolutionaries like Argentine-born Che Guevara and was
himself fluent in Spanish; he even bought textbooks in Spanish
rather than English (he believed its biblical translations to be purer).
But a year or so into major seminary, his West Coast province of the
Redemptorist order (based in Colorado) asked for volunteers willing to serve in Thailand. It had been several years since the
Redemptorists of the Denver Province had contributed a priest to
the Parish of the Holy Redeemer in Bangkok.

"In a moment of weakness," as Father Joe recalls it, he, a protester against the Vietnam War, had been seduced by a tactic per-
fected by military recruiters: the glossy flier. In a church magazine
lying around a seminary dorm in rural Wisconsin, he explained,
"little snotty-nosed Joey Maier from the wrong side of the tracks in
Longview, Washington" glimpsed all that he could be. "I was enam-
ored by a couple of priests in their white habits and black belts and

strings of rosaries, standing on a windblown hill reading a Thai newspaper. It all looked quite romantic."

Founding Redemptorist Saint Alphonsus Liguori had lived with squatters and worked with the homeless in eighteenth-century Naples. In creating the Congregation of the Most Holy Redeemer in 1732, he dedicated the religious order to the world's "desperately poor and most-abandoned people."

Father Joe had been both: poor (if not desperate) and abandoned. Growing up in blue-collar Longview and rural South Dakota, he and his younger sister and brother had their fill of government eggs and cheese and church-donated holiday turkeys after their dad left the family when the kids were still young. "I hurt a lot as a kid, and I didn't want other children to hurt the way I had," he says. "It's not very complicated."

Inspired by the socialist grit of Guevara and Catholic Americans like Tom Dooley, a former Navy physician from Saint Louis who in the 1950s built hospitals and medical clinics for the poor of Laos and Vietnam, he told the Redemptorists that he'd go. He pledged himself to the desperately poor and abandoned of Thailand.

The '60s were a heady time for an aspiring Catholic revolutionary. Pope John XXIII was trying to breathe new life into centuries-old orthodoxy and move Catholicism more toward the public square. The Second Ecumenical Council of the Vatican, held during four autumn sessions from 1962 to 1965, had begun with the popular church reformer, the "Good Pope John," as he was affectionately known, proclaiming that he wanted to "throw open the windows of the Church so that we can see out and the people can see in."

By the time Vatican II would conclude in December 1965, Good Pope John had died from cancer and the more socially conservative Pope Paul VI had replaced him. But true to the intent of Vatican II, the first of nine new decrees passed by the council was

Ad Gentes (To the Nations), known as the "decree on mission activity."

In effect, *Ad Gentes* encouraged mission priests to be more ecumenical and cooperate with denominations and organizations outside the church and to live among the laity (for Redemptorists, "the desperately poor"). This would enable priests to glean a fuller understanding of the cultures served and, more important for the church, vice versa.

That same year, Father Joe's Class of '65 would finish major seminary studies and receive its much-anticipated parish assignments. These were considered permanent deals. Or as Father Joe said, "You just kiss Mommy good-bye and tell her you'll call." Back in the day, he explained, meaning his era, Catholic priests posted overseas typically visited their families and home parishes once every five years.

The assignments for Father Joe and his major seminary classmates were taped one afternoon to a wall outside their classes at the Monastery for Redemptorist Fathers in Oconomowoc, Wisconsin, thirty-five miles west of Milwaukee. Father Joe scanned the list of twenty-one names and saw assignments to Detroit, Saint Louis, Chicago, Oakland, Seattle, and somewhere in Brazil.

Then he spotted "Joseph H. Maier: Parish of the Holy Redeemer, Bangkok, Thailand."

He shuddered.

Oh, yeah. *That.* He'd forgotten about the ruggedly handsome airbrushed priests atop a windblown hill. The photo and impulsive dare it elicited had faded into the monastic routine of pastoral theology, Gregorian chants, sacraments, creeds, Socrates, Plato, choir rehearsal, more sacraments, creeds, pizza, and beers.

"I was speechless," he recalled. "Well, almost speechless. I do remember standing there saying, '*Oh, shit.*'"

Over and over to himself. *Oh, shit.* He was still muttering it long after classmates left to celebrate their life's assignments with pizza and beer.

"I could have refused to go, I guess. I went to the superiors and sort of tried to talk my way out of it. . . . But in those days, you did what you were supposed to. You lived up to it."

⚜

Vatican II would never fully realize the liberal expectations raised by Good Pope John, but it would inch Rome away from biblical literalism and attempt to demystify the godlike reverence parishioners afforded their clergy. By encouraging priests to engage the modern world, the church hoped to fleck the rust off its antiquated image.

But in the Bangkok parish, there would be struggles.

The Reverend Harry Thiel, a former superior and mentor of Father Joe's in Thailand, told me that Vatican II loosed a freer breed of priests that arrived in Bangkok gung-ho and with a swagger. Thiel was a dozen years older than Father Joe and had been in Southeast Asia since 1958.

Late in 1966, after Father Joe completed an internship at Saint Alphonsus "Rock" Catholic Church in downtown Saint Louis, Thiel had begun training him in the languages and culture of northeastern Thailand and Laos. Like Tom Dooley a decade earlier, Thiel and Father Joe lived and worked among the durable, gracious Hmong hill tribe people, refugees caught in the crossfire of the Vietnam War and its "secret war" fought against communist North Vietnam, with tens of thousands of Hmong recruited by the CIA.

Memories from that time remain vivid, and in one of our first interviews, Father Joe recalled walking into a Tom Dooley Hospital in a Laotian jungle town near the Mekong River border with Thailand. "There were all these beds, no mattresses, just cots and bamboo mats. Kids wounded as soldiers were in them, bandaged up from bullets and shrapnel. They were ten, eleven, twelve years old and had M-16s—though a few had AK-47s. Those had been captured from the bad guys and were highly treasured. I'd never seen anything like it, and I just cried and cried and cried. Standing in a corner of that hospital, I couldn't stop crying."

The wounded children, trained in guerrilla warfare to be Ninja quiet, didn't even whimper. For several minutes, they silently watched him sob. Finally, a kid of about ten with a leg wrapped in bandages climbed off his cot and hobbled over to Father Joe. He smiled sympathetically, then patted the priest's hand in an effort to console.

"Here I am, this jock—this *jock* American priest know-it-all—and here is this bandaged up ten-year-old kid trying to help me. Comfort *me*."

About a year or so later, in 1970, Father Joe moved to his permanent assignment in Bangkok's Parish of the Holy Redeemer. His mentor, Thiel, had preceded him there by a few months and was entrenched as the parish rector.

Still emboldened by Vatican II, newly ordained priests were marching into the Holy Redeemer monastery eager to challenge its "very conservative old guard," Thiel recalled when I visited him in Seattle in 2005, where he was living in semiretirement. Even before Father Joe arrived at Holy Redeemer, old guard and new were clashing, and Father Joe's entry into the fray would only make matters worse.

"All hell broke loose," Thiel said, sitting in the staid parlor of the Sacred Heart of Jesus monastery in Seattle, a few blocks from the Space Needle. "There was so much that had been pent up and seething under the surface that when Pope John XXIII asked for this opening of the window, well, it just let loose a wellspring of, of . . . a *revolt* is what I guess you'd call it."

Curfews, mandatory noon prayers, rules about the length of hairstyles, the patronizing of bars, and the dating of women were all challenged by priests who'd come of age in the antiestablishment culture of the Vietnam War. Late-night carousing in the name of Vatican II's charge to engage the modern world became common. And as Thiel would say after shifting uncomfortably in his chair and pausing twice, it appeared that the new guys were having a closer association with women than Good Pope John had perhaps intended. "They were facing the real world and, um, maybe being of service to women, let's just say."

Dinnertime had become a minefield at the monastery, with Father Joe or one of the other half dozen new priests questioning American politics, the Vietnam War, the CIA-led secret war in Laos, and even the divinity of Christ and the existence of God—often for no other reason, Thiel suspected, than to inject some life into an otherwise quiet meal.

"I just think these young men who came over after the Second Vatican Council were uncertain of their foundations. Everything was being questioned again. . . . They were confused, and a few were rebellious and maybe a little flaky."

Even Father Joe? I asked him.

He smiled stiffly and then lowered his voice. "I wouldn't say he was *rebellious*. He was *searching*. He could be high-strung, like, 'C'mon, let's do this, let's go here, let's try this.' He could be off the wall, all over the place, searching, *searching*—trying to figure out where he fit in. He wanted to make a difference. . . . But there was, um, angst."

As a younger priest, Thiel had been hard-charging himself. Tall, slender, and regally handsome in his white cassock with black belt, he'd spent most of his adult life ministering to the Hmong. Photos of him atop a windblown hilltop in northeastern Thailand or Laos would have fit perfectly in the pages of the glossy magazines of the church. He identified with Father Joe and with "all of these young men full of enthusiasm," he said. But he sympathized with the conservative old guard, too. Thus he was the ideal rector for Holy Redeemer's civil war.

When the old guard decided by secret vote to appeal to the Bangkok diocese to reassign some of the more aggressive young priests, Thiel intervened on Father Joe's behalf. "I saw a lot of potential in Joe, in his energy," he said. "I'd like to think I saw myself."

To spare Father Joe "the knife," as Thiel put it, he secured the monastery's least desirable job for Father Joe: the Slaughterhouse parish. It was the largest slum in Klong Toey, and in 1971, its butcheries still worked through the night killing thousands of pigs, cattle, and water buffalo. Without the proper facilities and water hookups, animal remains and human waste flowed into a canal that doubled as a sewer. To Holy Redeemer priests, old guard or new, it was the Siberia of assignments, the sort rotated by seniority or draw of the shortest straw.

"If you can make it here, you've got it made," Thiel recalls telling Father Joe, not sure that he would. "But I remember *praying* that he would."

Thiel accompanied Father Joe on his first day there in 1971, and dozens of migrant families gathered on the catwalks to eye the church's latest offering. As Father Joe and Thiel approached them, Father Joe's knees were trembling. "*Literally*, they were trembling," Thiel recalled.

None of the Redemptorists had lasted very long. The previous Slaughterhouse priest had been out "sick" for several months. In alcohol rehab, Thiel whispered. This one was reed thin, built like a runner and looking anxious. But if Father Joe's legs quivered, he recovered well or pretended to. He proceeded to introduce himself to the locals in a jokingly bold manner intended to disarm them and him.

"*Fook* you," he said in Thai, smiling. "Here I am. Deal with it."

Unedited. Crass. A tad funny. Just like the slum residents, not stiff like a Catholic in a robe. Thiel said the Slaughterhouse residents were immediately smitten with Father Joe. And he with them.

In the evenings, Father Joe began hanging around the catwalks instead of returning to the Holy Redeemer dorm, preferring to work on his Thai language skills and learning slum slang. He stayed out late, drank backroom slum beer, and learned how to squeeze crap out of a pig's intestines (like wringing water out one end of a rolled-up towel). Then he'd eat the chitlins like everyone else, deep-fried in fat.

The monastery immediately saw less of Father Joe, and its dinner conversations resumed a quiet normalcy. By month two or three, they rarely saw him at all, except at noon prayers and Sunday Mass. The hotheaded priest who had been searching, *searching,* had apparently found something. He soon was scolding the old guard—and the new—in a friendly but accusing tone: "A *real* slum priest can't live uptown and work downtown."

When he'd leave, returning to the slums to sleep on his borrowed cot, they'd laugh behind his back. "They'd say, 'Joe Maier's gone native,'" Thiel recalled.

In other words, one of Holy Redeemer's own was acting like he was one of *them,* like he was no better than a slum squatter. Thiel smiled. "*Going native,*" he repeated. They used to say the same thing about him when he lived in the jungles with the Hmong.

"I'm afraid that was frowned upon," he explained, still smiling. "I don't really want to knock my congregation but, well, there were elements in the Redemptorist that just didn't look kindly on *too much* activity. I'm not talking about the social [carousing]. They didn't want you to do too much outside the traditional way. It frightened them. If you did it, they would maybe have to do it someday. It's just safer inside the walls of the monastery. It's comfortable. You don't have to make decisions."

Thiel paused, sagging a little in his chair.

"You're always going to have that element, I guess," he said.

The old guard wasn't too worried about Father Joe at first. They figured he'd last three months, then come back to the monastery defeated, Thiel said. He'd return to them tamed, housebroken, Thiel said. Then, maybe, he'd go along to get along.

Not long after Father Joe began sleeping on a Slaughterhouse cot, Mother Teresa visited Bangkok and ventured into Klong Toey's hard middle. It was soon after the 1971 release of her biography, *Something Beautiful for God* by Malcolm Muggeridge, but before she was a holy icon. Had she already been famous, chances are that the elders of Holy Redeemer would not have risked putting her in the unedited company of Father Joe.

Together, kindred spirits in poverty, slum nun and slum priest toured Father Joe's portside ghetto for three days, walking some of the same planks and catwalks I would walk with him a quarter of a century later. This was long before AIDS and yaba would mix and combust, and still, Mother Teresa pronounced the Slaughterhouse as sorrowful as anything in the gutters of Calcutta. "Spend your life working with these poor . . . if you can," she told Father Joe.

And with that simple, direct charge, it was as if he'd been anointed. "I remember thinking to myself that if this is what a Christian-Catholic saint is all about," Father Joe said of Mother Teresa, "I *could* and *would* spend all my life trying to imitate her."

He never asked to move back into the Holy Redeemer dorm, Thiel told me, smiling and sounding proud of his protégé. "I think Joe kind of found his niche in the Slaughterhouse, when he began meeting these very simple, honest, straightforward people. They weren't phony—and Joe's not phony."

In profiles I'd read of "Bangkok's Mother Teresa," Father Joe suggested that he was assigned to a slum in Thailand as a sort of punishment for being a war protester and hippie seminarian who counted himself a fan of the famously hallucinogenic rock band the Grateful Dead. But that didn't square with what his bosses in Denver had told me before I arrived in Bangkok. They gushed about *their* priest, like he was the pride of the order. Never a problem, a great guy that Joe, I was told by the provincial superior of the Redemptorists' Denver Province.

"Here is a man who has clout not because he has a lot of money but because he is doing what he thinks is right and other people are captured by that," the Reverend Richard Thibodeau told me in the spring of 2000. "Because of his results, the kingdom of God is that much stronger in an area of the world and an area of a country and an area of a city which we many times would like to ignore."

But on that first evening in the Slaughterhouse in 2000, Father Joe didn't volunteer stories about Mother Teresa, Vatican II, or even his banishment from the First World by priests who were supposed to be his brothers in arms in the Third. So standing on a catwalk with him, I had the same burning question any reporter or interloper would have after staring into a sewer masquerading as a canal, the place Father Joe called home:

Why in heaven's name live *here?*

He hemmed and hawed and then blurted his condensed standard answer.

"These are the people I was sent to. And them to me."

That's it?

"Yep."

It wasn't until several years later that Father Joe let me much closer. In Bangkok for my final visit in 2007, I'd asked him twice if he kept a journal of his thoughts and daily life, a diary by any other name. Thiel had kept voluminous journals detailing his philosophy and struggles and rugged life in the hills of northeastern Thailand, Laos, and Bangkok. But whenever I'd inquire about Father Joe's journals, he'd shrug and answer vaguely. "No, no, I haven't *really* kept any."

Nothing?

"Not really."

Then one evening in 2007, we were eating a dinner of vegetable stew at Mercy when out of the blue and completely unprovoked, he confessed.

"Upstairs in my office, you'll find a messy pile of . . ."

His voice had that promising tone fathers adopt when telling their son or daughter for the first time, OK, here are the car keys; don't put a scratch on it, and bring it back with gas in it and before midnight. He knew what he was about to offer me was equivalent to that, at least for a journalist.

". . . books, um, my journals, I guess *you'd* call them. You can flip through any of them, all of them if you like. Take them with you if it'll help. Whatever you want, they're yours to use."

Eighteen daily planner journals dating from January 1999 to March 2007 had been moved from a bookshelf to the floor, stacked in three knee-high, leaning towers. I immediately sat cross-legged in front of them, like a kid on Christmas morning, and opened the first my hand fell on. I began turning pages randomly, my eyes roaming and scanning, and on the third or fourth glance, I was drawn to a scribble in pencil. It was written sideways in a page's margins: "To be an outcast in a society where it's acceptable to be an outcast and an alien—so I came to Thailand."

☙

It was getting late in the Slaughterhouse in May 2000 when we arrived back at his car in a forest of tractor-trailers. The fickle weather had returned, with raindrops the size of marbles that drummed against the hood of his Corolla.

He asked me how else he could help, what more I might need. By the drag in his voice, I knew he meant, *What more do you want? C'mon, let's wrap this interview up.*

The mother in the portrait, I began, and the boy asleep beneath it.

He answered again before I could finish. The mother had lived on the streets with a push-cart junk collector. She slept in the red cart; he slept on a straw mat beside it. They were both heroin addicts, and when Det Dheo was born, he was one, too. Inherited the habit like he inherited HIV. In utero. The government hospital kept him for a while until he was weaned off it; then he was sent "home" to sleep on the streets with his parents. A few months later, the grandmother found him asleep in the mud, face down in the muck of a monsoon storm. She's raised him ever since. The father died a few years later when he fell drug-drunk on something sharp that punctured a lung. In short order, the mother died too. Police had found her asleep in the cart with a needle in her arm. She died at age twenty-nine, racked with AIDS and in jail. Before she died, she told her mother that if she had known she was infected with AIDS, she'd have killed herself before giving birth. "No one wants to give death to her baby," Father Joe said. "But she'd never known."

So like Nuth, Nong Bla, and Boi, a scrappy kid named Det Dheo entered this world at war with himself.

The grandmother supported the boy and her junk-collecting second husband with modest sales from a homemade sweet coconut candy and immodest sales of bootleg liquor. Times were tough, though. Yaba had cut into her liquor receipts.

But the questions Father Joe and Grandmom exchanged that day with frowns both ways had to do with more immediate concerns: What's the boy eating? How's his energy? How's his appetite? How many days each week was he making it to school?

Telling me this, Father Joe rubbed his temples as though his head was about to explode. "You put your fires out one at a time," he said.

And in the downpour on that catwalk, leaving a little boy asleep beneath the portrait of his mother, you could feel that fire still burning. "It's a totally different world where all the kids get hurt and no one gives a *shit!*" he snapped.

We sat silently again for several minutes in his silver church-bought Corolla, staring out at the long-haul trucks parked near a maze of catwalks that stretched into the darkness. With his elbows resting on the steering wheel, Father Joe's head slumped forward into his hands again. His fingers pressed into his temples.

"Take it all in," he told me softly. "Take your time. Write it down."

⚜

Leaving the Slaughterhouse, Father Joe merged with Bangkok's mainstream and a commercial district that looked worn by age and economic recession. Crawling in traffic past dry cleaners, coffee-houses, and fast-food restaurants, he pulled to the curb and jabbed a finger toward a complex that housed a Sizzler restaurant.

"That's where the asshole did it," he sneered, staring at a sign on the same stone facade as the Sizzler's.

"Rosser Music Studio," it read.

The concert pianist Eric Franklin Rosser of Bloomington, Indiana, was a big reason why I'd gone to Bangkok instead of Mumbai or Kolkata. A former keyboard player for John Mellencamp's band, he was perhaps the world's most notorious pedophile. On February 12, 2000, he'd admitted on the front page of Bangkok's English-language daily newspaper, *The Nation,* to molesting young Thai girls—but no more than five, he told the paper. Of the forty video-tapes and hundreds of photographs police seized from his Bangkok condominium and music studio, where he had cameras hidden in the bathroom and under the piano bench, Rosser could be seen molesting his ten-year-old niece, who lived with him and his Thai wife, Muay.

Rosser, in his late forties, balding, with a potbelly and a slouch, had taught piano to the children of Bangkok's upper class for a decade and played piano at a bar in the luxurious Oriental hotel. But after trading his pedophile porn back and forth on the Internet with a porn buddy in Bloomington, he was infamous as the first child pornographer to ever make the FBI's Ten Most Wanted list. By the time his trial arrived on April 18, 2000, he'd posted a bail of 1 million baht (about $25,000) and fled.

"A real slippery-slimy, that one," Father Joe said. "He's one of those who will come back in his next life as a worm—but not just any worm. Not a dirt worm that gets to wiggle into mud and get cozy. He'll be one of those—what do you call it?—"

He held two fingers a fraction of an inch apart and screwed up his face like someone had shoved a maggot toward his nose. "Uh, you know, the little worm that crawls around in shit. What is it?"

Hell, I offered. I think you're describing hell.

"Well, yes, yes, that too."

The day before, I'd interviewed Chitra Vanaspong in the Bangkok offices of an international nongovernmental organization called End Child Prostitution and Child Pornography and Trafficking (ECPAT). Vanaspong said that the financial crisis of 1997 was still being manifested in the sale and bondage of children into sex slavery and that parents in some areas of the rural northeast now celebrated the births of daughters more so than those of sons. For a patriarchal culture, it was a seismic shift. But, Vanaspong explained, "daughters can bring more income; they are very valuable now. Parents celebrate because in the next fifteen, eighteen years, she will bring a lot of money to you."

Father Joe believed that was true only for a few villages north of Chiang Mai, but he knew firsthand that parents would sacrifice their children to Thailand's poor economy. Police had asked the Mercy Centre to keep the niece of Rosser's wife for a few days until the girl's mother could retrieve her. She'd been allowing Rosser and Muay to raise the girl while she lived and worked in a bar a hundred miles away in Pattaya, a touristy beach town notorious for its strip clubs and massage parlors. When the mother saw her daughter for the first time after Rosser's arrest, Father Joe said she was furious—at her daughter. She scolded her and warned her to never, ever talk about the brooding pianist.

Rosser was the family's benefactor. He took care of Aunt Muay, paid for the girl's private schooling, and sent money regularly to Pattaya. At a custody hearing weeks later, a Mercy social worker overhead the mother telling her daughter in court, "'You're going to *ruin* this for us.'" She received custody of her daughter that day and then promptly returned with her to Pattaya.

We were still parked at the curb outside the Sizzler with the engine running. I took notes quietly as Father Joe told the story.

"'You're going to *ruin* this,' she said," Father Joe repeated, making sure I understood. "*Ruin* this. This little girl was the family's meal ticket. That *asshole* had been screwing around with her for years."

Rosser had evidently fed and dressed her well and kept her well groomed. She'd arrived at Mercy in clean clothes, with pigtails, even wearing a smile. She was a little chubby for her age, Father Joe said, which made her stand out noticeably around the AIDS kids, who lagged behind on the growth chart. "Totally trusting, totally naive," Father Joe said. "She didn't even know she was being abused. She's the type who believes everything and *does* every miserable thing that every shitty grown-up in her life has told her to do."

His head went slack. It drooped into his hands, and his palms clamped against his temples like a vice. He rubbed his temples like he was trying to harness racing thoughts. In my short time at Mercy, I'd seen him put his head in that vise several times. The first time was after he told me how Boi and her mother were kicked out of their slum home by Boi's father "because they were no *fun* any longer." Boi had been six months old.

He did it again after telling me how Nong Bla and her mother were forced from their slum near the airport. "The *dumb* ones get to keep living—out by the airport," he'd said, rubbing his temples.

And he did it again after leaving the bedside of a woman he said was the mother of Nuth, the boy who had crawled onto my lap to listen to me read from my notebook. She'd been in the adult hospice next door but could no longer read to her son.

"Her TB is *very* contagious," Father Joe had whispered to me just before introducing us. "Don't get too close."

Hearing his own advice, he took a discrete step backward. I scribbled notes at her bedside in the same notebook I'd just read to Nuth.

"As thin as kindling," I wrote. "Only possessions are tucked underneath her bed in a red bucket: bar of soap, toothbrush, toothpaste."

She smiled broadly at me through the surgical mask covering her mouth and nose.

Afterward, Father Joe stopped in his tracks, arched his head backward, and stared up at the rafters. He squeezed his temples and pressed with his palms—much as he was doing at this very moment, as traffic crawled past us on a fashionable uptown street.

That year and the previous few, Mercy had been averaging a half dozen deaths per month, mostly men and women dying with the Virus, but children, too. When its hospice first opened in 1994, taxis would arrive with AIDS patients literally taking their last breaths. One died before the cabbie could run around and open the passenger door; another fell on the steps leading into the Mercy

Centre. So many adults and children were arriving at Mercy in the late stages of AIDS that Mercy was recycling the lids of its donated kid-sized caskets.

Those caskets and lids are generally hard to find. "Kids aren't supposed to die," Father Joe explained.

The lids would be removed out of sight after friends and bunk-mates had a chance to tuck a stuffed animal or favorite something else next to the deceased, just before the temple monks would chant the last chant and light the pyre. Catholics typically bury their dead; Buddhists cremate. It just made sense to save the lids to use for the next cremation ceremony and the next and the one after that.

That's how Father Joe knew what he told me next. Something he assumed I already knew and something I felt sorry for his already knowing.

"Kids' bones burn up to almost nothing."

We were still at the Sizzler curb.

"With a kid, there just isn't much left after cremation. Their bones aren't real dense, they're not fully developed . . ."

He rubbed his forefinger and thumb together like he was feeling fine granules.

"There's just not a lot of ash. Not much to scatter."

They try anyhow, tossing flecks into the wind outside the Buddhist temple down by the slum bridge, into the dirty canal that goes to the river that flows into the sea—the idea being that all water, pure and polluted, flows toward the ocean, a metaphor for life and death and the oneness of all things. Rich, poor, saint, sinner, Buddhist, Muslim, Catholic, Protestant, Jew, agnostic, you, me. One big body of water.

Children's ashes, *damn*. I hadn't known. The hospice village, Soi Forty, my own kids, God forbid.

Father Joe had stopped rubbing his temples and seemed matter-of-fact about it. He'd been walking children through "these patches of trouble," as he called them, for several years. "We don't talk about it, but we don't *not* talk about it," he had said at Boi's bedside. "We walk through it with them, and you look for the joy in life."

I looked up from my notepad, and my shock must've shown. He changed the subject, even as he continued to absentmindedly rub imaginary ashes between thumb and forefinger.

"We all have common enemies—ignorance, greed, violence, hate. And we have common friends—love, mercy, compassion," he said gently, as if he wanted to reassure me that everything would be OK. "The Muslims, the Christians, the Buddhists, all of the religions, we are different. But we are all on the path. And we all meet at the end of the path."

⚜

From the Sizzler, we adjourned to the drink. Subjects like AIDS and kid caskets are enough to drive reporters and slum priests to an overcrowded O'Malley, O'Leary, O'Brian expatriate sort of place with requisite cloverleaves and dark draught.

I suspect it's where Father Joe's forbidden verbs received their shot of brogue.

When the bill came, I reached for it, insisting. I knew there was no jingle left in his pockets. We'd parked three blocks away, and a few of the desperate poor had trimmed the sidewalk, children among them.

Father Joe and a neighbor outside his second
Slaughterhouse shack in 1983

© 1983 Jim Coyne

SIX

Where Right Equals Might

This bit from Bush about whose side are you on (us vs. them) is no good. Now USA wants to bomb people. To terrorize = to join them. . . . Don't out-terrorize the terrorists. . . . Where will this all end?

—Father Joe's daily journal
in the days after 9/11

When I last saw Father Joe in 2000, he was slapping himself on the forehead, driving off after returning me to the Banyan Tree Bangkok.

"Ah!" he shouted, gunning his Toyota.

He still needed to prepare a sermon for Sunday Mass. It was nine o'clock Saturday night. I ordered room service from my posh fifty-first-floor suite where the view of Bangkok twinkled, looking more like Manhattan than Klong Toey. Father Joe returned to his lopsided shack perched an arm's length above sewage and then stayed up half the night writing metaphors about branches connected to the tree of life.

It was five years almost to that day when I'd see him again. Much had occurred during the interim: the Bush-Gore election; 9/11; the bombing of Afghanistan; the invasion and occupation of Iraq; the Bush-Kerry election. Those were the highlights just from my side of the economic divide.

Halfway around the world, Muslim separatists were terrorizing the Islamic provinces of southern Thailand. There'd been shootings, beheadings, and bombings of schools, offices, teachers, and civil servants. At the end of 2004, the deadliest tsunami in recorded history had killed or displaced thousands of villagers on the Andaman coast of Thailand's southern panhandle. And a typically reserved Thai citizenry was beginning to protest the suspect politics of billionaire prime minister Thaksin Shinawatra, who, by my final visit in 2007, would be deposed by military coup and junta rule.

Our meeting this time was on my turf, the capital of the free world. Father Joe had traveled nine thousand miles to Washington, D.C., to speak at a summit to raise money for victims of the Asian tsunami.

We agreed to meet in a conference hall of the Ronald Reagan Building and International Trade Center. Walking into the room, I immediately spotted a well-dressed priest leaning stiffly with arms

crossed, shoulders flush against a beige concrete wall. Deep fur-
rows in his brow were driving his bushy eyebrows into a distinct
and damning V.

"There he is, the man himself!" I offered midstride, a preemptive strike to loosen the ice. "Great to see you again, Father Joe."

"Hi, Greg" is all he said.

The Reagan Building is a colossal gray stone complex three
blocks from the White House. On surrounding streets are the similarly severe neoclassical gray stone red-tile-roof homes of the U.S.
Treasury, the FBI, the IRS, and the Justice Department. It's the
intoxicating center of global power if you're of the type who
believes that "might equals right."

Father Joe looked stone sober.

"You look like you've stayed well," he said flatly, staring over
my shoulder at several circles of small talk that form at every Washington function and were now beginning to orbit the large room.

I turned my head to look at what he was staring at, then turned
back and smiled. "I bet you feel like a fish out of water," I said, hoping to tease a smile from him.

"Ohhh, very much," he groaned.

The all-day summit was a chance for governments and charities helping with the tsunami recovery to solicit corporate America. The ruling class of Boeing, ExxonMobil, General Motors,
Coca-Cola, Pepsi, Chevron, Pfizer, Unocal, and Nike was present.
Father Joe had been invited as one of four representatives for the
victims of Thailand. He was dressed in his black clerical garb, the first
time I'd seen him in uniform.

"Dressed for battle?" I grinned and nodded toward the finely
pressed dark suit and clerical collar.

He smiled.

I'd left Mercy Centre in 2000 with a question that couldn't be
easily or directly answered. What was it about Mercy that had sick,

dying, orphaned, abandoned, abused, neglected, or otherwise broken children brimming with life? Crackling with it, practically. Hopping and skipping and laughing and playing. Father Joe once wrote in his daily journal, "You have to take the journey, take the journey and you'll understand."

I wanted to understand—at least as much as a newspaper reporter accustomed to good health, good family, and the comforts of a good home could understand. So in a volley of e-mails two weeks earlier, I'd asked Father Joe if he'd allow me to intrude on his time. Again. And for much longer. In a few dressed-up sentences, I explained that I wanted to write a series of books about modern-day prophets and that I needed the first of these prophets to cooperate. He agreed to discuss it during the tsunami summit in D.C., but the commitment he made sounded like one of those since-I'm-going-to-be-in-your-neighborhood-I-might-as-well sort of things.

At the Reagan Building, I pulled from my satchel a crisp white sheet of bonded paper. On it was the book's concept statement, a two-sentence "hook" used to chum for literary agents and publishers: "To know Father Joe is like having a light come on. He illuminates the shadows of our shrinking global community and challenges assumptions about class, culture, and religion."

I handed it to him and waited like the teacher's pet for a pat on the back.

He read it silently, glanced up, stared at the orbit of people behind me, and then looked back down. He read it without comment two, three, maybe four times. It felt sickeningly similar to the Polaroid moment in his hospice office the day I'd met him, and I could feel my stomach tightening. Standing to his immediate right was Tom Crowley, a fit Vietnam veteran and former executive of Outward Bound who split time between Bangkok and a home in Maryland. Crowley, like Father Joe, is proud Irish. Unlike Father

Joe, he's pleasantly reserved and soft-spoken. On trips like this, he served more or less as Father Joe's small-talk buffer and, in my case, book filter.

Father Joe handed Crowley the paper and returned to leaning hard against the wall. Crowley read it once, handed it back to Father Joe, who handed it back to me.

It felt like a shove.

Surrounded now by business suits and diplomats, Father Joe straightened off the wall and leaned slightly forward to deliver his critique in a whisper-bark.

"If we're going to do this," he began slowly, pausing for a split second to glance left and right, "we're going to do it *right!* People are always saying, 'Wow, what a success,' but any success I've had is all by accident. Anything I've ever done that's worth a *shit* I've had to be dragged into by the scruff of my neck, kicking and screaming and saying, 'Noooo, dammit, I don't want to do *thaaat.* . . ."

He paused for a breath, to reload.

"I might be the thread that runs through your book, but it has to be an honest telling. Tell it like it is, *dammit!* Tell the truth, warts and all! I'm no *fookin'* hero. And if *they* don't like it . . ."

They could have been the suits in the room or the cassocks in Rome. He lowered his voice another decibel but still managed to speak like he was jerking about at the end of a chain.

". . . *Fook 'em! Fook 'em! Fook 'em!*"

Best I can tell, the warts he speaks of stem only from that contrarian spirit that fires on a hair trigger. Foul moods and foul language dog him, but they're usually loosed only on narrow minds and dubious authority, doubly so on narrow-minded authorities.

So surely I could forgive his irritability in a building named for the poster child of trickle-down economics.

Father Joe feels estranged from his homeland. He curses the confounding might of the Christian Right ("What the hell is *right* about it?"), the "shitty" decision to invade Iraq, and "that damn idiot" Bush. "I don't think Bush is stupid," he scribbled in his daily journal during the summer of 2001, "but he sure seems to be on TV."

On occasion I've also sensed his passing of judgment on me. My birthright and leg-up on life are difficult to reconcile with the haves and have-nots and Mercy's avowed self-sacrifice—difficult even for me.

But as I worked on this book, I would come to sense Father Joe's loneliness and notice his eyes swim during the singing of "The Star Spangled Banner."

It was 7:35 in the morning in Bangkok (8:35 at night in Detroit) when Brian McKnight sang at the 2005 Major League Baseball All-Star Game. Father Joe and I were at Mercy with ESPN muted in the background. Seeing Alex Rodriguez with his Yankees cap in hand, Father Joe turned the volume up just in time for "Oooooh, say can you see . . ."

He didn't speak again until after ". . . and the hoooome of thuuuuhhh braaave."

"Do you miss it?" I asked.

He knew I meant America. He nodded yes in the way that suggested something was lodged in his throat. Moments later, he said quietly, "If I moved back, I'd be in jail. I'd be one of the guys hanging out with Roy Bourgeois and that group."

Father Roy Bourgeois is a Maryknoll priest who helped the poor of Bolivia before being deported in 1975 for opposing the alleged human rights abuses of the Bolivian dictator, General Hugo Banzer. Bourgeois is a former U.S. Navy officer and an outspoken critic of American foreign policy. In 1990, he formed a human rights group that attempted to close the U.S. Army's School of the Americas (SOA), derided as the School of Assassins. SOA alumni include General Banzer, former Panamanian military dictator Manuel Noriega, and Salvadoran military strongman Roberto d'Aubuisson, suspected in the 1980 death-squad killing of San Salvador archbishop Oscar Romero, one of South America's most prominent Catholic priests. In nonviolent protests, Bourgeois and his small group, SOA Watch, have trespassed on SOA property enough times to cost Bourgeois more than four years in prison.

"It's just better that I fight my war here. Try to help some damaged kids," Father Joe had said that day while millionaire baseball all-stars played on mute. "This is where I belong. Not there. I'm very much out of step *there*."

On May 12, 2005, *there* was the Federal Triangle.

⚜

The Private Sector Summit on Post-Tsunami Rehabilitation and Reconstruction lasted twelve hours. Following morning speeches from former presidents George H. W. Bush and Bill Clinton, panelists from the countries hardest hit by the tsunami gathered in conference rooms for direct appeals to corporate America. Father Joe was seated last on Thailand's four-member group, the only non-Thai and nongovernment representative.

The Mercy Centre had expanded to southern Thailand soon after the Indian Ocean earthquake sent a wall of the Andaman Sea rushing over Thailand's coastal south. That same day—December 26, 2004—Father Joe huddled with some senior staff to decide how or if Mercy should respond to a natural disaster a twelve-hour drive from Bangkok. No one yet knew the extent of damage or casualties, only that significant help would be needed.

The Human Development Foundation and its Mercy Centre were founded in and for the squatter slums of Klong Toey. For the children, primarily. To educate, to rehabilitate, and beginning with its hospice in 1994, to help HIV-infected kids and their parents.

"We don't do tsunamis . . . do we?" Father Joe asked the staff.

Fatalities and people counted as missing would exceed 220,000, the majority from Indonesia, Sri Lanka, India, and six of Thailand's fourteen southern provinces. Thailand's toll would be estimated at more than eight thousand dead and missing, but that counted only the most visceral losses. Several thousand more would lose homes and livelihoods, primarily migrant families from Malaysia, the southern tip of Myanmar, and the Lao-majority region of Isan in northeastern Thailand. Whether in Thailand legally or illegally, these were migrants employed in the tourist and fishing industries, living on low wages in low-lying fishing villages.

Mercy's work had always been concentrated in about thirty of Bangkok's worst slums, primarily in Klong Toey, the port area southeast of downtown. Its 2004 budget for just maintaining what it already managed was about $1 million, the majority donated by individuals, corporations, and governments in Europe and North America. It was barely enough for Mercy's programs in Klong Toey, much less the tsunami-wrecked areas of southern Thailand.

Crowley is responsible for managing Mercy's budget with the help of staff accountants and Mercy's primary business manager, Sister Maria Chantavarodom of Bangkok's Daughters of Queenship of Mary Immaculate. "Every month, I'm usually scared to death," Crowley would tell me later of Mercy's knack for budgeting from month to month. Then, speaking of Father Joe, he added, "He doesn't worry himself with the finances. He believes it's OK to hold out your bucket for donations during the day and, if at night there is enough left over after paying all the bills, you can go have a beer."

In the staff meeting on December 26, 2004, Father Joe walked tight circles and thought out loud. "We are a partnership with the poor," he said, reiterating Mercy's mission statement, repeating it several times as if trying to find an answer hidden in it. "*We* are a partnership with the poor. . . .We *are* a partnership. With *the poor.*"

Nowhere was it written that Mercy was exclusive to Klong Toey or even to Bangkok.

After an hour of walking and talking, Father Joe stopped abruptly. He sat, clapped his hands together, rubbing them like he was warming himself by a campfire, and then asked, "OK, what did we decide?"

"We agreed with you," Crowley answered.

"What did *I* decide?"

"Our mission says we are to help the poor. These people *are* the poor."

"Very well then!" Father Joe exclaimed.

And with that, Mercy expanded. In 2005, it would spend an extra $1 million, most of it coming in tsunami relief money given by Ireland's government, by an NGO called Trocaire, or "Compassion," the overseas emergency relief and development agency for the Catholic Church in Ireland and by corporations like U.S. tobacco giant Altria (formerly Philip Morris) and the United Bank of Switzerland. Mercy would repair roofs, water wells, fishing boats, sewer lines and buy school uniforms and lunches for hundreds of poor children in the southern provinces of Phuket, Phang Nga, and Satun. In villages where water wells and other infrastructure were destroyed, children had been drinking groundwater and complaining of kidney stones. So Mercy bought and delivered four thousand barrel-sized cement water jars, each large enough to collect four hundred gallons of rainwater from spouts rigged to roofs. In predominantly Muslim villages, Mercy asked the imams, village elders, and mosque counsels what they needed the most.

"The money pouring in from the [Thai] government and others was going toward repairing hotels, building new ones, all the touristy stuff," Father Joe said later. "No one went in on the ground and asked the people what is was that *they* wanted and needed."

The imams and mosque councils were unanimous in their reply. Public address systems, everyone said. So Mercy replaced fifty loudspeakers that delivered Islam's five daily calls to prayer.

"We're not always very good at planning," Father Joe said later, referring to Mercy's hand-to-mouth budget that keeps Crowley worried, "but we are very good at crisis management. We have stuttered and stumbled from one crisis to another until we have gotten quite good at it."

In D.C. to lobby corporate America for tsunami relief, Thakur Phanit, serving at the time as the deputy permanent secretary of the Ministry of Foreign Affairs, went first on the panel of four. He raced past details of a $10,000 child development program to get to his plea for $20 million to rebuild Phi Phi Don, a resort island near Phuket's famous nightlife of go-go bars and massage parlors. The money was needed for an electrical grid and a storm warning system. With a storm warning system, he explained, "we will all feel safer when you enjoy your vacation, enjoy the sun, the sea, and the Thai food. Or whatever that you like over there."

Father Joe had not looked up while Thakur spoke. He scribbled notes and played with a pencil, rolling it on the back of his hand, but when Thakur mentioned tourism, Father Joe stared at him.

The director of Thailand's international development, Piamsak Milintachinda, and the secretary to His Majesty the King, Kwankaew Vajarodaya, made similar pleas for money that would "encourage the return of U.S. tourists back to Thailand," as Piamsak said.

Then the microphone was passed to Father Joe, and he sat silently with it. He had no script, nothing more than what he had jotted while the others spoke. He looked down the length of the table at the Thai officials and drew a deep breath.

"With great, great respect to my Thai brothers and with apologies if I would say anything that might not be proper or fitting or might disagree with others here, but I think the reason we are all here is to try and do the best we can."

Earlier in the day, he'd prayed for the strength of restraint. He feared that his contrarian spirit might accidentally fire and maybe harm the fundraising effort. He paused once more and searched for Thakur's eyes. He waited until Thakur turned toward him.

"You know," Father Joe snapped, "I really think this whole idea of tourism is a pile of *crap!* The last thing we need is more tourism! We have this unbelievable chance in Thailand to now make tourism what it should be, as tourism is in Europe, as tourism is in other parts of the world. *Real* tourism. . . . We don't want a tourism where people come and *buy* our children. *Buy* our women. *Buy* our boys!"

His voice softened.

"That seems to be left out a bit. I really think if we talk about tourism, Mr. Ambassador, we must, must, *must* talk about *real* tourism and not cheap tourism. Not the tourism that doesn't cost very much economically. Because it doesn't cost much for the tourists, but it costs a tremendous amount for us and our children. So on tourism, we really have to think about that."

He paused to let this sink in.

"That is just an opinion," he said.

For the next twenty minutes, he looked out at corporate America but directed his words at the Thai panelists. He requested that the most urgent tsunami aid be directed toward the needs of villagers, not the profits of businesses and bureaucracies. He talked about the village children suffering kidney stones due to the lack of potable water and the remedy found in inexpensive four hundred–gallon jars. He talked about the need to ask community organizations and

village leaders what they needed rather than imposing bureaucratic will from afar. Mostly, though, he lobbied for the dictates
of reason—for leniency to be shown to undocumented workers
and squatters who'd become homeless and unemployed on the
same day.

"We've got all of these wonderful people who are the backbone
of Thai society, most of whom do not have proper documentation.
They don't have the proper papers. They don't have the proper birth
certificates. They do not have land titles. And they have been there
for sixty or seventy or eighty or ninety years, but they do not have
titles. They know a lot about fishing and about living, but they don't
know much about *titles*. . . . So we beg the Thai government—we
beg the Thai government—to deal with people who do not have
papers."

He apologized again "for anyone I've offended" and finished
with Shakespeare. "How will this all end? Like it always does. With
tears and a long journey."

He drew the session's only applause. Several people stood. The
moderator, William H. Itoh, a former U.S. ambassador to Thailand,
smiled and waited for the room to quiet.

"Well, that's why we invited Father Joe. I know from long experience, when I was living in Thailand and we used to have meetings with Father Joe, that I used to take about ten times as long to
say something as Father Joe did. . . . You could say he's pretty much
blunt and to the point."

⚜

Afterward, Father Joe, Tom Crowley, and I huddled as the
Scotch-Irish are wont to do, standing at an open bar. This one was
a bit high-class for modest tastes. We stood at a round glass table
beneath a one-acre skylight in the Reagan Building's atrium. It was

here that Father Joe granted me what I had come for—access to a life he calls barking mad and slums he deems holy.

He repeated his nonnegotiable condition: "Tell the truth," he demanded, "warts and all."

It is in that spirit, then, that I must recount what I saw next, though I'm not convinced of its crusty blemish. In that bar filled with newly formed orbits of small talk, a Catholic priest in full black clerical garb held a glass of Chardonnay in one hand and his middle finger aloft in the other. He said something to Crowley about "that asshole over there" and raised our universal gesture of contempt. He held it there for all to see.

The target, as best as Father Joe could recall when we rehashed that day much later, was a fundamentalist something or other who had refused to donate to poor children unless they were schooled exclusively in Christianity. To explain his disgust, Father Joe mimicked a Bible-thumping, holier-than-thou accent.

"*Yew* see, all children *mist* be taught *ooonly* to believe in *Jeeeezuz*. They *mist! Beeelieeeve!* In *Jeeeezuz!*"

He sighed. "Of course you can't say that though."

But I must.

TO PUT *the world right in order,*

we must first put the nation in order;

to put the nation in order,

we must first put the family in order;

to put the family in order,

we must first cultivate our personal life,

we must first set our hearts right.

—Confucius

Predawn walkers, joggers, and homeless in Bangkok's Lumpini Park

PART II
Manifest Change

Sunrise tai-chi class in Lumpini Park

SEVEN

Sticks, Stones, and Bags of Bones

*Sometimes they wait till everyone goes—
so they can die alone—cuz we won't let
them go and thus it makes the dying that
much more difficult.*

—Father Joe's daily journal, written after
Boi died alone in the middle of the night

I returned to Bangkok six weeks later, in July 2005, before Father Joe could change his mind. We met each weekday in the predawn of Lumpini Park, a tuft of sanctuary set like an island in the middle of Bangkok's surging traffic. Think Central Park but smaller, busier. Lumpini's 140 acres are cut with jogging trails that wind under the canopies of rain and bodhi trees, past elaborate Buddhist shrines draped in garlands, alongside artificial lakes and ponds, all within earshot of so much squalling, squealing, screeching fowl that a capital city of seven million registered residents (and almost as many unregistered) can seem muted.

Day and night, monitor lizards the size of small crocodiles stalk the park, hunting their next meal, and one morning, just as a lizard was ready to ingest breakfast, Father Joe couldn't help but to interject himself into park Darwinism. Picking up a small stick and striking the snoot of a four-foot-long reptile with a stick, he freed a frog, which hopped away excitedly but without so much as a glance backward.

Judging by the spring in their steps, the newly emancipated and the freedom fighter deemed the intercession righteous. For reasons no Catholic need explain, Father Joe believes the child-friendly amphibian to be infinitely more divine than the fork-tongued reptile.

"I can't stand those things," he said of the defeated lizard.

♲

During the five years I was away, the Mercy Centre had continued renovating, building, and expanding, completing $3 million of upgrades paid for by a devout Catholic from Georgia, John M. Cook, whose name was now emblazoned on the new two- and three-story cream-colored buildings crowding Mercy's half-block-long campus.

An international business executive and philanthropist, Cook had heard Father Joe speak in the spring of 1997 at the Holy Spirit Church, a parish in the leafy suburbs north of Atlanta. He'd left church that day as smitten with the plain-talking priest as the poor were in the Slaughterhouse. "If you're a Christian, be a good Christian. If you're a Buddhist, be a good Buddhist," Cook would tell me a decade after he'd heard Father Joe's ecumenical message, reciting almost verbatim the Mercy refrain of righteous conduct over pious devotion.

As founder and chief of an Atlanta-based auditing and profit-consulting firm with business in forty countries, Cook travels a great deal and frequently visits Asia. His schedule brought him to Bangkok a month after Father Joe had spoken at Holy Spirit during a brief tour of North America. To raise money for the poor, Father Joe had begun mingling with Western wealth, preaching, glad-handing, and basically collecting alms like a saffron-robed monk holding out a bowl for donations.

Cook, an easygoing, silver-haired grandfather of three, had told Father Joe to expect him in Klong Toey. But when Cook gave Mercy's address to the concierge at his usual Bangkok haunt, the world-famous Oriental Hotel, he was advised to stay away from that part of town.

You need to go where, sir?

Klong Toey, Cook said.

No sir, you don't want to go *there*, the concierge warned. It's as bad as anything you'll find in Calcutta.

The hotel's driver took Cook through some of the same winding roads and alleys that I would see in 2000. Arriving, Cook discovered what he later described to me as "just two shacks next to each other"—a children's hospice that accommodated dying adults when and if spare beds were available and a small preschool. Mercy's thirty or so other one-room schools were sprinkled throughout Klong

Toey's slums. In 1997, the main campus consisted of only two ram-shackle buildings set in the bowl of Klong Toey's floodplain. Small and worn, they were made of wood, tin, single-pane glass, and a bit of brick and mortar. They served modest goals. Walking through for the first time, Cook saw insect bite marks on several of the kids, scratchy red welts from "creepy, crawly things" that ride swells of water indoors when monsoon rains collect in low-lying plains.

That evening, over cheeseburgers and bowls of soup, Father Joe told Cook about his ambitions for Mercy, and as he elaborated about its potential and philosophy, he began to sell a fellow Catholic on the Buddhist concept of "making merit." Good karma, Father Joe explained, could spread globally and beyond their imaginations if First World currencies were exchanged into weaker currencies and invested in helping the Third World poor. Cook's money could sow positive change for generations to come. The idea gave literal mean-ing to Wall Street's definition of investing in futures.

Cook asked how much the projects would cost. Father Joe wasn't sure. Get the numbers and phone me, Cook said. Six weeks later, Father Joe gave him the estimates.

"I had given a good amount of money to Saint Louis Univer-sity," Cook said of his alma mater, home of the John Cook School of Business, "but now I was intrigued by what could be done with money internationally. By American standards, you can build a school overseas with twelve or fourteen classrooms without spend-ing an enormous amount."

In July 1997, a few months after their dinner meeting, the Thai baht collapsed, setting off the Asian financial crisis—further boost-ing the purchase power of the U.S. dollar in Thailand. Although Cook had founded two private charities in the United States, he was now a full convert of Father Joe's investment strategy. "If you earn your wealth around the world," Cook said, "I think it's unfair to give back only in the U.S."

By the time he began in 2000 pumping more than $3 million into Mercy's expansion, each dollar bought 40 baht. Thanks to Cook's backing, Mercy could complete its new and larger AIDS hospice where mothers and children could spend their dying days together (the nearly completed hospice I would visit in May 2000); add a preschool large enough for hundreds of students, a special-needs school for illiterate children too old for preschool, and another for delinquents and HIV-infected students deemed unfit for government schools; and also construct a gleaming new 120-bed orphanage. Most of it was built on the same squatter plot as the old Mercy campus, just a little higher and with better drainage. This thwarted the creepy-crawlies that surfed indoors.

"I really thought I'd go down there, buy the guy dinner, and that would be the end of it," Cook told me of that first meal with Father Joe. "But from Klong Toey the world looks different than from Rome or elsewhere in Europe."

Cook had attached one nonnegotiable condition to Mercy's expansion: Father Joe could no longer live in a lopsided shack downstream from a city sewage pump. Slum life racks the health. With no drainage system or wastewater treatment plant, the air breathed in and around the Slaughterhouse was a noxious potion: the effluvium from humans and the few remaining butcheries mixed with the diesel fumes emitted 24/7 by long-haul trucks. The racket from the slum's emerging night markets of yaba and prostitution didn't help. Father Joe wasn't getting much rest. He'd been sick a half dozen times the previous year with colds, flu, pneumonia, and such. Although he often slept at the Soi Forty orphanage, he still called his hovel in the Slaughterhouse home. Cook said that the director of an expanding, dynamic charity would need to remain on campus and in full stride. That meant living as healthfully and comfortably as orphan kids and runaways, safe from bed-bugs and the shantytown rats, which were notorious as much for their size as for their skill at sneaking past mosquito netting to lick salt from the hair of sleeping squatters.

In the summer of 2005, the first time I saw the new-millennium-styled Mercy, I did a double take. Anchored at one end was a three-story director's house with gated driveway and carport, air conditioning, dial-up Internet (wireless broadband today), full kitchen with laundry room attached, and just outside the upstairs foyer where a small statue of the Virgin Mary stood sentinel, a balcony overlooked a large Malaysian redwood deck. The deck stretched to a koi pond and Mercy's new four-hundred-seat preschool.

After three decades of living on a Slaughterhouse catwalk, Father Joe was living relatively large. For Klong Toey, it was upper-crust. Pangs of guilt over the newfound comfort supplanted his bouts with cold and flu, and he thought briefly about moving back to the Slaughterhouse. He'd maybe use his fancy new digs in the same way American presidents have employed the White House's Lincoln bedroom. "The ultimate executive retreat. . . . Bring in rich people to spend a week here in this house," he wrote in his journal during the summer of 2001.

On another page that same season, he wrote, "Mercy is now physical and existent and outside of my head."

⚜

When I returned, Nong Bla was still at Mercy, a member of its modern Thai dance team. She looked fairly healthy, helped along by her daily dose of two government-bought antiretroviral cocktails and Mercy's mandatory three square meals a day. Same with Nuth, who received antiretrovirals through Mercy and was healthy enough to move home to a slum shack, and Det Dheo, who had quit school and made himself over with several tattoos of dragons and snakes. To ward off the bad luck, Father Joe explained, and I wondered how much worse his luck could get. His drug-addled dad had died from a punctured lung, his mother had died with AIDS and a heroin habit in jail, and he was born infected with the Virus. He still lived just a rung or two up from the mud his grandmother had found him face-down asleep in as a baby. But he was scrappy. Det Dheo graciously accepted his antiretroviral medicines and took life day by day. Before he quit school, some of the healthy kids had made fun of him for being one of *those* kids who had to take medicine every day. He pointed and laughed back, telling them they were just jealous that they weren't special like him.

What would've cost Mercy 40,000 baht ($1,000) per child per month several years earlier—in effect bankrupting it in the B.C. era ("Before Cook," Father Joe jokes)—was now given free by the government. (In 2007, the Thai government would ignore objections from the World Trade Organization and manufacturer patents to produce generic copies of Kaletra and Efavirenz, two powerful HIV/AIDS antiretrovirals.)

A charity that had bribed, connived, and constructed itself illegally, often building or renovating on squatter land in the cover of night or behind curtains of tarp, had moved comfortably onto the government dole. School milk was supplied to Mercy's preschools free of charge by the Thai Ministry of Education, and antiretrovirals came compliments of the Ministry of Public Health.

It helped that in 2004, on the seventy-second birthday of Her Majesty Queen Sirikit of Thailand, Father Joe was recognized by the monarchy as a national hero. Her Majesty had presented him with the award for "foreigner who has contributed the most over the long term to the protection of women and children." During the ceremony, Her Majesty had broken from tradition and descended the stage. She walked smiling to Father Joe, grasped his hand, and whispered, "I thank you for the women and children. I thank you for His Royal Majesty the king. And *I* thank you."

In the kingdom of the world's longest-reigning and most revered monarch, there is no higher honor. Mercy may have been illegal, but it was no longer illegitimate.

⚜

As good as this all sounded, however, the news wasn't all good.

Boi had died alone at Mercy between one and two o'clock in the morning on April 24, 2001, six days after her twelfth birthday. Her heart was enlarged, and tuberculosis raged inside her, just as it had her mother.

Toward the inevitable end, when she was vomiting scraps of food and blood every day, Father Joe knelt at her side for hours at a time and combed two fingers through the fuzzy soft spot on her forehead, the silkiest smooth part at the front that the Thai call *boi*.

"We dressed her in a new pair of red tennis shoes so she wouldn't be embarrassed when she went to heaven. We didn't have any children's caskets; we had only the big adult-sized donated casket, made of pressed sawdust. But that was OK. We put her in a big casket, and that way she would have a bigger room in heaven. That's what we told the kids," Father Joe said in a voice that cracked. We were in a Lumpini sunrise, and I could see his eyes begin to water. If he hadn't changed the subject, I would have.

"Look over there," he said, pointing. "Isn't that neat?"

It was a large class doing tai-chi, spread out on several acres of grass, much like several other tai-chi classes we had passed that very morning.

⚜

Viewing the world from another's perspective can make your own appear decidedly less definitive. In returning to Mercy, I had hoped Father Joe and his slum utopia might grant some clarity to my post-9/11 America and to our shared new millennium. One week after Muslim terrorists had flown jets and travelers into the towers of the World Trade Center, the Pentagon, and a rural Pennsylvania field, six hundred people braved a lightning storm to pack into Bangkok's Holy Redeemer Church to hear Father Joe warn against fear and the hatred begotten by hatred. In his sermon that night, he drew from Martin Luther King Jr., Abraham Lincoln, John F. Kennedy, and Psalm 23 ("He guides me in paths of righteousness. . . . Though I walk through the valley of the shadow of death, I will fear no evil"). He ended with the universal wisdom of the Jedi master Yoda, who tells Luke Skywalker in *Star Wars,* "Fear is the path to the dark side. Fear leads to anger, and anger leads to hatred, and hatred leads to suffering."

Considering the events since 9/11, I found the sermon profound. The next morning, the *Bangkok Post* reported that the city's first memorial service for 9/11 had filled the Holy Redeemer Church from its pews to its portico with parishioners of various nationalities holding hands and praying. In his sermon, the *Post* said, Father Joe Maier had criticized the news media for describing the World Trade Center and the Pentagon as the symbols of the United States. "American symbols are our *homes,* our *schools,* our *churches,* and no one can ever destroy those," he'd said.

⚜

I would return to the Mercy Centre three times between 2005 and 2007, traveling twelve time zones from Washington, D.C., to hang out with this Catholic who hangs out amicably with Buddhists, Muslims, and Jews—and now with me, a native Southern Baptist.

But as the go-to guy for an expanding empire of schools, hospices, orphanages, safe houses, and such, Father Joe had no time to spare. Others had dibs, usually children or matters that involved them. So he manufactured an artificial block of free time. We agreed to begin each weekday by meeting at six in the morning at Lumpini Park, unless his schedule was extraordinarily hectic. In that case, we'd meet an hour earlier.

Five o'clock became our standard starting time.

Named for the Himalayan foothill region where the Buddha, Siddhārtha Gautama, was born in the sixth century B.C., Lumpini's 140 acres are lush with mature trees—pine, palm, jackfruit, and the sacred bodhi, under which the Buddha is said to have received enlightenment.

Bangkok's largest park is wildly popular on weekday mornings with the city's ethnic Chinese, and at sunrise, long lines of high-end sedans creep through the entrance and triple-park as if at a college football tailgate party. And like ownership of a Mercedes or a BMW for Lumpini's morning faithful, park exercise is apparently mandatory: walking, jogging, weightlifting, aerobics, badminton, tai-chi, and ballroom dancing—outdoors. All of it commences at dawn. I've seen families carry party tents and color TVs onto a park lawn to watch Chinese operas, alfresco, with their morning tea. On a weekday.

The ensuing chatter crackles, and a park that was midnight-quiet one hour earlier fills with static. "Ohhh, I'm usually gone by now," Father Joe sighed one morning. It was half past six.

Twenty yards in front of us was an aerobics class of a hundred or so people in shorts and sweats jumping, stretching, running in place, and twirling to the pounding, throbbing dance music of the American '80s.

"It's really a very pleasant place," Father Joe said in defense of his favorite park. "Early. Early it's very nice."

It's in the quiet of Lumpini that Father Joe maintains his sanity.

An hour or so before the sedans trail through the gate at Rama IV Road, Father Joe finds a dark corner. Street prostitutes are receding from the night and street vendors are emerging when a white guy in white Nikes, dark blue tennis shorts, a golf shirt, and a white floppy hat stops inside the main entrance. Father Joe stands with his hands in front of him, closes his eyes, and inhales the morning air. In his hands he holds an imaginary bag, the size of a laundry duffel. He opens it and exhales like he's blowing out birthday candles.

Out flows the grief that travels fist in glove with memories of Boi and the smiling children in fading old Polaroids. Inhale, exhale, and out flows angst attached like barnacles to the care and concern of Nong Bla, Nuth, and any small children sleeping on floors beneath portraits of their dead mothers. Again, inhale-exhale, trying to purge the fear and angst that accumulates when you build a sprawling charity in the open and against the rules. Despite Her Majesty's blessing, Mercy's land is still owned by the Port Authority of Thailand. Like the poor they serve, Mercy and Father Joe are, in effect, squatters. Schools, orphanages, safe house, and hospices could be shut by bureaucratic whim or a military coup.

Three or four more times he inhales and exhales, ridding himself of the concern that builds so fast there's never enough time to explain it all.

"How are you, Father Joe?" someone in the park might ask.

Invariably, he tries to keep walking but responds, "Ah, busy, very busy. Lots of stuff, you know. Et cetera, et cetera."

He places all of the et cetera, et cetera into that imaginary burlap duffel. Inhales, exhales one last time, and slowly the wounds that burn like ulcers burn a little less. He pretends to tie the bag closed and drops it in the shadows, not far from Rama IV Road.

He jogs away.

⚜

Anyone who witnesses this pantomime might think the American with knobby knees and calves of cordwood is just another tourist. Or as a writer in the *Bangkok Post* once jokingly remarked in reference to Father Joe's Lumpini Park routine, "The Loony of Lumpini." They'd not see that the nutcase is really just a Klong Toey Catholic practicing the lessons of old mystics from all of the teachings, Buddhism, Catholicism, et cetera, et cetera.

"Twelve times a minute you breathe in and you are filled with God," Father Joe explained.

He drew a breath, swept his arms upward.

"Twelve times a minute you breathe out and you expel all the bad stuff."

His arms came down slowly.

"Breathe in and you are born. Breathe out and you die. Twelve times each minute we are born and we die."

The idea is that we are cleansed, forgiven, and recycled in every breath of every moment of every hour of every day. Consciousness is motion, the perpetual sifting of choices and perspectives that perpetuate and balance yin and yang. We're vessels of energy and its filters, too. That's the belief, anyhow.

"You pass energy on in every word and every thought and every action," Father Joe told me one morning, just as a deafening squawk from a large raven-looking black shag sitting five or six feet overhead screamed its Maori given name: kawau (*kaa-WOW!*).

I jumped, startled. Father Joe was unfazed.

"This whole thing of life is not ours, not ours to *keep*," he continued. "You pass it on; you're giving it away—constantly, always, whether you're conscious of it or not."

Until the ninth or tenth century, some monastic mystics believed that if your worries and angst were chronically backed up, all you needed to do was empty your bowels. Literally, go to the john and rid yourself of the polluted energy.

This reminded Father Joe of a favorite quote from *Monty Python and the Holy Grail,* and as he recalled it, I could see Lumpini's medicinal effect on him. The line is from a scene in which the French guard taunts King Arthur from outside a Scottish castle: "I don't want to talk to you no more, you empty-headed animal-food trough-wiper. I fart in your general direction! Your mother was a hamster, and your father smelt of elderberries!"

Father Joe repeated the line—"I *fart* in your general direction." He laughed so hard, his body bent and convulsed, propelling him in a semicircle of tiny stutter hops.

And like worries and angst and foul moods, his laughter was contagious.

Jogging in Lumpini's predawn, you eventually grow accustomed to the black shag's first squawks. You relax into the rhythmic slap-slap-slap of sneakers on pavement. Feeling jettisoned of Mercy's burdens, Father Joe moves gracefully on the balls of his feet, an athletic gait for a man in his sixties.

Twelve breaths per minute become fourteen, then sixteen; the pulse, the sweat, the endorphins begin to crest. The breathing is relaxed, the stride stretches comfortably, and eventually the shag's cry of *kaa-WOW!* sounds muffled. After about a mile and a half, a sense of peace washes over Father Joe, and the boil of worry is noticeably lanced. After four, five, maybe six miles, he's drenched, sweaty from the floppy hat to the knobby knees. Slowing to a walk, he often stops to smell the flowers, drawn by the come-hither scent of the night-flowering jasmine. Its popcorn-colored buds bloom in Lumpini and in the *feng shui* of Mercy's new courtyard.

"Smell this. These are just *lovely.*"

He stopped and pinched a stem. Pulling it close, he inhaled the jasmine's sweetness as though it were a balm.

He waved me over. I gave a half whiff.

"No, really, you need to get close."

I leaned in.

"Closer. Now smell. Really smell it. . . . Ahh, isn't that lovely?"

Lovely. I hadn't heard him use that word. But in that park and in that moment, it fit him. Leaving the park that day, he had the spring in his step of a frog just freed, and as we neared the exit, he breezed past the shaded corner near Rama IV Road.

"Aren't you forgetting something?" I said.

He stopped like he wasn't sure what I meant. I nodded toward the spot where he'd dropped his imaginary duffel bag.

"Oh, *Lord, no.* I don't pick it up. I go out a different way."

Mercy preschoolers arriving for classes on the new campus

EIGHT

Dead End or Turnaround?

We are what we think.

—Father Joe's daily journal

Father Joe typically arrived for our interviews at Lumpini around four o'clock in the morning. That way he could unload his bag of worries and jog alone before I intruded.

I always arrived at a quarter to five, fifteen minutes early, just to impress. (I'm not sure he ever knew.) Sitting and waiting on a park bench wearing blue jeans or khakis with a collared button-down shirt and a work satchel strapped across one shoulder, I must've looked oddly out of place. Predawn joggers would eye me curiously, and I'd immediately scribble drivel in my wallet-sized notebook, as if that somehow explained who I was and what I was doing in the park at that ungodly hour, dressed for work rather than exercise. At the precise appointed time, Father Joe would emerge from a park lamp's yellowish glare, and he'd look at me oddly, too, his face slightly strained, unable to force a smile. He looked like a man arriving for a dentist's appointment.

Following our perfunctory "good morning" and "howdy-do," I'd stick an iPod-thin recorder into his sweaty front pocket. He'd wince, as if it were intravenous, then grit his teeth and soldier on. A devout introvert, Father Joe is great with kids and a charismatic speaker and fundraiser when needed or called upon, but he avoids the topic that pains him most: his own life. In a collection of two dozen of his *Bangkok Post* columns that were published later that year by Asia's Periplus Books, readers hear only about the poor of Klong Toey. Beyond the foreword, nothing much about the priest is told.

I'd been warned that he would initially dodge my questions into anything personal.

"Be patient," Tom Crowley advised me the first afternoon after I arrived back in Bangkok, a rainy Sunday, July 3, 2005. "It will take a few days for him to warm up."

In the first minute of our first Lumpini Park walk, Father Joe welcomed me with this: "You know the reason I come here, other than it's outdoors? No one knows me here. Out here, I'm just a fat old bald guy. Nobody bothers me here."

I knew he was referring to me, already regretting the access he'd granted.

Ten minutes later, two middle-aged Asian men approached him like a long-lost favorite uncle. Father Joe responded in kind. They asked how he was and how often he came to the park. Did he walk here or did he drive? How far had he run? How were his Mercy kids? They spoke in Thai, and Father Joe translated into English for me. As they walked away, he said matter-of-factly, "I don't know them. . . . I don't have the slightest clue."

Each morning, we'd walk for an hour or two and then drive to Mercy for mugs of squatter's blend (coffee beans ground with rice, cinnamon, and acerbic unknowns that can stretch one pound into two). Lumpini is only two or three miles from Mercy, but in the weekday traffic, we'd crawl, sometimes taking thirty minutes to travel a distance that could probably be traversed more quickly on foot.

During my five years away, Klong Toey hadn't changed much. Roofs were still rusty and corrugated, roads rutted and congested, and a 20-baht fare straddled to the back of a motorbike was the best way to cut through the gridlock—a risky veer through four lanes of traffic, a brush past long columns of pockmarked low-rises, then braking, appropriately enough, at a dead end.

That's where Mercy with all its expansions and renovations was anchored. A gleaming new orphanage; three-story preschool; three-story director's house; computer, art, and music labs; and a large, windswept hospice opening to a courtyard shaded by palm trees and scented with the night-flowering jasmine, the same come-hither scent that had pulled Father Joe off the beaten path in the park.

At a dead end.

"Pretty neat, huh?" Father Joe said. "At a turnaround."

Looks like a dead end to me.

"Can you turn around?"

Sure.

"Then it's a turnaround."

⚜

There was a buoyancy to him some days that defined Mercy and befuddled me.

With John Cook's backing, Mercy's preschools had expanded their reach, and a few had been rebuilt or renovated. Several had morphed into full-fledged schoolhouses, made of cinderblocks, mortar, and single-paned glass. On a wall in Mercy's new community room was a multicolored poster board with photos of nearly three dozen schools taped up in a zigzag pattern across a map of Klong Toey, like colorful pins marking the fifty-five Starbucks franchises in D.C. Printed beneath the snapshots was Mercy's slogan spelled out in red, its blood oath: "A partnership with the poor."

But the environment around many of the schools was no better than before. In some cases, it was worse. Two years earlier, a Mercy preschool in the Slaughterhouse slum of Rong Khoi was scorched when debt collectors burned three drug houses surrounding it. Five- and six-year-old students had been inhaling secondhand methamphetamine smoke for days, vomiting occasionally, so in a way, the bonfire was a blessing. But Father Joe was furious that the ecogangsterism that had exploded during the Asian financial crisis now dared to encroach on a Mercy school. The next day, he wore his white Catholic robes—battle regalia, he called them—to a community meeting held near the remains of the drug houses and charred, drenched shanty school. More than one hundred families were present.

"Enough!" he shouted. "This kind of *shit* will not be tolerated! This is war!"

Slum families could enlist themselves or not, he said, spitting an ultimatum, but anything less than a full resolve to safeguard the teacher and children would cost the slum its school. If the drug dealers were allowed to move back in to rebuild and reopen their drug dens, Mercy would pack up desks, chairs, and textbooks and move its school to a different slum.

The families present immediately drafted a manifesto declaring the area around the school drug-free and warning the residents of the burned homes never to rebuild there. It was a gutsy move for a slum where ecogangsterism had become law. But of the 114 homesteaders present, 103 signed. Illiterate parents scrawled illegible signatures or dipped fingers in ink and pressed them to paper. A village leader pricked a finger and put his blood to the declaration. In 2005, the three lots were still vacant and no one was selling drugs next to the school, Father Joe said. Cement had been poured over the lots and a chain-link fence erected. It was an open space used for community weddings, celebrations, and preschool graduations.

"The most important thing about that story is the message that the community sent," he said. "By dealing drugs and smoking drugs right next to our school, the bad guys had told the kids that this education stuff isn't worth it. School is *not* important. *That* was the message. They disrespected us and they disrespected the school and they disrespected sacred Klong Toey. But it backfired. The grownups stood up to the bad guys in a way they'd never done before, all because of the school. . . . *That's* a powerful message."

Mercy's newly expanded hospice for mothers and children with HIV/AIDS was a grand addition, completed the summer after I'd left in 2000. Her Royal Highness Princess Galyani Vadhana, the elder sister of His Majesty the King, presided over its ribbon cutting. But the new beds had filled up almost immediately, no differently than after the opening of the original hospice in 1994. Taxis dropped adults and children off and then left. One man died en route to his bed, others the same day they checked in or the day after. And Boi's passing had left Father Joe feeling guilty because he wasn't there when he felt he should've been. He'd told her he was going out to a dinner fundraiser, but he'd be back to check on her that night. It was late when he came home, so he figured he'd check on her first thing in the morning.

She'd died without him. The look on his face when he told me this suggested he had not forgiven himself. He was sobbing when he phoned his younger sister, Kathy, a palliative care nurse in Oregon. "She told me, 'You arrogant S.O.B. She didn't *want* you there. You wouldn't let go; you didn't want to let her go.' And she was absolutely right, of course. My ego thought I could control it. 'How dare you die without me there.' She didn't want me there because I wasn't ready to let go."

Meanwhile, yaba and prostitution had remained staples of the black market despite draconian arrests, prosecutions, and alleged police-enforced curbside executions of addicts and dealers. The guilty or the suspicious (a few of them probably innocent) bled to death on slum sidewalks—Father Joe counted at least six from the Slaughterhouse. The police crackdown had succeeded in diminishing the supply but not the demand. So with yaba's heightened risk, the price shot up sevenfold, from 40 baht to nearly 300 hundred baht per pill. For Klong Toey, this meant that drug-addicted prostitutes—a younger crop of them now, Father Joe said—had to hustle more deals inside and between long-haul rigs parked less than ten feet apart, twenty or so to a lot. Also, the notorious Bang-Kwang prison was more infamous than ever. With new arrivals from the government's drug war, it was now housing twenty-five inmates to a cell. Dealers guilty of selling yaba were sentenced to life in Bang-Kwang or, perhaps more mercifully, death by lethal injection.

Yet Father Joe behaved as though he were encouraged. He drank squatter's blend every morning and declared the day glorious. I wanted to shake him and shout, *The sky is falling! The sky is falling!*

On July 7, 2005, he looked at the brilliant orange sunrise over Lumpini and dared to say, "Ah, this is great." It was the first day-break in Bangkok after Muslim terrorists had indiscriminately killed fifty-two commuters in London. But Father Joe stretched his arms overhead, opened his hands toward the heavens.

"We're *winning*," he said, even as London sorted its dead.

By "we" he meant Mercy and Thailand and America and Iraq and Israel and Britain and Pakistan and all the others. He meant good versus evil. He'd just finished a spirited four-mile jog. I suspected he was delirious from the rush of endorphins, and I told him so.

I reminded him of 9/11 and of the ongoing stream of civilian and military deaths in Iraq. My country—his country, too, though it seemed an odd thing to say—had led a large-scale preemptive military strike that counted civilians as "collateral damage."

"Shock and Awe," I said, referring to the arcade-sounding name the Pentagon and talking heads had given the U.S. invasion of Iraq, a war that as we spoke was grinding on and on at the cost of civilian and military lives and hundreds of billions of taxpayer dollars, roughly $200 million per day.

And despite all of the bombing, shooting, killing (or maybe because of it), our shared planet had grown more prosperous than ever while the economic divide had only grown wider. One hundred million of the world's poorest children at that time still didn't have access to formal primary education. These children are the seeds for our future, I told him, as if he didn't know.

And you think we're *winning*?

"Yes, yes, we goof up a lot," he said, agreeing just to appease me and shut me up, I thought. "We goof off. We goof up. We all have those tendencies, don't we? We get lazy with this stuff. We lose focus."

But we are redeemable, he added. "To quote somebody, 'Many people who have run away in battle have come back to be flag bearers.'"

Sounded like wishful thinking to me, though I didn't say that. I'd said enough.

"If your idea of God is that he is totally *out there*," he said, motioning toward the palm shade and grassy lawns of Lumpini, "then you will probably be fine and lead a pretty cool life, . . ."

In front of us were several manicured acres filled with a hundred or so early risers spread several yards apart in a tai-chi class. They stretched and flexed and took deep breaths, emitting loud grunts and groans. About twelve breaths per minute.

". . . but if your idea of God is that you are totally filled with God in *every* thought and *every* breath and *every* heartbeat and that you are reborn in every breath, twelve times each minute, then you are with God all the time," Father Joe said. "He is in you, and He is wrapped up in everything you do. He *is* you. God is energy. God *is* life."

And when He's not?

The four suicide bombers in London had chosen the busiest traffic of the workday to effect as much carnage as possible. As Father Joe and I spoke, we didn't yet know the extent of the damage. We hadn't seen the day's headlines, only breaking news on TV.

"We know not what we do. We forget, don't we?" he said. "We forget Him."

Or we reject Him?

"Yes, and that's scary. These terrorist guys are breaking all the rules. They are breaking the Muslim rules, the Christian rules, the Buddhist rules, the sheiks' rules, the abbots' rules, all of the rules. But you have to say that Jesus died on the cross to forgive their sins too."

I stopped walking.

"You can't say He died only for fifty or sixty or seventy percent of the population. You can't say He died for this one and not for that one. Like rain and sunshine, it's for everybody, not just *some* people."

For Catholic, Muslim, Protestant, Buddhist, Jew, . . . agnostic?

"Jesus said that anyone who is doing good stuff is on our side. *Anyone.* He is our example. The way to the Father is through the Son? He's saying to follow His example, follow His ways. Do good stuff."

And the terrorists?

We began walking again.

"Well, they decided to walk a different way."

✤

We were greeted at his house that day with 9/11-sized headlines. The *Bangkok Post* stretched two words across its front page: "London Bombed." Bangkok's competing English-language daily, *The Nation,* looked similar: "Terror Strikes London."

We retrieved the papers from the carport and proceeded inside, as though the outside world remained outside. Everything was as usual. We opened the blinds, turned on the lights, brewed coffee, and scared up a plate of fruit or chips or cereal or whatever was around. One morning, our shared breakfast had consisted of a bulky family-sized bag of Cheez Mania Cheez Balls. We sat in comfortable silence reading the news, trading sections back and forth.

The reports on July 7 supported my skepticism, I insisted. I understood how we could be vessels for God and how the Holy

Spirit often stirred the devout from the inside out. A Southern Baptist perspective of heaven and hell, God and Satan had been drilled
into me nearly every Sunday of my childhood, dragged as I was to
Sunday school and church in a kid's suit and clasp-on tie. But I'd
also been at work within a bird's-eye view of the Pentagon the day
America was attacked; was dispatched to Ground Zero, where I
watched a charred corner of Manhattan smolder; wept as I walked
two blocked-off miles down West Street into the face of billowing
smoke. I'd attended a church service with the last victim pulled
alive from World Trade Center and interviewed wives of firefight-
ers who never emerged.

Father Joe sipped his coffee silently, listening, never interrupting.

Less than two years later, I continued, I was treated graciously
on the streets of Baghdad one month before our nation—*his* and
mine—invaded and occupied a sovereign nation. I had sipped
sweet hot tea with Sunnis and Shiites in their simple homes, but if
they were still alive, I doubted they would welcome me back. Even
in his own backyard, I told him, I'd witnessed the wretched poverty
that's allowed to fester in the widening gaps of our economic divide.
And I'd seen some of the consequences. In about the time it took a
college freshman to graduate, the Mercy hospice could nearly
empty and refill.

His face revealed no opinion; he nodded like he understood,
and of course he did.

So what on earth makes you think goodness is *winning?* I asked
as politely as possible.

My filibuster and question had been blurted entirely from the
heart, not from some Protestant-knows-all perspective. I knew he
knew far more than I, and I wanted to know too. This was exactly
the sage-atop-the-mountaintop sort of thing I'd returned to
explore. It was this energy and optimism of Mercy's that I'd felt
years earlier but had been unable to interpret or explain. I'm a

believer and live among the faithful, but it seemed to me that society overall was *way* out of sync with God's intentions.

That's what I told him as London struggled for its bearings and we sat there with plates of sweet papaya and a pot of slum blend. I had thoroughly ignored the universal unspoken rule of morning newspaper time. Silence; we were supposed to read silently. I knew I was breaking the rule, and still I couldn't help myself.

He put the *Bangkok Post* down, abandoning any hope of reading it. "No, not out of sync. In sync," he said quietly. "Most of society most of the time is *in* sync."

The night before, while coverage of the bombings played live on CNN and the BBC (London was six hours ahead of Bangkok), Father Joe gathered students and staff from the Mercy grounds to watch it. Some of the students were teenagers from the Mercy Travel Team, the Soi Forty teenagers who'd endured unspoken abuses and risen from the squatter slums to find Mercy and, now, scholarships abroad.

"They needed to see the news; they want to understand this stuff. They are worldly now. *Worldly*," he said. "Poor kids from the Klong Toey slums have entered this parallel universe that they used to see only on TV. Kids from the Slaughterhouse."

He shook his head and laughed. He waited for me to grasp the significance of such a change.

"Do you see? *This* is what it's all about. You win your wars a little bit at a time."

You lose them the same way, I said. And it's not just the terrorists who lose focus and break all of society's rules. We all forget in ways large and small. The Golden Rule had been shredded like confetti.

"Yes, I know, I know," he said. "Why is that one so hard?"

It had been five years since we'd discussed the simplicity of treating others as you'd like to be treated. The first time was when I stood in the echo of Soi Forty's two-thousand-square-foot bedroom.

Things had not improved much in the world since then. More than one billion people—about one-fifth of the world's population—were surviving on the equivalent of one U.S. dollar per day or less while the world's wealthiest 10 percent accounted for more than half the world's income.

That fall, the 2005 United Nations' *Human Development Report* would put our economic divide in terms that I, a slave to Starbucks' Caramel Macchiato, could easily grasp: "One-fifth of humanity live in countries where many people think nothing of spending $2 a day on a cappuccino. Another fifth of humanity survive on less than $1 a day and live in countries where children die for want of a simple anti-mosquito bed net."

When I first read that, I thought the UN sounded alarmist. At the time, each of my dollars in Thailand converted to 40 baht, and meals could be purchased curbside for half that amount. A plate of chicken and rice sold for 20 baht, if you dared purchase it from vendors beneath streetlamps. A slim fold of U.S. twenties wrapped around the American Express card in my money clip felt like a fortune.

But two pages later, the UN crunched the data in real terms. If rich nations didn't own up to their pledges of financial help to the developing world, the "human cost gap" of the unmet goals was projected to equal death on a scale greater than three Holocausts. By 2015, the UN warned, forty-one million children under the age of five, primarily from sub-Saharan Africa and South Asia, could die from things preventable or treatable: pneumonia, diarrhea, measles, malaria, tuberculosis, and lack of access to clean water and sanitation. The gap between the current pace of change and the world's broken promises could equal 4.4 million additional deaths of kids under age five in 2015 alone.

Killed by "the most readily curable of all diseases—poverty," the report declared on page 5 of the 353-page report.

In my profession, we'd say the UN buried its lead.

The report's biggest understatement was on the same page: "This is an outcome that is difficult to square with the Millennium Declaration's pledge to protect the world's children."

The Golden Rule, I said to Father Joe, shrugging and shaking my head. We preach it, we hear it, we understand it, we accept it, but then we don't live it. I wasn't recusing myself. With 10 percent of my family's gross divided between Sunday offering plates, NGOs, and charities, I could sip the caramel foam off my $3.65 venti-sized espresso without a trace of guilt. One-tenth, and I could sleepwalk and still feel damn good about myself.

"We know not what we do," Father Joe repeated softly. "We forget. Every day. You, me, *we* do it too. . . . We all struggle with this."

I was surprised he included himself, but he was saddled with guilt for living in a house with state-of-the-art appliances, Internet, cable TV, and a glorious bed that didn't bite. Judge not lest ye be judged. That's about our opinion of ourselves. All his life, he'd held the sissy comforts of others in disdain; now he found himself in his own crosshairs.

"Oh, yes," he agreed, looking toward the rattan blinds, raised halfway to allow the sun to stream in from off the Malaysian redwood deck. "This love of comfort is the love of self. Same as the love of money. Love of *things*. It's nice, *very* nice. . . . Ahhhhh."

He leaned back with his hands behind his head, mocking the lifestyle. In such comfort, it's easy to sleep.

"It's about selfishness and greed, isn't it?" he asked. The satisfaction we get from material things is supposed to fill the void. That's the gospel today. Consumerism. Materialism. These are our idols. We're told that these *things* will bring you happiness. It's everywhere in the West, but it's here now too. Klong Toey kids see this and they want *things* too."

Sounding determined to squeeze some optimism from its '05 findings, the UN advisory and consulting team of world-class economists, statisticians, and analysts—so many names they filled two pages—described the upcoming UN World Summit in New York City as "an opportunity to chart a new course for the next decade."

Of the world's twenty-two richest countries in 2005, three of the elite Group of Eight (G-8: United States, Canada, France, Germany, Italy, Japan, Russia, and the United Kingdom) were giving the smallest percentage of their gross national income to poor countries. They were Japan, Italy (the capital of Catholicism); and the largest Christian nation, where all currency bears the words "In God We Trust." The UN report scolded, "While rich countries publicly acknowledge the importance of aid, their actions so far have not matched their words."

None of this would garner serious media attention at the World Summit in September 2005. Two weeks earlier, Hurricane Katrina had exposed America's dirty laundry.

Father Joe nodded, yes, yes. "We forget. We wipe out the lessons. Or as the storybooks say, 'Their mommies really didn't love them very much. Now they've gone to the dark side.'"

How, then, can we say *goodness* is winning?

He thought for a moment and told me to turn off my recorder. "Save your batteries."

I read the sports section quietly. Lance Armstrong was leading the Tour de France (again), and if not for the day's front page, it seemed like a typical July morning. The morning of September 11, 2001, had felt the same sort of way: a normal, pleasant football-season day.

Father Joe contemplated the question quietly and poured more coffee. Outside, the children of Mercy were awake, and the courtyard had filled with the light pitch of tiny voices. At eight o'clock, public address speakers played the Thai national anthem, a daily ritual that brings all conversation to a halt. I sipped Klong Toey blend, read the paper quietly, . . . and waited.

Father Joe crossed his arms, closed his eyes, leaned his head back, resting it on the cushions of his brown leather couch. Minutes passed, and I worried he'd fallen asleep.

Finally, he stirred, opened his eyes, and locked his hands behind his head. "It's difficult to explain . . . ," he began.

I put the paper down, punched the recorder.

"Christ says, 'I am here; you are my brothers and you are my sisters; you are my family, and I fill you *totally* with my spirit. I am totally *with* you.' And He is. He's in every breath. And He's not a capricious God—which is most important. He's not a God who changes his mind on Fridays or Mondays or every other Tuesday."

He thought about that for several seconds; then he seemed to read my mind. He sat up and leaned forward, staring toward me but through me, like he might be contemplating all of this for the first time.

"But then, of course, I understand what you're saying. It seems like a contradiction, doesn't it? If we are *totally* filled with God, why then do we act so . . . selfishly?"

He took a sip of coffee. A bite of papaya. I waited.

"We are really just fighting against *ourselves,* aren't we?"

Ego versus the Spirit. Life's duality.

And maybe we *aren't* winning? I suggested, feeling certain I had won the point.

"No," he countered gently, sitting back again. "We're just having a bad week."

An HIV-infected child eats a dinner of chicken and rice alone, apparently
the only HIV/AIDS child at Mercy with an appetite that night.

NINE

The Sanctity
and Sanctimony
of Life

*AIDS kids and really all small kids have no
self-pity—they have to be taught this
terrible quality.*

—Father Joe's daily journal, quoting
Mercy senior adviser John Padorr

One week after Muslim terrorists bombed London, members of a Red Cross chapter in the world's most populous Islamic nation, Indonesia, visited the Mercy Centre, taking a tour of its AIDS program and meeting the sick, dying, orphaned, abandoned, abused, neglected, or otherwise broken of Klong Toey.

The dozen or so Indonesians mingled pleasantly with the children; they smiled, scribbled notes, and spoke to one another in a language that sounded like gibberish to the kids, who smiled in return, bowed the *wai,* and spoke to one another in a language that sounded like gibberish to the Indonesians. It was all Greek to me.

Later, Father Joe asked the children, "Do you think God speaks Indonesian?"

Yes, of course, they replied.

"Filipino?"

Yes.

"English?"

Of course.

"Thai?"

They giggled and looked at him like he had gone mad. Of course, of course, you silly old man.

Father Joe laughed until he was bent over and hopping in tiny stutter steps.

"See, *see?*" he asked me, straightening to raise his voice above the children's cackles, which had amplified on the back of his. "Children know. They get it. God is not something *out there.* God is not something to be owned. Not by one group or one religion or one nation. Not mine, not yours, not theirs. God speaks all languages."

We were in Mercy's main breezeway, but there were no breezes, and the temperature had raced beyond 90 degrees Fahrenheit, rounded the turn, and made a mad dash toward the triple digits. Father Joe wiped his brow with the back of his hand, slung sweat to one side, then rested his forearms on that Buddha belly. Just like the first day we'd met in the hospice five years earlier. Standing there, he looked exactly the same. Cuffed slacks and a sweat-splotched cotton shirt hanging loose, loafers worn sockless with the leather backs smashed flat from being slipped on-off, on-off, always in a rush in a culture that rarely wears shoes indoors.

"God speaks *all* languages," he repeated, this time with Southern Baptist certainty. There was a shine to his eyes, a gloss, I suspect, polished by the children's laughter. He floated in that lightness for several quiet seconds and then punctuated the point for me: "God. Is. Everywhere."

I nodded enthusiastically, affirming, yes, yes, yes, I understand, but he stared at me like I still didn't. "Ask your children," he said, sighing but smiling. "They'll explain it."

⚜

From its inception in 1973, the Human Development Foundation and Mercy Centre functioned like a new religious order, swimming in such a blend of Buddhism, Catholicism, and Islam that no one dared color it the sunny yellow of the Vatican flag. Buddhist, Muslim, Catholic, Protestant, Jewish, something else, anything else—it didn't much matter to the priest who burned joss sticks and kept shrines to the Buddha on the deck of the Mercy house.

Sanskrit or Scripture; Buddhism's Pali Canon, Judaism's Torah, Islam's Koran, or Father Joe's tattered King James—its black leather worn by use and age—all point in the same direction. And as he was telling me all this, Father Joe began pointing there too. He raised his right arm like a rifle, squinted down the barrel of his forearm, and used his index finger as the front sight.

"This is what you and I are supposed to be," he said, holding the pose. "We are to be a finger pointing toward the moon. We can't let ourselves get distracted looking at the elbow. Don't focus on the hand. Don't get hung up staring at dirt under your fingernails. Don't do anything except point toward the moon."

So the moon is . . . what? Our universal expression of light and goodness?

"Don't worry about that now. Just focus. Point toward the moon. Don't allow the other stuff to distract you. You have to concentrate on form, practice form, maintain form, keep your focus, keep your form. . . . Just point toward the moon."

I was jotting notes, and when I looked up, his arm had dropped. He was staring at me.

Oh. You mean me?

"*Point* toward the moon."

It was a weekday morning, and we'd just lingered over our customary pot of Klong Toey blend discussing Mercy's "passive" (his word) promotion of condom use. I'd seen condoms taped to Mercy's office windows in arrays of color and design—a smiley face, a tree, and what appeared to be a flower. The ones we'd just passed after a brisk walk through Lumpini were arranged to look like a caterpillar: blue condom, orange condom, green condom, red condom, yellow condom, pink condom, lined up and taped across an office window off the main breezeway, a broad, busy stretch teeming with Mercy's own and Mercy's visitors. Rubber bands served as caterpillar antennae, a pencil eraser for an eye. It was a silhouette.

Seeing this, I'd suggested that Mercy's promotion of condoms was an *aggressive* campaign. He flinched as if it was an accusation and then began stepping lightly. It was an odd gait for him. "No, no, we don't *push* them and we don't *endorse* them," he'd said.

I thought his tone was harsher than the observation warranted. So I, too, began stepping lightly.

"We just put the information out where it needs to be," he added. "It's there. If it's needed."

Condoms should be slung by the fistful into Klong Toey's slum streets, I said, like candy in Macy's Thanksgiving Day parade. All the better if it were done with the explicit consent of clergy—the imam, the abbot, the priest, whomever. He searched me like he was trying to decide if I was friend or foe on the issue. Or maybe he just didn't agree. But at the time, Mercy was caring for some fifty orphans infected with HIV/AIDS in utero, a number that fluctuated depending on the newly arrived and dearly departed.

Also, Father Joe had told me earlier that morning that he could count six Mercy teenagers whom he thought were determined to work in Thailand's sex industry. Some had friends and relatives already in it who could flaunt the latest Wi-Fi-compatible cell phone, iPod, Blackberry, et cetera. Others had gambling- or drug-addicted relatives who needed money or family members sick and dying who needed the same. Whatever the reason, they were headed for an industry that promised fast cash.

"Massage places and karaoke bars, whatever else they call themselves. That's what they'll do, and that's just an effing fact," he'd said earlier that morning in Lumpini Park. It had been a few minutes past six, and we'd just passed a group of girls (or boys—it was often difficult to know) in tiny shorts and halter tops head-ing home from work.

Back at his house, I told him that during my twenty-one-hour pilgrimage from Washington to Chicago to Tokyo to Bangkok, United Airlines had broadcast a video discouraging passengers from having sex . . . with children. "I am a *child*, not a tourist attrac-tion," the film's young Asian girl implored. The World Vision Inter-national production had been shown only on the trip's final leg.

In my opinion, I told him, whether or not to promote the use of condoms in Thailand—or anywhere—seemed like a nonissue to me. When he didn't respond, I did what I thought one was sup-posed to do when a priest sits quietly. I confessed. In two or three long breaths, I told of how I knew from my own hormonally charged youth and two glorious summers spent as a beach lifeguard that if a condom isn't in the pocket or wallet at three pints and a few minutes past midnight, it doesn't rank as a priority. And I'd come from the privileged stock that all of behavioral science calls low-risk: two-parent home, devoted mom and dad, mandatory Sunday school and church attendance with boilerplate warnings about something worse than AIDS: eternal damnation. I'd been risking my inheritance of the hereafter. But at the precise moment when matters of gratification needed deciding, the meticulously planted fear dissolved right along with my self-discipline. For me, every time. In my moderate Baptist church that straddled the Virginia-Tennessee state line, the best ministers could spit more than Old Testament fire and brimstone. They preached New Testament forgiveness. Said God had an infinite supply. Convinced me of it. So despite the distractions of a pretty girl and all the blood drained from my brain, I always recalled *that* lesson. At the line of scrimmage at a quarter past midnight, it had been the only dog-eared lesson of my upbringing.

Father Joe's silence made my face flush. I'd said too much. Again.

His posture shifted from reclined to sitting up. He placed a mug of that bitter slum blend on the coffee table and leaned forward on the couch, elbows on knees with a finger pointing.

"That thing on?"

He was looking at my voice recorder.

Thank God, I rejoiced. I had no bait left—at least none I was willing to share.

"On strictly moral issues," he began, "there can be *no* give-and-take. I'm with the Church on that. Murder is murder, and killing is wrong. I'm against abortion too. I should be clear on that. These things are wrong, . . . just *wrong*. Now maybe it's a case where the mother's health is at risk or maybe you had to kill an intruder or kill to protect your children or whatever. But you feel bad afterward. That's different. These were choices forced on you. . . . But does the sun come up in the morning and go down at night? Yes, yes, of course. Some things do not need debating."

He paused, staring at the silver recorder with its glaring red "on" light.

"Now," he continued, taking a deep breath. "Is it wrong to use a condom?"

The old Catholic popes and the newest old one too—a conservative theologian steeped more in biblical curriculum than Third World slums—had maintained a ban on contraception that predated latex prophylactics and HIV pandemics. The Holy See has forever considered the seed of man holy. To divorce it from propagation by any method other than the careful navigation of menstrual cycles was the same as tying God's hands. The pill, the diaphragm, the condom—these are cheating. Thus sayeth Rome, as mandated by God.

Liberal Catholics had hoped that Vatican II, which culminated in 1965 with Good Pope John's nudge of the church to loosen up, would end its ban on birth control. Instead, Pope Paul VI, a son of Italian nobility who'd taken a solemn oath against the heresy of Modernism, reaffirmed it with an encyclical titled *Humanae Vitae*. He described the "conjugal act" as the ordination of man's highest calling—fatherhood. Thus, he declared, all men must be called back to the norms of natural law. He concluded that "each and every act of marriage must remain open to the transmission of life."

This interpretation of "natural moral law" was God's indisputable will, Pope Paul VI wrote in that controversial encyclical. His immediate successors, John Paul I and II, carried out his wishes like marching orders to the end of one century and the beginning of the next. Meanwhile, HIV burned through much of

Asia and sub-Saharan Africa, and hospices like Mercy's became expert at marrying last rites to the realities of AIDS and poverty.

Conserving the lids of caskets the size of Radio Flyer wagons, for example.

⚜

Father Joe scooted several inches closer to the recorder. He spoke slowly, enunciating each syllable so that every word registered.

"Condoms are what I call a doubtful moral issue. Go ahead, write it down. This is a *doubtful* moral issue. It's not murder; it's not abortion. *Doubtful. Moral. Issue.*"

He stopped and waited until I wrote it.

"Now, for me to tell people they must follow my religion and my religious beliefs on a doubtful moral issue that can put lives in danger—*does* put lives in danger—well, *that* is the height of arrogance."

He paused, determined to maintain a cool demeanor and damp down the worst of the cursing.

"The height of arrogance, isn't it?" he continued, starting to nod his head more vigorously, grinding his teeth, squinting. I could see the pot begin to simmer.

"Little Joey Maier from the slums of Longview, Washington, is going to tell these fervent Buddhists of Thailand that they cannot, will not, shall not use condoms? Who am I? The Spirit speaks to them as well as He speaks to me. No more, no less, no better, no worse."

One week earlier, three of the six teenagers whom he feared would eventually work in strip bars and massage parlors had run away from Soi Forty. They were back the same day, but for how long? Like all the kids, they hungered for independence or material gain or whatever satisfaction and hip comfort the culture, the TV, and the Internet promised that fast cash would purchase. It doesn't matter how many Saturday Masses the kids of Mercy attend or how many different ways Father Joe tells the parable of mustard seeds falling on gravel and ground; some kids are going to find the short-cut. Thailand's tourist economy and black market depend on it.

"So what do you do?" he asked. "Do you just pretend that all will be fine and they'll always listen and that they ultimately will make good choices? No. No! You bring a bunch of sex workers in here and let them talk to the girls, let them tell the girls about *every* detail of the business. These are the facts—listen up girlies. Maybe *they* talk some sense into them."

He thought about that.

"Probably not."

He started to stand but sat back down like he'd been pushed. Then he began tapping the coffee table with one finger, hard, like he was punching a number into his phone.

"But at least the girls will have been told that *this* is the way it is and *this* is the reality of it and *this* is what you have to do if you're going to survive this shit, and *this* is how you protect your twat if you want to live, and *these* are the rules, and *this* is how it is, *this* is the game you're getting into."

All of *this* had come out in a single gust. He stood to refill his lungs, and when he did, his cool resolve fell like a costume back-stage. If he had stepped lightly before, he stomped now.

"Use a condom? You asked me whether or not we should tell those girls to use *condoms*?"

Well, not exactly. I started to correct him but thought better of it.

"We damn well better tell them to use condoms! Not only that, we better tell them the whys and the hows and the whens. . . . What a *sin*! What an effing Catholic sin to look the other way, to pretend this shit ain't gonna happen if we don't say so."

He'd been attempting to curb his coarsest language, but restraint was now in that costume heap on the floor. His tone turned mocking; high-pitched, and holier than thou.

"'*Noooo,* I don't want them to be sex workers. I don't approve, so I'm not going to tell them *anything,*'" he said, shaking his head and a figurative finger at Rome.

"What a fookin'—*fookin'*—Catholic sin!"

He sat down, deflated, and fell silent. I scribbled that exact description in my notebook, then looked up, expecting more. He'd leaned forward to rest his head in his hands, his fingers pressed into his temples. It reminded me of the night five years earlier in the Slaughterhouse parking lot, when slumped against the steering wheel, he told me, "Take it all in. Take your time. Write it down."

He sat up, his hands still at his temples.

"You see," he concluded, so quietly the recorder barely picked up his voice, "if I ignored it, I'd be an accomplice in their deaths. Wouldn't I? I would've killed them."

He sighed.

"So . . . what was your question?"

⚜

Following Pope John Paul II's death three months earlier, April 2, 2005, advocates of birth control had hoped Pope Benedict XVI might reconsider Paul VI's interpretations and prohibitions. As yet, that hadn't happened. (A year later, after news reports that the Vatican was rethinking *Humanae Vitae,* Rome would deny it had ever considered altering its ban—not even for cases of marriage where one spouse is infected with HIV.)

Like American liquor laws in the 1920s and '30s, the Vatican's prohibition was firmly entrenched against the opposition. That would make a slum priest with condoms taped to his windows a bootlegger of sorts, I joked to Father Joe.

He didn't laugh.

Next thing I knew, my right arm was aimed like a rifle toward the sky, my finger pointed toward the sun or moon or whatever.

Condoms arranged to look like a caterpillar taped to a Mercy office window

TEN

Wars on Terror

Christ was the highest evolved Buddha.

—Father Joe's daily journal

I squinted.

"Really? You want me to look into the sun?" I asked.

"Not directly," Father Joe said, and from his tone, I could tell without looking that he was staring at me again like I was one of the dumb ones allowed to live out by the airport.

"And it's not the sun," he added gently, as if he regretted thinking that about me. "The moon. We're aiming toward the moooon."

Members of the Indonesian Red Cross, dressed business casual and looking collegiate with backpacks and notebooks, walked past the office toward the breezeway without noticing the silhouetted caterpillar that could have been an artfully arranged package of glow-in-the-dark Trojans. Father Joe was just beginning to explain to me this philosophy of "pointing toward the moon" when he was interrupted by a Mercy staffer. Could he please give the Indonesians an impromptu lecture on how to care for children living with HIV?

He thought on it for a few seconds before launching into a ten-minute lesson about the threat of tuberculosis, the medicinal value of food, and his personal definition of the human immunodeficiency virus—or lack thereof.

"There is no HIV. Let's call it what it is," he said. "It's AIDS; it's all AIDS."

⚜

For Mercy, it had seemed like it was all AIDS for much of the last decade. In the initial two months after it opened Thailand's first free AIDS hospice in 1994, Father Joe had recited last rites over the emaciated bodies of sixty Buddhists who'd gone toward their fate on nothing stronger than painkillers and Catholic prayer. They were primarily men and women from the surrounding slums, but several had come from as far away as the airport and even from the subdistricts farther out from the city, such as the slums that had chased dimple-cheeked Nong Bla and her mother away. Bad karma, the Buddhists call it, chasing children away.

The Indonesian Red Cross had gathered in a loose semicircle around Father Joe when he asked a question that everyone understood to be rhetorical.

"What is the most important AIDS medication?" he said, looking at each member and repeating the question slowly and several times. "What is . . . the most important . . . AIDS medication?"

Implied in this was the absence of antiretroviral medicines. Mercy had begun receiving generic antiretrovirals from the Thai Ministry of Public Health two years earlier—about three years after the hospice for mothers and children opened in 2000—and all of Mercy's HIV children and at least half of its HIV adults were receiving the medicine. However, many of the adults and some of the kids were too far gone by that time, and Mercy's march to cremations at the Wat Saphan (Temple by the Bridge) was still steady. Looking at the children, you could usually tell who was in a losing fight with TB or Kaposi's sarcoma or drug resistance and whatever else could piggyback on HIV.

That morning, as I'd watched children pick at bowls of rice congee thickened with eggs and chicken, I could spot the weakest without staring. It wasn't just the stick figures or arms, legs, and faces marked by lesions. It was the noise and the lack of it. Dozens sat side by side at long wooden tables in an open-air mezzanine. Elbow to elbow, and they were well behaved. The loudest sound wasn't even from a child. It came from a drug-resistant strain of TB, its cough a wrenching hack, repeated again and again. A tiny girl and her pathogen were eating alone, one picking at congee, the other at lung tissue.

Fern, eight years old and a Mercy newcomer, was semiquarantined at a kid-sized plastic table where she ate in small bites and spilled her milk once as I watched. She cleaned the mess without crying, whining, looking around, raising her hand, or otherwise asking for help. Watching her and the calm village of small AIDS victims, it was obvious that chronic disease and its medicines stunted physical growth, but it seemed perhaps to accelerate other things, such as maturity and responsibility. Fern got up, refilled her mug with white milk, threw away the wet napkins and replaced them with dry ones, and returned to her seat unnoticed. She never uttered a whimper. At her fingertips, dampened by the spill, was a girl's zippered change purse, burgundy trimmed in gold. Mercy kept a few purses and wallets handy, weighted always with heavy Thai coins. Father Joe said that the extra heft made the sick beggar kids feel a little more secure.

And Fern had been a prolific beggar on Bangkok's streets, especially as HIV advanced its well-trodden path: informal job sector to father to mother to newborn to full-blown AIDS.

When Fern's growth slowed, then stunted, then her weight receded, her eyes had seemed to grow larger, buggy, like dark olives. She could look sad and pleading without acting. There was real profit in that.

In Lumpini the previous day, Father Joe and I saw a one-legged cripple who'd been carried to the edge of a jogging path and placed flat on his stomach. He was propped on one elbow with dirt streaked on his forehead and cheeks, and a baseball cap was flipped upside down on the ground near his nose. On the second or third lap, Father Joe said quietly, speaking almost to himself, "Tsk, tsk, tsk, look at that poor fella." He dropped in the morning's first cash donation and then ran a finger along his own face.

"Why the dirt?" Father Joe asked politely, speaking in Thai, "Why not clean up before you come out here?"

He'd asked for my sake, I'm sure. Any slum priest or slum any-body knows the answer.

The man smiled broadly, probably because of the 20-baht bill that had just fallen into his upturned cap, and answered cheerfully, "I get more money this way."

Fern, too. Her father had recently checked her out of Mercy like a library book. To go for a walk, he told the staff. Later she was heard bragging of the bounty she'd collected for him.

⚜

"Food!" Father Joe shouted. "Food is the most important AIDS medication." A member of the Indonesian Red Cross was filming the lecture with a handheld camera while the others nodded politely—yes, yes, we understand—and took mental and written notes.

"You must feed them. You must fatten them up. Food—food!—is the most important AIDS medication."

Since its first case of HIV/AIDS was diagnosed in 1985, Indonesia had survived relatively unscathed. Even as AIDS burned in neighboring Malaysia and Thailand, the island nation seemed immune. It was as if the Indian and Pacific Oceans served as Indonesia's buffer. But sometime after the millennium, as the Indonesian economy continued to reel from the effects of the Asian financial crisis, an overlap of intravenous drug users (heroin mostly) with sex workers had lit a match. It was similar to the yaba-prostitution one-two that had ignited the ecogangsterism in Klong Toey. Indonesian authorities were estimating in 2005 that half of the country's 160,000 drug users were infected with HIV, despite a government campaign promoting safe sex and condoms. Just as Father Joe had said about the Slaughterhouse parking lot ("In the slums, if the money says, 'No condom and I will pay you more,' then it's no condom"), a 2005

UNAIDS study concluded that condom use among Indonesia's high-risk population—prostitutes and johns—was "infrequent to rare." In the red-light district of the capital, Jakarta, 85 percent of sex workers polled by researchers said they hadn't used even one condom with clients in the week preceding the poll.

A special edition of *Far Eastern Economic Review* published to coincide with the 2004 International AIDS Conference in Bangkok depicted Thailand as the poster child in AIDS prevention and declared Indonesia on the "cusp of a crisis." In the same issue, a feature on Father Joe showed him smiling and looking relaxed in his black priestly garb. He was posed alongside an HIV-infected child who ate intently from a cup of noodles.

"Sanctuary for Bangkok's AIDS Orphans," the headline read.

But if the Indonesian Red Cross came to Mercy looking for good news or an HIV Holy Grail, Father Joe didn't offer much of either.

"You *will* have AIDS," he said to the group, nearly shouting. "AIDS is coming. AIDS is not going away. AIDS is here to stay. It will be in all our families. All our families. Christian, Muslim, Buddhist. No family is exempt."

He began to fumble with his gray collared pullover, groping his stomach and chest. I had no idea where he was headed with the demonstration, but I was enjoying watching the faces of visitors who'd not been baptized into Father Joe's unorthodoxy.

"TB is your biggest problem right now. TB spreads easily, not like AIDS."

He continued playing with his shirt until it rode far enough up for us all to see the oblong scar of what appeared to be an appendectomy but in fact was the result of a near-fatal case of diverticulitis twelve years earlier.

"With AIDS, you have to do all this funny stuff," he said, squirming suggestively, imitating the mad lust of two lovers or a quickie between a prostitute and a john.

He stopped suddenly. A couple of the Indonesian women were grinning; another had pursed her lips.

"But TB," he warned, deadpan and loud again. "TB! That spreads easily."

⚜

The Indonesians thanked Father Joe and filed out of the breezeway so quietly I wasn't sure if they were digesting the lecture or just shell-shocked by it.

Without missing a beat, Father Joe resumed our conversation, but now he wasn't pointing toward the moon. He gripped an imaginary golf club—a driver, it appeared, from the full-body backswing and follow-through. It resembled Arnold Palmer's punchy stroke, choppy but effective. More oomph than finesse. (He's never been a big fan of golf, despite an annual charity fundraiser in Bangkok named Father Joe's Charity Golf Classic.)

He bent his knees and dipped into another shot. "It's all about form," he said, swinging again. "Maybe Tiger Woods starts hooking the ball, slicing it, doing whatever. If that happens, he'll reexamine things, take an inventory. OK, then, how's the posture? How's the swing? How am I holding my hands? What is my stance like? What has changed? If things aren't right, you go back to the teachings and to the teachers. You review the lessons." That week, Tiger Woods was leading the 2005 British Open at Saint Andrews in Scotland, a venerable course and tournament that he would dominate.

"It's no different with you and me. If we start slicing and hooking it, we need to check ourselves, take inventory, review the old lessons," Father Joe continued. "We need to check our form."

As he spoke, Mercy's children moved in between and around us like a stream around rocks. We were still in the breezeway thoroughfare, and Thailand's school year was one month old and going full bore. Without interrupting a sentence or a thought, he reached out and tapped fists with several of the kids, eliciting grins and giggles.

"Maybe sometimes you're short-tempered with your bride, your children, whatever. Maybe I fall asleep during my prayers night after night. Whatever it is that's going on when we find ourselves slipping, that's when you stop everything and assess your form. You review the lessons—the lessons that we're all taught."

They're in Buddhism, Islam, Christianity, Judaism. They're in any home where children matter and grown-ups care, he said.

He raised his arm again, briefly this time, pointing toward the sky, the sun, the moon . . . whatever.

"Good form. You get back to good form."

So you're saying that good form is like the Golden Rule?

"Not like. Is. All of your religions and all of the great musicians talk about it."

Treating others with respect and behaving in a way that's humble and good? Do not kill. Do not steal. Do not burn, pillage, plunder, pollute, or abuse children and cute, fluffy animals?

"Yes, yes, exactly, all that and more. It's this way of living that produces the fruit of the spirit. . . . It works. But we can't get caught up looking at the finger. Look toward the moon. The mooon. To God, the good examples, the prophets, the wise teachings."

The founder of Buddhism and the first Buddha, Siddhārtha Gautama, is said to have told his followers, "All instruction is but a finger pointing to the moon; and those whose gaze is fixed upon the pointer will never see beyond. Even let him catch sight of the moon, and still he cannot see its beauty."

The slum imam had told this to Father Joe. A Muslim cleric sharing Buddhist wisdom with the slum's Catholic priest. Who had now shared it with me; a Southern Baptist, give or take a few Sundays and several liberal leanings. Quite the ecumenical relay.

⚜

At the precise eureka moment the baton was handed to me, Pope Benedict XVI was making news for opposing contemporary fiction's most popular protagonist, Harry Potter. As a Western journalist looking for ways to translate and put into context these matters of mental focus, fingers, moons and such, I felt profoundly blessed by the timing and odd criticism. God bless the pope.

The *Bangkok Post* and the *Nation* were reporting, along with the rest of the mainstream press, that two years prior to becoming pope, then-cardinal Joseph Ratzinger wrote to a German sociologist named Gabriele Kuby, who in her recent book *Harry Potter: Good or Evil?* had concluded that he was evil. Kuby believed J. K. Rowling's fictional goblets of fire and witchcraft were subtle lures that could lead good Catholic and Protestant children to the occult. "It is good that you enlighten people about Harry Potter," the future pope wrote to Kuby, "because those are subtle seductions which act unnoticed . . . and deeply distort Christianity in the soul before it can grow properly."

Or rather grow with church provenance.

The letter coincided with Rowling's sixth book, *Harry Potter and the Half-Blood Prince,* which was breaking all sales records for fiction. Father Joe is a fan of Harry Potter, reads all the books, and sees the movies. I'd asked why he read serial fiction for children, and he shot me a look like I'd asked why he showered.

"Potter sells millions of copies. This is what the kids are reading. Millions and millions of them. Hundreds of millions! If you want to know what's going in the minds of children, you damn well better read any book that that many kids are reading."

He wondered if the pope had actually read them. "Potter is about the battle between good and evil and about making right choices. It's about all the very things you and I are discussing. In the end, the good guys in Potter make some good choices. The good guys win! Isn't that what it's about? That's what Potter teaches: making good choices. Is that wrong?"

Kuby, a Catholic, saw in Rowling's fiction a threat to the Church specifically and Christianity in general. In an interview with ZENIT, a news agency that reports only on the Vatican, Kuby read from the cardinal's letter with the new pope's permission. The man who was now the leader of the world's largest religion had told Kuby that Harry Potter books cut children off from God and could steal their "spirit of discernment between good and evil" in such a way that "they will not have the necessary strength and knowledge to withstand the temptations to evil."

Back at his house, Father Joe read the letter on the front page of the *Nation,* shook his head, and smacked his lips together like he'd just tasted something sour. He attempted to put it in context for me.

"Parturient montes et nascetur ridiculus mus," he said.

I stared at him and shrugged. Latin is Greek to me.

"Parturient montes et nascetur ridiculus mus," he repeated slowly, as if that might jar a memory from the high school elective I'd in fact never selected.

"It's from the ancient Latin poet Horace, who said something like 'The mountains are in birth labor, and a tiny ridiculous mouse is born.'"

He put the newspaper down and began swinging his imaginary golf club again. Looked like a sand wedge this time; he dipped low and swung like he was digging out from a bunker.

We're talking about form?

"The Church is focusing on the finger," Father Joe said. "We have parts of this world going to hell in a hand basket, and this new guy is worried about Harry Potter. Condoms and good ol' Harry Potter."

He rolled his eyes.

"The real issues are that religion has dropped out of the critical stuff in culture and has banalized God, and the clergy have become caretakers stumbling along with no real leadership. And any leadership they get from the Church is, 'Don't do this, don't do that.' The great prophets are not being listened to, the moral high ground has been given up, and we're all told to just hide out like the rebel force against the empire (in Star Wars). Except we can't win it back by violence. We can win only by prayer and doing the tiny day-to-day things that generate good energy. Like helping some throw-away slum kids."

By telling them about condoms?

"That's a small part of it. Yes."

One month earlier, speaking to bishops visiting the Vatican from Africa, Pope Benedict XVI had acknowledged the "cruel epidemic" of HIV/AIDS and said it "seriously threatens the economic and social stability of the continent."

He concluded, however, that the Church would stick to its ban on birth control. To Rome's way of thinking, condoms were a symptom of the ill, not the cure. In other words, antidotes couldn't be part and parcel of the poison (never mind the makeup of all successful vaccines).

"It is of great concern that the fabric of African life, its very source of hope and stability, is threatened by divorce, abortion, prostitution, human trafficking, and," the pope concluded, "a contraception mentality."

This was about the same time Fern's father decided he could no longer care for his daughter, so he brought her to the orphanage/hospice/preschool anchored at the end of a busy slum street. At the dead end, some parents were still hoping for a turnaround.

Even if the sign promised only Mercy.

But Fern's father wasn't among the hopeful. "He brought her here," Father Joe had told me earlier, standing in that crowded breezeway, "because he knew she would die easier with us."

As Fern walked reluctantly away from her dad and toward a dormitory with dozens of frilly bedspreads and stuffed animals sprinkled on pillows, her father turned to leave.

Father Joe stood in the breezeway watching. Trembling, one father approached the other and began sobbing—a Buddhist confessing to a Catholic.

"I've killed my family, I've killed my family," Fern's father stammered to Father Joe, who later said to me, "Yeah, the asshole did."

Father Joe and the "AIDS brigade" say morning prayers over a breakfast of rice congee at the Mercy Centre. (Joop is the tallest girl at the far end.)

ELEVEN

Religious Medal, Spiritual Mettle

Kids need us when they *need us, not when we have free time.*

—Father Joe's daily journal

Fern was immediately embraced by the Mercy village, and by the time I saw her, she was roaming the campus with a small pack of girls, veterans her age who showed her the shortcuts and hiding places and how best to strut your stuff when you're pulling an oxygen cart that feels like a collie fighting its leash.

You skip. The harder, the faster, the better. It's all about momentum.

A week or so after I'd met Fern, Father Joe and I dodged an approaching storm and ended our talk-walk in Lumpini Park early. It was a few minutes past six in the morning when he headed full stride into Mercy's outdoor cafeteria, where dozens of HIV/ AIDS children had lined up lazily for the daily regimen of breakfast and meds—one and the same if you believe congee to be medicinal.

The kids were dressed in school uniforms of royal blue shorts or skirts with white button-ups and blouses or Carolina blue pullovers with taffy pink sleeves. (Pink? I took my sunglasses off, just to make sure. Yep. Pink.) The sickest AIDS kids were dressed more casually, in blue jeans or mesh basketball shorts with T-shirts or soccer jerseys, like it was Saturday instead of Monday. Like they'd be watching cartoons instead of learning math and the Thai alphabet.

Father Joe was still in his Lumpini uniform—white Nikes with reflective stripes, Converse ankle-length white socks, blue tennis shorts, and a golf shirt, this one beige with checks. Despite the abbreviated workout, the shirt was see-through sweaty and sagged at the chest because we'd forgotten to remove my voice recorder from its front pocket. A week into my return, he was so used to the recorder, he forgot it was there.

Earlier, in Lumpini, when his Nokia tweeted, he excused himself to step out of my earshot and speak to his younger sister, Kathy, calling from Oregon. (She's the palliative care nurse who later told me that she never called Father Joe an "arrogant S.O.B." when he phoned her about Boi's death. That was only Father Joe's self-deprecating recall. He'd told me, "My arrogance—such *effing* arrogance—that I thought she would wait on me, wait until *Joe Maier* was ready for her to die." Kathy did, however, explain to her brother that people near death will often wait until loved ones leave the room before passing away. The dying are often ready to go, but family, friends, and occasionally a slum priest aren't willing to let go. "It's why we all the time hear people say, 'I stepped outside for a smoke, and when I came back, Mom had died.'")

I'd phoned Kathy the day before to arrange visits and interviews with the Maier family in Washington State. This morning, she was phoning her big brother to check up on me. *Who's this reporter from Washington, D.C., and what's this book he's talking about? Friend or foe?* The most basic of background checks.

"Yeah, yeah, yeah, he's cool. I'm completely frank and on the record about everything. *Everything*—Dad, Mom, all the shit, so talk, talk, talk. *Talk* to him. I have no secrets," he told Kathy.

My thin recorder was still resting against Father Joe's chest, light as a stethoscope, when he took the call. I felt decidedly guilty listening to his side of their conversation later. (Of course, he might've been aware all along.)

"It'll never get published anyhow," he'd told Kathy about this book. "Who wants to read about an old fart in Klong Toey?"

He was laughing when he said it, doing that little half circle of stutter steps. Even on a morning when menacing dark clouds threatened to cut short his time in Lumpini, a jog in nature was clearly his congee. An hour earlier, he'd dumped his bag of woes in the patch of shade near Rama IV Road, then raised a thumb to his nose, waggled his fingers, and spit out, "Nanny, nanny, boo, boo," mocking everything that stalked him 24/7. Then he'd jogged away.

Maybe not *literally* and out loud, *nanny, nanny* and *boo, boo,* he explained, but that was the general tone running through his mind. Some days he saluted the cursed bag with his middle finger. On others, he taunted it playfully.

Entering Mercy's mezzanine dining hall that morning, he called out, "The AIDS brigade, the AIDS brigade!" sounding like one Sigma Alpha Mu spotting another. He greeted the chow line by tapping fists lightly with kids the same way ballplayers greet one another, keeping the mood light because, as he routinely points out about such matters, "What's the alternative?"

The children stirred and began smiling, confirming what I'd already suspected. The greatest contagion at Mercy wasn't Fern's TB. It was the positive air blowing that very moment through the cafeteria. Moving child to child to child, the crazy American with knobby knees and calves of cordwood shuffled sideways, almost skipping. Little shoulders shuddered in fits of giggles.

⚜

Monsoon clouds as large as cruise ships had followed us from Lumpini, bringing with them a gust that carried the day's forecast and brushed three-story-tall palm trees against a cafeteria wall, causing a rustle that sounded like joggers in corduroy. The air that morning tasted clean, almost lemony, and like Father Joe, it carried a charge. The AIDS brigade stirred playfully in the wind, but there was still no pushing, pulling, teasing, tugging, fussing, fighting, shouting, or wrestling. As on previous mornings, they mingled elbow to elbow and without an apparent care. They laughed in cliquish circles and played slow-motion tag while some of the sickest yawned and waited patiently for breakfast. Fern abandoned the charade of quarantine to huddle in a scrum of girls. Through a blue surgeon's mask worn over her mouth, she giggled and whispered about whatever girls that age giggle and whisper about. Every few seconds, the scrum would spring up at the precise same second, look around like they'd discovered a secret, and then sink down again into their huddle.

In the column Father Joe writes for the *Bangkok Post,* he once noted, "You want to know something interesting? Kids with AIDS don't fight each other like other kids, even when they're feeling okay."

You could imagine him scratching his head.

"I don't know what that means," he finished.

Crowding again into the tight quarters of those two enormously long tables—more than thirty feet each, at least—kids infected with HIV/AIDS then did something that I sometimes allow myself and my own healthy sons to forget. They gave thanks. Recited in unison and in a nasally Thai singsong, they prayed for mercy and for Mercy. They prayed for each other and for Mercy's teachers, cooks, nurses, house mothers, and the steaming bowls of breakfast that most of them would only pick over. They concluded with supplications pitched softly—to God, to the Virgin Mary, to the enlightened nature of the Buddha residing within—asking that "bad people become good" and that their moms and dads please, please, please remember them, wherever they are—in prison, in hiding, in hock, or in the flecks of ashes tossed into the canal that flows to the river that goes to the sea.

And dear Lord, thank you for your bountiful blessings.

That's what the Buddhist kids prayed, even (or especially) the children dying, their cheeks already sunken.

Amen.

On cue, the monsoon clouds answered with rafter-rattling thunder. I jumped and looked around. No one else appeared startled or even aware of the clap's ironic timing. The kids picked at their food quietly, Fern alone at her kid-sized table, the rest complacently elbow to elbow. Then they lined up for school or cartoons—whichever their health dictated.

Standing away from everyone, dressed for class but looking hesitant, was a girl of ten or eleven, by my best guess. A sheet of rain floated toward her on the cafeteria's balcony, looking in the distance like a cloud of locusts, yet she leaned into its breathy approach, braced by the mezzanine's chest-high railing. Any second, I expected to see her lift her arms to her sides and fly like DiCaprio on the bow of the *Titanic*.

⚜

"*Phe long maa? Taan long maa?*" a child shouted to her.

Then another. "*Phe long maa?*"

Are you coming down? Are you coming down?

After breakfast, the children began moving toward the stairs that led to the downstairs breezeway, and the girl had returned to Mercy's balcony bow, which was wet from the storm that had arrived like a marching band. She stared into the sky and didn't reply to the children's question. She stared without ever once turning her head.

"Joop Jang," Father Joe said, to me, not her.

You mean *the* Joop? *That's* Joop? Throughout breakfast I had not recognized her.

Father Joe looked at me like I suddenly spoke fluent Thai.

"You *know* her? You've met?"

He was being sarcastic. He knew I didn't speak a syllable of Thai outside of a Bangkok taxi and I was lost in most parts of Klong Toey without him. How could I know Joop or even *of* Joop if he hadn't introduced me to her or at least her story?

About a week earlier, Tom Crowley—Father Joe's right-hand man—had let me tag along with him to a government hospital where Mercy's sickest go when they need the kind of medical care a hospice can't provide. Mercy's staff of course bonds with the kids, and by default they sometimes assume extra responsibilities for this one or that one. Tom felt responsible for Joop, the smart, lanky big sister of the AIDS brigade. Joop had come to Mercy very young, left for several years to live with a grandmother, and then returned at age ten. Grandmom had died, and no other relative, including a rich auntie, wanted her, Father Joe told me. And just as Tom now looked out for Joop—bringing her a yogurt drink and fruit at the hospital—Joop was emotionally attached to a five-year-old girl, Puh, who'd arrived at Mercy in the late stages of AIDS, blinded by cytomegalovirus retinitis, a by-product of the Virus.

"That's what family does," Father Joe explained to me later: the older generation helps the younger, and the younger helps the youngest, all the way down the line.

In recent months, it had been Joop who needed extra attention. Whenever she caught a fever, flu, or cold, she'd ask to go to Bangkok's "poor-person hospital," as Father Joe called it, a second-rate facility a couple of miles from Mercy. Illness filled Joop with a dread of imminent death, and since hospices are where people often die and hospitals are where they often recover, the choice for her was a no-brainer.

"This hospital will always keep her alive—that's what she thinks," Tom had said, leading me into Joop's hospital ward, a dormitory with about half the square footage but twice the musk of a middle school gymnasium. Adults and children were side by side and a few yards apart in a room where walls, doors, chairs, and plastic bedpans were various shades of blue. As if blue was the antidote to feeling blue. And maybe it was, because as Tom walked toward Joop, her smile curled until it pinched the oxygen hose that was stuck up her nose. Days earlier, she'd been coughing and wheezing so hard, she couldn't catch her breath. Now she drew comfort and breaths from a hospital oxygen tank. She was anchored to a corner bed with oxygen on one side, an intravenous drip of saline on the other, and at her feet, a plastic bedpan half full of liquid that looked stale and pale yellow.

A Thai variety program reminiscent of *The Carol Burnett Show* played loudly on a small TV propped on a metal equipment cart, but all I could understand was the perpetual laugh track (same in any language) and what sounded like the theme music to *The Wild, Wild West* (duuuh, duh, duh, duh, dummmmmm).

As government hospitals go, I'd seen worse—in the impoverished Shiite areas of southern Iraq, for example. After a decade of UN economic sanctions and weeks prior to the 2003 U.S. invasion, the fly-infested Basra Hospital for Maternity and Children had seemed to me more deteriorated than this. But not by much.

Tom leaned close to plant a peck on Joop's forehead and then lingered for two or three seconds, his face lightly brushing her cheek. He inhaled, looking like Father Joe in Lumpini savoring the scent of a night-flowering jasmine. Tom pulled a plastic chair close and sat, then motioned—sit, sit—for me to do the same.

"We'll be here for a while," he said. "I don't want to short-change her."

There were no vacant chairs nearby, so I sat cross-legged on the floor, using my satchel as a cushion between the small of my back and the wall. Tom shook his head discreetly. "No, no, she'll think you're uncomfortable," he scolded, his voice calm, the only tone I'd ever heard him use.

I was pretty comfortable, so I shrugged him off. No problem, all's good, relax. "You can't," he said more sternly, but still Zen-calm. "It will make *her* uncomfortable. *For* you. She'll be uncomfortable because you're *having* to sit on the floor."

I looked up and directly into Joop's kindly, coffee-colored stare. A Saint Christopher medal on a silver necklace dangled over the top of her blue hospital smock. She'd been scribbling on a notepad with a pencil topped by a large Teenage Mutant Ninja Turtle eraser, but the de facto leader of the anthropomorphic crime fighters had now stopped bopping his head. It seemed like Leonardo was staring at me too. Joop forced a smile, then looked at Tom, then at me, then Tom, then me. Tom and I sprang up and seconds later returned with an armless plastic chair, the kind you'd find poolside at any municipal rec center. It was blue, of course. Leonardo's head began to bob again across the page.

The Saint Christopher pendant swayed, too, slightly and with each turn of Joop's head or shift of her oxygen hose.

The patron saint of travelers?

As a teenager, I, the native son of Bible Belt Baptists, went through a Saint Christopher phase. It's not like I had read up on Catholic martyrs; I didn't even know back then that the saint around my neck had been famously persecuted for being a Christian, circa third-century Rome. It didn't matter. I'd seen peers wearing a pendent that sounded oddly pleading—"Saint Christopher, Protect Us"—but looked fashionably cool, as if Nike had endorsed a saint with its swoosh.

But why would a Buddhist child in a Buddhist nation hitch herself to a Christian martyr?

Evangelism per se isn't on Mercy's program. Or so I'd been told.

❧

One year earlier, on June 4, 2004, PBS had broadcast a short documentary titled *Father Joe: Slum Priest*. An irreverent Third World Catholic planting preschools, orphanages, and hospices in a city of Buddhists while decrying the follies of Catholicism made for a good story. PBS reporter Phil Jones had walked some of the same Slaughterhouse catwalks as I had four years earlier. After staring into and smelling the open sewers, he'd also had similar, burning questions.

Why Thailand? And why in heaven's name *here?*

"To become a missionary priest and to work with the people and to convert them to Christianity and become holy, I guess," Father Joe told Jones on camera. "*They* converted me, though."

"Who converted you?" Phil asked.

"The Buddhists and the Muslims. I've only learned to be a Christian by learning from the Muslims and Buddhists of tolerance and calmness and peace."

Such a pronouncement was still bold in the "you're either with us or against us," Judeo-Christian-versus-Muslim post-9/11 era. Some conservative Christians responded predictably, the only way the Internet-savvy can when they don't have a public broadcasting crew trailing them. They blogged. In one rant headed "Catholic Sell Out," a conservative whose Web page listed 1 Timothy 2:9–15 (A woman should learn in quietness and full submission.) cited Jones's documentary and said of Father Joe, "It's priests like these that give conservatives hesitation in supporting the Roman Catholic Church, especially in its work in the Third World. . . . Rather than do the hard work of fighting local religion, many priests just incorporate large parts of it into Catholicism, and thus create problems for years to come and undermine the name of Christianity and confuse it with some bastardized version."

PBS showed Mercy's children singing the Thai national anthem as Jones intoned, "It's how their school day begins. After the anthem, it's time for their prayers led by the teachers. 'Bow once to the Buddha. The Buddha is great.'"

Long lines of dark-skinned children were filmed praying in unison in a nasally singsong language foreign to the majority of American TV viewers. "What's so unique about this scene is, the kids are praying to Buddha in a *Catholic* school," Jones continued. "But that's just fine with Father Joe Maier, who says he doesn't care if the children say their Hail Marys to a statue of Buddha as long as they know some prayers to help them deal with life. They live in Klong Toey, amidst poverty, drugs, gang violence, and child sex abuse."

To some of the fundamentalist and conservative bloggers, such tolerance was the cause of social ills, not a remedy. "This sort of thing typifies the problem: taking a positive experience with a spiritual element and relabelling it 'Christianity' by mixing in a couple of elements of Christianity and ignoring doctrine so that everyone is happy. While Christ came so that the world could be saved and came in love, He is not weak and willing to submit to other religions just so that their supplicants can feel free to be Christians without any discomfort."

Father Joe never saw or heard the criticism and didn't appear bothered when I told him of it later. He chuckled as though I were reading from the Sunday comics, then responded using the accent he adopts when mocking sanctimony. The tone is high-pitched, with the rich twang of my southern heritage: "*Yew mist* believe in *Jeeeezuz!* All of *hew*-manity *mist beeelieeeve* in *Jeeeezuz* and only *Jeeeezuz.*"

He doesn't spare Catholicism either. By the summer of 2005, Pope Benedict XVI was being dismissed by Father Joe as "Pope Eggs Benedict" for his condemnation of Harry Potter. This was long after the Vatican had become "just another government" to Father Joe. "No better, no worse, no more moral, no less moral" than the might-equals-right corridors of Washington, D.C.

Why, then, the Saint Christopher medal around Joop's neck? I asked him. If the paths of Buddha and Muhammad lead to tolerance and calmness and peace (which sounded like heaven to me), why advance the cause of *Jeeeezuz?*

I said it just like that: *Jeeeezuz.* Born in Tennessee (native pronunciation "*Ten-Seeee*"), I can effortlessly stretch the televangelist *eeee.*

We were still watching Joop. She had followed the AIDS brigade downstairs and was lingering in the breezeway. Father Joe stared at her for a few seconds, as if trying to come up with a good response, then turned to answer me. I could sense the wheels of self-editing turning, could almost hear the rusty axles grind.

There was a hint of a smile. I immediately thought of foxes and henhouses, even jotted exactly that in my notebook.

⚜

He began his answer with a story. Several years earlier, at the dedication of a new Mercy Centre school and several offices and a courtyard, across the street from where we now stood, the imam who'd opened the first school for Klong Toey's Muslim kids three decades earlier pulled Father Joe aside and whispered into his ear.

"The sign, Joe. *We* forgot to bless the sign."

Klong Toey's leader of Islam was the elderly cleric of a small mosque favored by the slums' Muslim minority. Two of his daughters were among the first teachers in the squatter schools, and they still worked for Mercy's 4,500-student preschool system. One would become the headmistress of the neighborhood's school. Mercy's bounty of John Cook's philanthropy had never been regarded by Mercy or its community as Mercy's alone, Father Joe explained. It belonged to everyone—the majority Buddhists, the minority Muslims, and the few Catholics who stayed behind after the butcheries fled. "A partnership with the poor" was Mercy's promise. Saint Christopher medal or Buddhist amulet, it didn't matter. You only needed to be *poor.*

Imam Selep Develah, seven inches shorter than Father Joe's five feet nine, was humble and soft-spoken. Whenever he spoke, Father Joe would lean close to catch each measured word, out of genuine respect and interest. He valued the imam's opinion. The day of the dedication ceremony, the imam squeezed Father Joe's shoulder gently, like a father to a son, and suggested that they correct the error immediately. *Inshallah.*

"Yes, yes, yes," Father Joe answered. "I understand. *Inshallah, inshallah.*"

The imam's comings and goings and all future plans, whether for dinner that night or travel abroad the following month, carried Islam's qualifier: *inshallah*—God willing. It wasn't a perfunctory utterance. He mouthed it silently, never out loud or intrusively, but always with keen intent. He'd look you in the eyes whenever he spoke, the way Father Joe was looking at me now, studying me to see if I understood.

It was the same with the blessings. The imam lingered over each one as if inhaling them, drawing the moment into his lungs, cleansing it, releasing the words purified. Like the twelve breaths of the mystics, deeply in, slowly out. Twelve per minute.

"I've learned many things from the old imam," Father Joe told me. "In everything you do—every time you pray, everything you bless—in all of this, you should be *totally* filled with God. *Totally* tied up with God. Totally. *Inshallah, inshallah.*"

Twice during Father Joe's days of living on a Slaughterhouse catwalk, he'd been hospitalized with serious illnesses: first pleurisy, in the early 1990s, and a few years later, diverticulitis. During both hospital stays, the imam visited Father Joe and brought with him a dozen imams from Bangkok's southeast district. Imam Selep walked through the antiseptic-scented hospital ward smelling like rose perfume and carrying a vial of rosewater, which he used for Islam's prayer cleansing ritual. He sprinkled Father Joe and the whole crowded room of holy men and then prayed over Father Joe, speaking slowly and intently, asking Allah to return the slums' fiery Catholic priest to good health. *Inshallah, inshallah*—never spoken, only mouthed.

"When my guts went bad (from diverticulitis) I thought I was going to die. Of course, when I didn't, I thought of it as a rebirth, and I promised to never, how does it go, 'curse or chew or go around with boys and girls who do.'" He laughed, then shrugged. "Yeah, well . . ."

Telling the story of the imam, Father Joe took a deep breath, filled his lungs as the imam would have, and let the air hiss slowly out.

"We really are *all* 'people of the Book,' you know—the Jews, the Muslims, the Christians. The Koran or the Torah or the first five books of the Bible, we are all the same there. . . . Their saints and our saints are basically the same. You might have to tune your ear to it, but you or I would say *Abe-ra-ham* or *Say-ra,*" he said, injecting a strain of Southern twang. "The imam would say *Ah-bra-Him* and *Sah-Ra.*"

He studied me, staring into my eyes to make sure I understood. I jotted notes without looking down, stared straight back at him, nodding yes-yes.

"But they're the same, you know," and he sounded convinced that I did. "They just *sound* different."

On that day in 2000, when the new Mercy buildings were blessed, Imam Selep explained to Father Joe that the Mercy Centre sign, written in Thai and English, read by people needing help and wanting to give it, was comprised of much more than letters and syllables. Names and words are vital, meaningful things. The Egyptian playwright and author Ali Salem, a controversial figure in Islam for advocating peace with Israel, had expressed something similar to me soon after 9/11. We were drinking tiny cups of espresso in a crowded café in Cairo when he leaned dramatically across the table. "Woooords," he intoned, making the word sound majestic. "Words are *real.* Words are *things.* Words are *actions.*" The baritone of his voice was as rich as James Earl Jones's, and the lecture, like the smoke of his cigarette, carried through the din. "Good things start with words. Bad things start with words."

Salem was referring specifically to the rhetoric of jihadist terrorists and fundamentalist politicians, a division widened after 9/11 by the reckless use of language like "evil infidels" and "axis of evil." Lines in the sand are easily drawn but difficult to erase, he warned. "When you speak, you have to be responsible for your woooords."

It was this life breathed into a word that Imam Selep Develah had stressed to Father Joe. The word *mercy*, the name Mercy, the granite sign engraved "Mercy" represent the essence of everything behind the sign. Ignore the sign, Joe, he said, and you ignore the word and the powerfully apt name of a slum oasis.

In his daily journals, Father Joe quotes the great thirteenth-century Catholic theologian Saint Thomas Aquinas, scribbling his words in blue ink across a page: "Mercy is the highest attribute to God." Next to this he's drawn a triangle with one word at each point. *Love* at the lower left, *Forgiveness* at the lower right, and set atop the triangle like a star on a Christmas tree, *Mercy*. "Mercy is the highest attribute of Christianity. It is also the highest attribute of Buddhism and Islam," Father Joe told me.

If you skip blessing the sign and just bless the campus as a whole, Imam Selep had whispered, you're only blessing glass, brick, and mortar. Leaning down, listening, Father Joe nodded yes-yes, I understand. "Let's do it," he said; "let's bless it now."

So two old clergymen of religions that share prophets and familial roots, the two biggest tents of Abraham that seem to feud nearly everywhere but in a cordoned-off corner of Klong Toey, clasped hands. And together they prayed that the new Mercy buildings—and its new granite sign—would serve the Buddhist slums for many generations to come.

"*Inshallah*," Father Joe said, finishing the story. "*Inshallah*."

❦

Great anecdote—gave me chicken skin. But I didn't see how it answered the question about Saint Christopher medals being worn by Mercy's Buddhist children. I was about to rephrase the question when Father Joe nodded toward Joop. From the breezeway, she was looking at the storm clouds still overhead. They looked larger than the *Queen Mary.*

"She will never grow up. She will never menstruate. She will never experience life as a grown woman. That's a fact."

Hearing his monotone, you'd think we were discussing the weather, not Joop. His voice sounded dry and resigned.

"She has cycled through all of the medications," he continued. "She is not going to make it much longer."

I stopped jotting notes and looked over at him, checking—not so discreetly—for any pulse of emotion. He shrugged as if to say, *What? You want me to lie?*

But what about the antiretrovirals? I asked.

"Those buy us a few more years, but the children develop resistance. The drugs are good for an extra two, three, four, maybe five years. Right now, that's about all."

We'd followed the AIDS brigade downstairs, trailing behind Joop, the tallest and obviously the big sister of the line. She lagged several paces behind the others, several paces in front of us.

"They all *die.* Eventually," Father Joe said. "That's the battle I have with my ego. I want to save them all. I want to keep them forever, watch them grow up, and watch *their* children grow and the children of their children and so on and so on. That's the American dream, isn't it? To kick back in your old age and thumb through the old picture books, sit in the rocking chair, gather the family at your side, sip hot tea from cups of fine china while

the grandkiddies play. That's the dream; that's what we *want.*
Right? *Right?*"

He rolled his eyes.

The first of the rain had arrived in sheets, blowing several feet
into the breezeway, licking at Joop's heels. She'd stopped while the
others walked on and then turned to face it. Father Joe and I
stopped too, still several steps behind her. She stared into the storm,
studying it as though she were charting water's binary compounds.
Her newest best friend was five years old, blind, and dying, and
she'd already watched friend after friend wither slowly away until
all that remained were bones, skin, and temple cremation. Father
Joe said Joop knew that the odds were heavy against her ever growing up. That's why she was clinging every few weeks to a poor person's hospital with pale blue, stale yellow bedpans.

"Of course I don't want her to die," Father Joe said. "I won't let
her die."

His voice cracked like an adolescent boy's, and this time I didn't
need to check for a pulse. He paused for a second, probably to collect himself, then returned to his monotone.

"But that's my ego talking, isn't it? She *will* die. That's just
a fact."

⚜

Boi had been the elder and the big sister of the children's hospice when I visited Mercy in 2000. Joop was at the head of the class
now. The girl I'd thought was ten or eleven when I met her at the
hospital with Crowley was in fact fourteen. A diminutive fourteen.
Antiretrovirals inhibit HIV, but they also keep "fourteen-year-olds
looking eleven," Father Joe explained.

The first time I'd seen Boi on her double-sized bed "listening"
to a radio with no batteries, I wrote in my notebook, "Skinny

seven- or eight-year-old girl." I found out later she was eleven. She hadn't taken antiretrovirals, but full-blown AIDS can have the same stunting effect. It's why Father Joe preached the gospel of congee. "You have to feed them good food, try to keep their appetites up, try to keep them eating, always, always, *always*," he said, sighing. "They don't always eat though—doesn't matter what you put in front of them. That's a fact."

Before the Thai government began giving Mercy free antiretroviral medicines in 2003, a British expatriate had tried to rescue Boi. He donated thousands of baht for her antiretroviral medicines. Her health rebounded, and she returned to Mercy's school for AIDS kids (Thailand's government schools didn't accept them), Father Joe said. In an e-mail dated June 27, 2000, about a month after my first visit to Mercy, Father Joe wrote to me sounding optimistic but realistic about the newest miracle meds:

Dear Greg,

This morning I was at the AIDS hospice and our favorite girl "Boi" was there—perk and almost chipper—not totally, but on the way with the new medicine, which she will take everyday till she dies.

She's better, but that's a funny word with AIDS. Her legs still look like she has spent six months in the trenches of some epic battle of WWII . . . but she smiles and talks a lot now.

Also she is back to her habit of reading the Thai newspaper each morning—yes, reading the Thai Rath newspaper each morning. She has graduated from the third grade and is exceptionally bright . . . and she is reading a book about Tigger—as in "Ru" and his mom Kanga and Pooh and Eee-aweeee and the folks in A. Milne's story. She even knows about the game . . . Pooh sticks . . . that Pooh and Christopher Robin used to play off the foot bridge over that gentle stream in Sussex in the 100 acres wood.

But she said that what she wants most of all, more than the newspaper or books, are hugs. No one really hugs her anymore, she said. . . . grownups hesitate when children are so sickly and small that it looks like they could break. So I promised—really promised—this morning that I would always be there to hug her, and she asked, "Even if I get funny looking again?" Yes, I promised. Had tears in my eyes. But all in all, through the tears and everything else, Boi is an ode to joy.

. . . prayers. fr joe.

She died ten months later, a year shy of reaching her goal of being a teenager—a universal milestone for children rich and poor, sick and healthy. In his *Bangkok Post* column, Father Joe wrote of Boi's last days. "She asked, 'When is my mom going to come and take me home?' Her eyes had that final knowing look—comfortable, secure, memorizing everything within sight, taking in every last detail one last time."

She had set the bar for the AIDS brigade life span, raising it by a couple of years.

Joop had already raised it again.

A few feet from where Joop stood watching the rain was a small gold-leaf Buddhist shrine angled prominently at the front of the breezeway. Behind her, in Mercy's main courtyard, was a life-sized bronze of Our Lady of Guadalupe set in a pond of lotus and goldfish in the direct path of the rising sun. On clear days, the statue reflects everyone: Catholic, Buddhist, Protestant, Muslim, Hindu, Jew, Mormon, agnostic, atheist, me, you.

Mercy's version of Mexico's most beloved religious icon is a deliberate melding of cultures and peoples, a sculpture designed and cast by Easterners and Westerners living on both sides of the economic divide. Like 95 percent of Thai, the affable caster was Theravada Buddhist. For a century, he and his father and his father's father had declined to mold any statue that wasn't a Buddhist shrine. But after hearing the story of Buddhist orphans, sick Buddhist children, and thousands of Buddhist students in schools built by a defiant Catholic, the family made an exception for the mother of Christianity.

Our Lady of Klong Toey—the name given to Mercy's interpretation of Latin America's interpretation of the Virgin Mary—was forged in fire and poured for free, aside from the 80,000 baht (about $2,000) outlay for the bronze. "We didn't want anything cloyingly Catholic, but at the same time, it had to be something the children could be comforted by," Father Joe said. "We tell them that Mary is like their mother, and she is soft and loving, and they can go to her with anything."

So two years ago on a monsoon morning like the one Joop now lingered in, Father Joe had taken a large umbrella and his favorite rosary to a crude centuries-old outdoor foundry sixty miles away. Praying beneath the foundry's tin overhang amid the pots-and-pans clatter of another day's downpour, he'd thumbed the dark beads of a special rosary strung by a friend during his novitiate forty-five years earlier. He'd carried it that day only because it was something he carried, like a wallet. He hadn't planned to use it in the statue's ceremony, but when asked to give a blessing alongside the huge vat of molten metal, he stepped toward the log fire that had been heating the bronze for the better part of three days. Staring into the bubbles, which had turned emerald green, he bowed the *wai* and prayed for

Holy Mary to imbue Our Lady of Klong Toey with the same magnanimous energy that had carried Mercy this far. Then, without
even a twitch of hesitation, he'd dropped his rosary into the boil.

A half-blind orphan boy nicknamed One-Eyed Jeip had gone
next. He'd tagged along for a joy ride because he'd been hanging
out bored in the main breezeway when Father Joe, Sister Maria
Chantavarodom, and a vanload of others had left for the foundry.
Jeip pulled a penny-sized medal of the Buddha from his jeans
pocket. It was a treasure, the only thing his dying grandmother had
left him. Clenching his one good eye shut, he'd made the sign of
the *wai,* held a fist over the hot bronze, then dropped the coin in.
He'd smiled, satisfied as he'd watched it vanish. Another neighborhood tagalong, a haggardly slum grandmother who'd been visiting one of the AIDS brigade kids, took an earring out of her ear
and dropped it into the boil. Sister Maria whispered a prayer to
herself in one or all three of her languages and dropped in a medal
of the Holy Virgin Mary.

Tai-chi master Tew Bunnag, a Mercy adviser and volunteer from
one of Thailand's oldest and most respected families, was the one
who'd convinced the foundry to cast the mold. He'd stepped
toward the boil, bowed the *wai,* then donated two coins from the
Thai monarchy. His wife, Denys, an English sculptor who'd
designed the statue and its eighteen-inch clay model for the foundry
to work from, had waited with a heart-shaped plastic bottle from
Sacre-Cœur, the Sacred Heart Basilica of Montmartre, the consecrated Catholic church whose 270-foot-high dome overlooks Paris.
Dropping the bottle into the boil, a gust of black smoke billowed
off the tin overhang.

"*That* was her heart," Father Joe said of Our Lady of Klong
Toey.

The rosary Father Joe gave away that day had traveled with him
from major seminary in Wisconsin to training with the Reverend

Harry Thiel in northeast Thailand and Laos to the Holy Redeemer monastery in Bangkok and finally into the Slaughterhouse shacks and new Mercy Centre house. For nearly three-quarters of his life, Father Joe had slept and prayed with it. It was his most sacred possession. But giving it to Our Lady of Klong Toey was an easy decision, he said.

Recalling the ceremony now, in the fresh air of another morning rain, he began slapping his lips together, like he'd just tasted an executive chef's finest broth.

"It felt like the thing to do." Smack, smack, smack "It was just one of those moments when you *know* you're supposed to do it. The rosary belonged *there,* in Our Lady of Klong Toey. I knew what I needed to do; I could *taste* it." Smack, smack, smack. "Sometimes you know because you *feel* it"—he backhanded my paunch—"right there."

He searched my face to see if I grasped the significance. "You need to understand, this is real stuff. This is about auras and energy fields, about all the good stuff that we all have. You don't throw just anything into that molten metal. It needs to be something near and dear, your most prized trinket."

He searched my face again. I was hunched over, leaning against the breezeway wall jotting notes. I nodded yes-yes, I understand.

He half-frowned and continued. "For you, the trinket might be the cross on your necklace or the entire necklace or your wedding ring . . ."

My wedding ring? I stopped nodding, raised my eyebrows.

"OK, maybe not *that.* But your necklace. You get the point, right? You're giving away something that means—really, really means— something to you. You're throwing a piece of *yourself* into that boil."

Either the wind or the story of blessed molten metal had caused tiny bumps to rise on Father Joe's arms, and when he held his forearm up for inspection, he looked like he was again pointing toward the moon.

"What do you call these? Goose bumps?"

⚜

The mascot of Mercy is a woman because the savior of humankind came from a woman, the Virgin Mary. Her presence in drawings, paintings, statues, and since 2003, a golden bronze, is all over the Mercy campus. Only the men who penned and translated the world's big-tent scriptures endowed the features of the Deity—God, Allah, Yahweh, Jehovah, Whomever—with male features, Father Joe explained. It granted dominion over religion and, by extension, over culture to man. "But we sure goofed up on that one," Father Joe said. "Salvation passes through the woman. We've *all* come through the woman."

He is also She. Jesus Christ, all twenty-eight Buddhas, Muhammad, Gandhi, Confucius, you, me, and the fourteen Dalai Lamas all spent the first months of life suspended in amniotic fluid, connected to female biology, part and parcel of woman.

When Our Lady of Klong Toey shed the mold four days after the ceremony in 2003, she weighed five hundred pounds and looked perpetually nine months pregnant. She had a large belly, wide hips, big shoulders, and a halo over her head. "We didn't want a Barbie doll. She had to be a big mama, able to carry many births," Father Joe said, staring now at the bronze awash in rain. "Someday we'll add a plaque with that line from Shakespeare—how does it go? 'The quality of mercy falleth like gentle rain.' It's this whole thing again about how the rain and sunshine fall to everyone. Like God's mercy. To everyone. . . . Remind me to do that—don't let me forget; remind me, remind me."

He held out his hand like a pushy valet. "We'll collect a fund for it, and you can contribute the first ten baht. As a gesture, you know. That way you'd be a part of all of this."

The outstretched paw looked like my First Baptist Church collection plate. I scratched my head and looked away, no different than when I was a teenager expected to tithe on the minimum wage I earned slinging grease at McDonald's.

You want me to put *my* aura into Our Lady of Klong Toey?

I didn't feel worthy, but I did feel conned. Then insulted. I'd done the math in my spat of head scratching.

Ten baht? You think my aura has a value of only twenty-five cents?

"Symbolic, it's all *symbolism*," Father Joe said, smiling but sounding exasperated. "You'd be joining in this *with* us . . . and that's worth a lot. That's really cool, man, don't ya think?"

࿓

It took two dozen Buddhist men to carry the mother of Christianity onto her rightful perch: in a pond of sacred lilies set in stone arranged to symbolize Buddhism's circle of life. The church's symbol of universal motherhood was oddly bowlegged. Each foot pointed outward and upward like two ends of an anchor. "Early Christianity said we are always in a boat and the world is the ocean and life is a storm," Father Joe explained. "To thwart the storm, every boat needs an anchor. We are grounded by our faith."

He nodded toward the Virgin Mary. "That's a five-hundred-pound anchor."

Every wedge of sunshine buffs her bronze golden, the color of the aura of saints. She wears a halo but no expression, no eyes, ears, nose, mouth, just a smooth globe head that reflects what others see in her. Deity and thyself, man and woman. Her sun-dappled cheeks adapt to all. Except on monsoon mornings. Today, water runs off her back.

Joop left the breezeway walking slowly past us like we weren't there. One week earlier, in the barren blue hospital ward, she had been tearing sections from a tangerine like they were strips of cotton candy, savoring each intensely when she waved instructions at Tom. "Here," he'd said, taking a section from her and handing it to me. "She doesn't want you to feel left out."

Today I was invisible. She was damp and tardy for class, yet she lingered again, staring into the rain at the opposite end of the breezeway, a stone's throw from Our Lady of Klong Toey.

"Does she know?" I asked.

"What? That she won't graduate, grow up, get married, be a mommy, a grandmamma, rock grandbabies on the front porch?"

His brow was crooked. He didn't say it, but I knew what he was thinking: *Where have you been? Haven't you been paying attention? We're burning so many caskets that the lids are saved.*

Even as I'd asked the question, I knew it sounded rhetorical.

He must've agreed. He never answered.

Our Lady of Klong Toey, anchored in the Mercy Centre's main courtyard

TWELVE

Forged by Mercy and Mary

To know Jesus is to love Jesus. Know him and you will love him.

—Father Joe's daily journal

I 'd like everyone to believe what I believe because I believe some *good shit,*" Father Joe said, and in the shade of the next day's sunrise, I couldn't tell if he was sneering or grinning. "We'd all like to think that we believe some good shit, and we want others to believe *our* good shit instead of *their* good shit."

It sounded like the beginnings of a George Carlin routine.

I'd waited until after his morning jog to make another run at the Saint Christopher question. It was still the summer of 2005, less than halfway into the Thai school year, and I'd been intruding on Father Joe's schedule for about two weeks. I figured it best to let the endorphins soften him up, then rush in when I saw the all-clear. Be direct, be polite, proceed with caution; never inflict irreparable harm on the reporter-subject rapport—at least not early on. Journalism 101.

Our Lady of Klong Toey, I began, the pendant of a Christian martyr, Buddhist "prayers" directed to the heavens and to the Virgin Mary—isn't this stuff just camouflaged Christianity or covert converting?

The timing was perfect. A sherbet-orange Lumpini Park sunrise peeked over a ridge of downtown high-rises. Park lamps had begun to fade. Father Joe was sopping sweaty from a three-mile jog and still light-footed, walking with the same spring that had foretold our best interviews. That was my all-clear. His latent ire at middle-class outsiders asking presumptuous questions would be evaporating that very moment in the colored cotton of his gray shirt.

You're really in Thailand spreading the gospel of *Jeeeezuz,* aren't you?

I laughed.

He didn't.

Perhaps it was *Jeeeezuz,* the way I said it, as if mocking his mocking of my Southern Baptist roots, but he stopped walking and stared at me or toward me, and in the orange-yellow glare of reced-ing park lights, I couldn't quite see his face. When he responded with the cursing that sounded like my favorite agnostic comic, I suspected endorphin failure, so I braced for the worst. Asking the questions head-on like that had felt risky, like jumping off the Route 421 bridge into South Holston Lake. As teenagers, if my friends and I stood and stared, we never dared. But if we closed our eyes and went on the count of three, we'd find an immediate answer to a hot summer day.

I counted to three and dared again.

You don't really believe all that stuff you told PBS, do you, Father Joe?

He was wearing a floppy white hat to block Bangkok's searing sun, and together with the fading fluorescence and brilliant sun-rise, a shadow covered most of his face. I couldn't tell if I was about to experience a gust of Old Testament Joe or the breezy New Testament version. Yin and yang, they both have critical roles. The former gets things done even if it means stomping, screaming, cursing, and breaking laws that stand in the way of slum children and the schools, hospices, orphanages, homes, and help they need. The latter walks hand in hand with sick kids toward their inevitable end, falling in love and being hurt again and again, but kneeling each time at their bedside to caress with two fingers the softest of the soft spots at the front of their heads.

Several seconds passed before he answered my question about PBS. I saw his teeth bared.

"Maybe you're right; maybe I got carried away with PBS," he said, smiling broadly, chortling just enough for me to relax. "I'm an activist, a rabble rouser, and sometimes I have to be harsh and make a lot of noise to make people listen. The danger with that, of course, is that you get people so angry they say, 'Eff you.'"

I exhaled. He resumed walking.

"But I *have* learned from the imam and the abbot, from Buddhism *and* Islam. We all can. And we *should,* we need to."

Learn from Buddhists and Muslims?

"Yes, yes. And *they* should learn from us. From the gospels."

That sure *ain't* what you told PBS.

"Maybe that part was cut out. Or maybe I just forgot it." He smiled to indicate otherwise. "Really, though, we should all learn from each other, take the best lessons from all the great prophets. Don't waste any of it."

He was springing again from the balls of his feet, invigorated by the topic.

"But," he said, louder now and breathing harder, "I think they've got it wrong and we've got it right."

I slowed down and looked over at him. He kept the pace. I caught up.

They? We?

"Basically."

⚜

For Buddhists, God neither is nor isn't. Siddhārtha Gautama lived five to six centuries before Christ. The calendar on this day in Thailand reads 2548, not 2005; dates are calculated from the birth of Siddhārtha. The Buddha, the Awakened One, is said to have attained enlightenment on how to end human suffering, or *dukkha,* while meditating under a fig tree. Twenty-five centuries later, these bodhi (enlightenment) trees trim Lumpini Park's 140 acres. Their leaves are heart-shaped, identical to the ceremonial funeral fans carried by Klong Toey's Buddhist monks, inscribed front and back with the same sutras they chant at funerals:

Nee mai pon. To run and there is no escape.

Bhy mai glap. To go and not return.

Lap mai dhern. To sleep and not wake up.

Fern mai mee. To not return to consciousness

Those are the lessons greeting Mercy's orphans, giveaways, run-aways, and AIDS brigade at Wat Saphan (Temple by the Bridge) cremations. If they thought life couldn't get any worse, they now see friends and relatives in unzipped red plastic body bags and read the sutras waved on the fans. *There is no escape.* After three consecutive days of the sutras chanted by monks and a monk's tolling of the temple bell, many of the kids will tuck coins, trinkets, candy, food, stuffed animals, and flowers into or around the caskets that will burn in the crematory furnace at 2,000 degrees Fahrenheit. Friends, siblings, classmates, and bunkmates reduced to ashes, like the cheap fiberboard of the donated coffins.

Nee mai pon.

Father Joe veered off Lumpini's asphalt jogging path and picked a bodhi leaf.

"There is *no* escape," he repeated, translating *nee mai pon.* "Pretty upbeat stuff, huh? There's no prayer, no 'Lord Jesus have mercy on us,' nothing like it. One-third of our children don't know their mother's name; another one-third were sold by their mothers and daddies or were abused by them or other adults. . . . Now they're being told, 'There is no escape.'"

The 2002 documentary *Mercy (Med-Dah)*, filmed over the course of two years at Mercy Centre, follows Luk Nam, a healthy eleven-year-old girl evicted from a rural Thai village and school after her father died with AIDS. Luk Nam's mother had been infected by the father, and Luk Nam's younger sister, Nam Fon, was infected in utero. It wasn't the same "slum of the dumb," as Father Joe called it, the one out by the Don Muang airport that had years earlier evicted Nong Bla and her mother. Just the same prejudices and paranoia.

Luk Nam, five years older than Nam Fon, had escaped HIV's infection but not its collateral damage. Her mother and father had already died, and in the film, her best friend is Boi, the twelve-year-old elder of the children's hospice who would die eleven months after my visit in 2000. In the first few minutes of the fifty-minute documentary, Luk Nam tells filmmaker Jeanne Hallacy, "I'm the only one left to tell the story."

At Boi's funeral, Hallacy shows Father Joe sitting where Catholics sit during ceremonies in a Buddhist temple: with the laity. His brow drips sweat, his eyes water, and when he talks about Boi, he bites down so hard on his lower lip, I'm sure it left a mark. "It tears your guts out," he tells Hallacy. Then, biting down harder, "It. Just. Tears. Your. Guts. Out."

During the filming, Nam Fon ages from about five to seven years old, and the destructive progression of AIDS is visible in the shrinking of her face, arms, and legs. At Boi's funeral, she sits on the lap of tai-chi expert and Mercy adviser Tew Bunnag, and her arms are so spindly, they look like legs on a spider. Expressive brown eyes bulge from her skinny face, staring directly at Boi's adult-sized casket. At the last minute of the body's viewing, Nam Fon squeezes Bunnag's arm.

"Do you want to go up?" he whispers to her.

She squeezes again, harder.

Bunnag carries Nam Fon up to the edge of the coffin, where she leans draped over his arms to peer downward, as if staring into a well. "I felt at that point her great strength . . . and I kept asking myself over and over, '*Why* would she have wanted to be taken up?'" Bunnag tells Hallacy. "The only answer I kept getting was that she wanted to *see* where *she* was going to be."

⚜

Father Joe turned a perfectly heart-shaped bodhi leaf over twice and pointed to its center, where the sutras would be inscribed. *Nee mai pon.* To run and there is no escape.

"So we give them Mary." He shrugged as if to say, *Sue me.*

"The Virgin Mary becomes their second mommy," he continued. "We say, 'Mary is our mother and your mother and she loves you. She won't curse you, she won't sell you, and she's not going to leave you. She is always there *for you.*'"

As if he'd just heard himself, he smiled approvingly.

"Hey, man, that's good stuff! We *all* need three or four anchors in life, and this is one. Prayer. It's one of our best tools. It's a step along the path. You pray to Saint Mary."

Christ never said there wouldn't be suffering, but *all* of life is not suffering, as formal Buddhism teaches, he explained. "We have this tendency in us to goof off, and we have a tendency in us to do really dumb things—in some of us, that tendency gets really strong. But life is *not* about suffering. Jesus came along and said, I will give you a way of thinking and a way of acting and a set of ethics, and if you live this way, yes, shit is going to happen, but you will basically be happy. If you live this way, act this way, treat people this way, it will all be OK."

Five centuries before Christ, the Buddha taught that nirvana—blissful emancipation from the carnal desires and attachments that lock humankind to perpetual suffering and rebirth—is found only through a learned, diligent mind and a compassionate heart. It's the same basic lesson that ran through Christ's teachings, and

Muhammad, who showed up about five centuries after Christ, said many of the same things. Renounce material gain and selfish comfort in favor of selfless action.

All three—the Buddha, Jesus, and Muhammad, in that order and historical symmetry—warned of the cravings that blind and bind humankind to ignorance, greed, lust, jealousy, anger, apathy, fear, hatred, and so on. It's the poison pumping through the veins of narcissism. Or as the pastors of my youth might call it, Satan's side of the street. The Buddha didn't discuss goodness and evil in the scare-the-devil-out-of-you way of a Southern Baptist, but he spoke of the Truth, or *Dharma*, as a spiritual awakening ushering us into eternal peace.

It seemed to me that our differences were semantic. At the very least, this nirvana stuff must be close kin to the paradise promised by the Christian resurrection. But at the Wat Saphan, children don't hear the resurrection's promise of salvation or sing from the Book of Revelation, "Holy, holy, holy is the Lord God Almighty—the one who always was, who is, and who is still to come."

The Buddha was born a prince and died a prophet, but like Muhammad, he never claimed to be a messiah. There's no theism in Buddhism. There's nowhere to hang Eastern shame or Western guilt, no absolution granted by a monk, priest, or baptism. Thai Buddhists will safeguard their houses, streets, cars, and nearly everything else with elaborate shrines, and they will ante up alms like the Christian tithe, giving charity in the hope that good karma is for sale, but there's no savior to absorb or pardon their sin and guilt. You own the karma you sow—or purchase. Its consequences and rewards are reaped in this life or the next or the one after that, and if you're born desperately poor or with the Virus, you might be getting what you deserve. The Buddha doesn't possess the power to forgive a debt.

According to Pali canon, the Buddha said he was neither alpha nor omega. But he foretold the coming of another prophet, a fully enlightened Buddha endowed with perfect wisdom and conduct, who would light the way to a purified, righteous life. And, just as the Buddha had warned of his own teachings, he said that the validity of any lesson proclaimed by prophets or messiahs had to be tested in the living of it. Nothing should be taken at its word.

If in my Bible Belt hometown "believing is seeing," then in Father Joe's squatter slum "seeing is believing." Buddhism is more experiential philosophy than orthodox Christian theology. Nothing is really faith-based. If you experience God, then God is real. For *you*. But Buddhism as a whole does not believe in a benevolent, omnipotent, omniscient supreme deity. Father, Son, and Holy Ghost burn internal, one with enlightenment. The Buddha said all dharma lies within.

This is where I see Christian belief merging with Buddhism but veering from Islam, which follows the first five books of the Christian and Hebrew Bibles. For Muslims, Allah is *out there,* the lone omnipotence on which to hedge all bets. The five daily prayers of Islam include its boilerplate: "There is no other god but God, and Muhammad is His prophet." To suggest that God is Father, Son, and Holy Ghost is heresy to Islam. God is love and burns internal? The warm flush of agape might be wonderful, but Allah doesn't travel in blood-red veins. Not even Muhammad's, and not in those of the prophet Jesus.

So maybe I'm a Christian Buddhist, I told Father Joe.

He twisted his eyes and nose like he'd smelled something sour.

"We have to take some things from Buddhism, yes," he said, "but Buddhism basically says God is *not* necessary. And you and I, in our teachings, say we can't even have a good thought without God blessing us. That is the scary thing about Buddhism. It says all of this is totally possible by yourself."

But if God is also the Holy Spirit living within us and Buddhism's goal is simply to return to the light or the dharma within, couldn't that be the same thing?

He screwed up his face again but clearly didn't want to argue the point. "Yes, yes, well, . . . OK." His voice trailed off, and I knew he meant, *Yeah, whatever.*

I tried again. Well, then, if Buddhism doesn't believe God is necessary, that makes it atheistic or agnostic, doesn't it?

"No, that's too harsh. It's better to leave those types of words out of it. Buddhism just doesn't concern itself with God. Everything in it revolves around *you.* The teachings are that *you* must calm yourself down. *You* must meditate. *You* must control your anger, your hate, your greed. *You* must do this and this and this. *You* must be cool, live cool, keep a cool temperament."

He handed the bodhi leaf to me.

"See? Looks just like the funeral fans. No escape, no God, no need for Him. Do it yourself. . . . But the West does this now too. It's taken God out of it. The religion of the United States today is materialism and commercialism, and it spreads this new religion throughout the world, proclaiming that *this* is what will bring you joy, *this* is what will bring you peace. The Supreme Court is going out of its way to remove God publicly and officially. Eventually it'll take God off the idol of all this worship."

I looked up from the notepad, waiting for him to finish.

"The dollar," he said. "Your *almighty* dollar."

The sun was fully awake now, and we were in the shade of a bodhi tree. It was nearly as tall as the Route 421 bridge was high, and around its trunk, roots had collected like the decorative skirt of a Christmas tree. The arch of my foot rested on a root with the girth of a fire hose. For the sacred tree of Buddhism, I said, its roots are *shallow.*

Father Joe studied the ground, then glanced around at several other bodhi trees.

"Hmm. Yes, yes, you're right. This *one* has shallow roots." He pointed to other bodhis scattered through the park. "But take a second look. You have to look *all* around, see more than just *one* tree. Look closer. They're different . . ."

Some had yellowish leaves, like the one Father Joe had picked; others were plain green. Some were taller or leaner or fuller. Some had roots spread above ground; many, however, did not. Like the Theravada and Mahayana schools of Buddhism and their various branches, the trees had unique characteristics.

". . . and the same," he finished.

All of Buddhism's branches connect to the Buddha's Four Noble Truths and the Noble Eightfold Path, studied by Buddhists in much the way Christians revere the four books of the Gospel that recount the life and teachings of Christ. And although Muslims, Jews, Protestants, and Catholics share the same Old Testament bipolar God of Abraham, Noah, and Moses—forgiving one day, condemning the next—Islam teaches that the Koran is the *only* uncorrupted word of God. That is not much different, really, from the fundamentalist Christians who swear by Testaments Old and New. Or Judaism, which dismisses the New Testament as a misguided attempt to erase God's rules as set forth in the Torah—setting Jews apart as God's chosen people.

I quoted for Father Joe as best as I could recall from the U2 song, "If God Will Send His Angels." The lead singer and songwriter, Bono, an Irish Catholic, sings about how Jesus used to show him the score but now Jesus is in show business and it's "hard to get in the door."

Everyone just wants to *own* God, isn't that it? I asked Father Joe.

He smiled and nodded yes-yes. "Write that. *Write that down.*"

He stopped walking and waited for me to do exactly that.

"I know you were raised Baptist," he said, "and we've the whole Protestant-Catholic thing supposedly working against us, but I think your idea of God is about the same as mine. You believe

Christ died on the cross for our sins—and he died for *everyone's* sins, no exceptions. And if he beat the rap and rose from the dead or God rose him from the dead, then that is an *unbelievable* energy field. Enough good energy to overcome all the bad energy, which you can call sin, Satan, evil, whatever."

I nodded yes-yes, even though I don't believe the Bible—with its many translations, interpretations, and scribes—is infallible. Its wisdom can be profound, but much of the text doesn't resonate with me as nonfiction. I suspect that as in certain memoirs, parts should be preceded by this author's note: "Names have been changed, characters combined, and events compressed. Certain episodes are imaginative re-creations, and those episodes are not intended to portray actual events." Nor do I believe that God compiled one mega-best-selling anthology and dropped out of the book biz. My spirituality is fed by the stories of the gospels as well as the inspiring prose of native Baptist Rick Warren and of New Age apostles Paulo Coelho, Neale Donald Walsch, James Redfield, and Marianne Williamson. The book of Proverbs informs my integrity and compassion, as does *A Course in Miracles*. The counsel of the Apostle Paul ("the fruit of the spirit is love, joy, peace, patience, kindness, goodness, faithfulness, gentleness, and self-control") feeds me no more, no less, no better, no worse than that of Honolulu physician and Native Hawaiian healer Kekuni Blaisdell, who once gave me this prescription for a full and spiritual life: "Pray every day, meditate every day, laugh every day, spend an hour with someone you love, and fill your life with purpose."

Why would the Almighty have dictated life's most critical lessons only to people writing two thousand years ago? I can't recall a time beyond the age of ten or twelve when I wasn't convinced that this fundamental "fact" was in fact a fundamental error. Jesus loves me, this I know, for *the Bible* tells me so? A cute song for children's church, maybe, and one that went unquestioned by me for the first several summers of vacation Bible school, but no amount of preaching could later convince me that the Bible's word was God's *final* word. I would always need additional sources.

However, in my opinion, there's enough corroborative history to establish the general biography of a Galilean Jew named Yeshua who became known as Jesus of Nazareth. He worked among prostitutes and the poorest of the poor, he coolly defied Rome, he healed the sick and the dying, he sacrificed his life for humankind, and he was resurrected in me and you. Buddhist, Catholic, Protestant, Muslim, Hindu, Wiccan, Pagan, Jew, agnostic, atheist, saint, sinner, the holy baptized and the holy not. And yes, I believe he beat the rap and rose from the dead. If he was not the physical manifestation of the deity, he'd have to have been a con man or a crazy man. As C. S. Lewis wrote in *Mere Christianity,* "A man who was merely a man and said the sort of things Jesus said would not be a great moral teacher. He would either be a lunatic—on a level with the man who says he is a poached egg—or else he would be the Devil of Hell. You must make your choice."

The preponderance of evidence to me isn't weighted toward egg or devil. So I look a priest confidently in the eyes while walking a mile loop around Lumpini and answer completely and honestly. Yes, yes, of course, I *do* believe.

"OK, then, if you look at this energy field and see God the way some of the physicists do—as pure light and total understanding—you can see that virtue is its own reward," Father Joe says. He repeats it slowly: "Virtue is its own reward. Buddhism says this. Christianity says it too. This isn't about believing or not believing. You don't need to. You can test this stuff. If you work out, you will feel better—your mind works better, your body works better, you're in a better mood. If someone needs your help and you volunteer it, you might be tired when the day is done, but you feel good. It felt *right*. It was the right thing to do. Your spirit is lifted."

So tapping into the energy is about living *selflessly* rather than selfishly?

"Yes, *that,* but it's a lot more than just that. It's not like mathematics: if I do twenty-seven good things and only twenty-one bad things, I'll get what I want or my prayers will be answered or I can make merit and that will be enough. It's not about checks and balances, though of course that is part of it. It's about *living*. It's about loving and forgiving and living in the same way Christ did and in this great energy created by Christ, by the resurrection."

I can pray, as I often do, for God to grant me patience and a holy perspective, but if I'm not living in a way that reflects the self-discipline taught by Jesus, the Buddha, Muhammad—if I'm not pointing toward the moon—I won't see what He sees. Or feel what He feels. Right?

"You would need to check your form," Father Joe said, mimicking a golf swing again.

If I goof off on my job, I fall behind in work. Eventually, I face deadlines unprepared, and the resulting anxiety makes me moody and agitated. At that point, I would feel nothing of what the Apostle Paul describes as the "fruit of the Spirit"—love, joy, peace, patience, kindness, goodness.

Father Joe was nodding yes-yes.

Two of the most vexing questions I recall from my childhood deal with God and Santa: How could God listen to billions of prayers every night? How could Santa make a billion or so house calls in the course of one night? I told Father Joe that I believe I could answer the first question. The second one still had me stumped. When my two young sons rush through their nightly prayers, I caution them to slow down, take a deep breath, and then listen, really *listen* to themselves with the sort of ear lent by priests, therapists, and first dates. If you don't hear your prayer, God doesn't hear it, I tell them. By now they know what I mean.

Where is God? I'll ask them. They tap their chests.

"Good, good, yes, yes," Father Joe said. "And if you are filled with God every second, every heartbeat, every breath, like you and I believe, then you are totally filled with Christ, and everything you do then is tied up with Christ. If God is in your actions, in your motions, in your thinking, then God *is* life."

He was talking with his hands, and his step was invigorated again. The sun had risen over Lumpini, and the park was full of people jogging and dancing and lifting weights and playing badminton. This was the morning I'd see a family carry a TV onto a park lawn to watch a Chinese opera under a party tent while drinking hot tea. It was a weekday morning.

"Now," Father Joe continued, "is every word of the Bible true? Is every word of the gospels entirely accurate? Was Christ born of a virgin? Did he ever get married?"

He shrugged.

At the time, Dan Brown's 2003 novel *The Da Vinci Code* was still breaking sales records everywhere, with its depiction of Jesus as a married father of one and the Christian canon as mostly fiction. The Vatican had condemned Brown's novel as heresy and would later ask Catholics to boycott the movie.

"Are these the things that are most important to us right now? Is this where we should be focused? Is this how the church can best spend its time, its resources, its energy? The Vatican isn't doing anything about the Muslim (terrorism) situation in the south (in Thailand); it hasn't done anything to help with the tsunami victims. We've a war going (in Iraq) where Christians and Jews are killing Muslims, and Muslims are killing Christians and Jews. . . . AIDS is killing mom, dad, and girlfriend. And the Vatican is worried about a Tom Hanks mystery thriller?"

It's staring at dirt under the fingernail?

"Exactly! We need to be looking at where Christ pointed. The teachings—the teachings!—*those* are what's important. Talking about all this other stuff is a distraction; it's a lot easier than focusing on the real problems."

Live the lessons.

"Yes, the Buddha was absolutely right. Christ said it too: I am the way. Jesus came to show us the way. When he got right down to it, he said, 'I am it. You have to be me. You have to think the way I do. You have to love and forgive—you have to accept it and give it.' . . . Do I have an obligation to teach Catholicism to these kids? No. But I do have an obligation to teach the lessons of the gospels, the Ten Commandments, the beatitudes. Those need to be here. We need to teach these lessons. It's not about *wear* this, stand *this* way, *bow* like this, *eat* this, *drink* this. Christ wiped out those rules."

Yet churches still cling to them.

"There's comfort in ritual."

Discomfort too.

⁂

For as long as I could remember, I'd remained quiet during the Apostles' Creed in churches I visited or attended. A few nights earlier at the Holy Redeemer Church, I hadn't said a word of it, didn't lip-sync or cover my mouth either. I was grateful Father Joe hadn't been watching me. In church, I always listen silently while congregations recite the declaration of faith, which sounds to me a little too much like "bubble, bubble, toil and trouble":

> I believe in God, the Father almighty, creator of heaven and earth. I believe in Jesus Christ, God's only Son, our Lord, who was conceived by the Holy Spirit, born of the Virgin Mary, suffered under

Pontius Pilate, was crucified, died, and was buried. He descended
to the dead; on the third day he rose again; he ascended into
heaven, sits at the right hand of God, the Father almighty; and he
will come to judge the living and the dead. . . .

I don't join the chorus because of the absolute authority it pro-
claims, but I'm also leery of the subtle peer pressure to go along,
get along, play along. I didn't join a college fraternity for that reason. I don't vote along party lines. And I stubbornly decline to
recite Christian incantations just because the well-dressed, well-
meaning faithful might glance curiously at the tight-lipped guy in
khakis and loose tie who didn't join the circle at the cauldron.
According to my baby book and Mom's neat cursive hand, I began
questioning this *Jeeeezuz* stuff pretty early in life. On a brittle yellow page, it reads, "About age 4 or 5 Greg asked his first unan-
swerable question. 'If God made everything then who made God?'"

Just because two or three years later, I would be dipped backward into the chest-high baptismal of my religious tribe doesn't
mean I walk in lockstep with it. My sister was baptized on the same
Mother's Day as I, and afterward our father took us down the road
to Bassett's Dairy for chocolate malts. Just like he'd promised.

So you see, Jesus and I don't have any problems.

Jeeeezuz, however. I've long had my doubts.

Father Joe nodded halfheartedly.

"You didn't ask this, but I'll tell you anyhow. Does Joe Maier
believe in the Vatican? No. *No!* Does he believe in the pope? I don't
not believe in him. But that's not important. The teachings—that's
what we need to focus on. The lessons in the gospels are really
good and they're pretty simple. *Love* one another. *Forgive* one
another. Your preachers all talk about this, and you and I go, 'yeah,
yeah, yeah'"—his head wobbled like a parishioner half asleep—
"but this is important stuff. We need to pay attention. The loving

goes on every second, and the healing extends into every breath. It doesn't turn off. If your kid breaks your favorite fishing pole, you don't curse him every time you look at that fishing pole. Forgiveness blooms eternal. Just because you haven't thought about your wife for the last three minutes doesn't mean you stopped loving her. It goes on. The love is continuous. That's the Father and that's Our Lady of Klong Toey. Those are great images."

But if you want the children to be the best Buddhist, the best Christian, the best Muslim, or the best whatever that they can be, I asked, referring to his earlier suggestion that all righteous paths lead to God, why then not have the kids focus on the lessons of the Buddha and the slum abbot?

They do, he explained. Mercy's children attend mandatory weekly services at the Wat Saphan as well as a mandatory weekly Mass in Mercy's small chapel.

"We often tell the kids that Mary is a wonderful grandmother, the kind who always has warm cookies waiting for you. Kids and cookies, man, that's a universal combination. No one religion can own that."

He began to say something more but stopped and then started again.

"You can never say this out loud because the church gets upset," he said, pausing again. "But what we've done, really, is take *practical* Buddhism—not *formal* Buddhism—and put some Christian spin on it."

The best that both offer, I suggested.

"Yes, yes, you could say that."

But you said we could never say it out loud.

He laughed.

"Oh, what the hell. Write it."

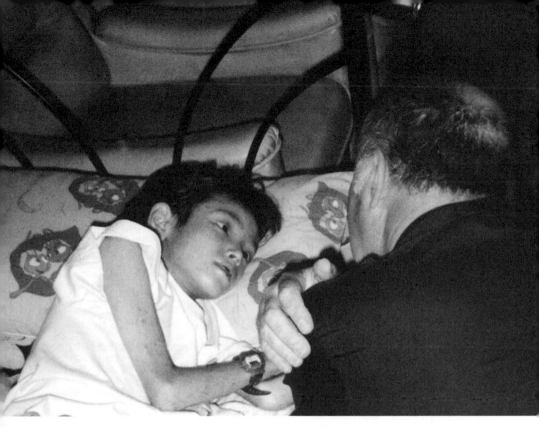

Father Joe bedside with Boi in May 2000.
She died April 24, 2001.

THIRTEEN

Any Dream Will Do

Our kids can sing Bach.

—Father Joe's daily journal

Two weeks after arriving back in Thailand in 2005, I thought I was beginning to know Father Joe about as well as any Protestant and Mercy outsider could. Yin and yang, Old Testament and New Testament, happy days, sad days, euphoric, melancholy—he was bipolar like me. The only difference was that he had good reason to be. And where optimism buoyed him, skepticism dogged me. He looked up and saw the heavens. I still saw the sky falling, though I was becoming less convinced.

My flight home was scheduled to leave Bangkok around midnight on a Sunday, and we'd made plans to meet that afternoon at his Mercy house and share an ordinary pot of slum blend during an extraordinary hour or two. That was my hope. Extracted from the literal and figurative fog of Lumpini's predawn, the questions, answers, and priestly retorts would rise into a cognizance of such wondrous give-and-take, the afternoon might exceed a week's worth of holy wit and wisdom.

But for the first and only time since I've known him, Father Joe reneged on a deal. He arrived a little late (another first), stammering apologies and appearing more sluggish than I'd ever seen him. If I hadn't been waiting, I'm sure he'd have proceeded straight to bed. He'd just returned from conducting two Sunday morning Masses (one nearly an hour's drive away), checked on Mercy's hospices/orphanages/safe house/et cetera, and succumbed to the twinkle-eyed panhandling of two Klong Toey kids who evidently made compelling arguments for a handout. As he shuffled toward me at 12:23 P.M. on that Sunday, he gave away his last 20 baht and grinned, looking giddy from fatigue. "Just a sucker, I'm always a sucker," he chuckled, unlocking his downstairs door, removing his loafers, flicking on a lamp, opening the blinds, then enduring the deafening whirr of his electric coffee grinder.

Late the previous afternoon, the Holy Redeemer parish had phoned at the last minute requesting a sermon for the evening

Mass, and he'd composed it—or most of it—in his mind on the way to church. Sweat dripping from a knitted brow, he'd then made a few hundred parishioners sing "Blest Be the Lord" twice, the first time to warm up and the second so they'd "sound like you mean it." To anyone who'd known that the night's sermon was being edited at that very moment in his head, it was an obvious stall, but none of the faithful crowding the open-aired chapel seemed to mind a rousing extra chorus of "God of mercy, the God who saves, I shall not fear the dark of night, nor the arrow that flies by day."

Everyone had then sat, hands in laps, waiting to be spiritually served. But Father Joe isn't much for spoon-feeding. He'd told the congregation to sit up straight, *straighter,* and take a deep breath, *deeper,* about twelve per minute, in and out, in and out. "You breathe in God," he'd said, repeating the lessons of the mystics he taught me in Lumpini. "You breathe out fear and ignorance and sin." Again, in, out, *deeper,* in, out. "You breathe in through your nose, out through your mouth. . . . You breathe in and you are born, you breathe out and you die."

Except for the oscillating breaths of a dozen floor fans, the only noise in God's house had been the collective sighs of an obedient congregation. The renowned Most Holy Redeemer Church of Bangkok, which regularly attracted tour buses and taxis ferrying camera-wielding Catholics from afar, sounded like a class of Lumpini tai-chi.

It was the first day of the waning of the moon in the eighth lunar month, Father Joe told the congregation, preaching alternately in Thai and English. The middle of July marks the beginning of a three-month-long Buddhist Lent known as Wan Khao Phansa, which traditionally coincides with the yearly monsoons and begins one day after Buddhism's most important holiday, Asarnha Bucha, the commemoration of Siddhārtha's first lecture as the enlightened

Lord Buddha. In effect, it marks the birth of Buddhism. "So let us celebrate our brothers and sisters of *other* religions as we celebrate our own religion," Father Joe said, nodding his head and mouthing *amen, amen.* Or maybe it was *inshallah, inshallah.*

Following a sermon about the divine lessons evident in the fiction of Harry Potter—in direct rebuttal to the pope, who was still in the news for objecting to Potter—and in J.R.R. Tolkien's *Lord of the Rings* ("Do the bad guys win?" he'd asked. "No! Goodness prevails."), Father Joe had served Holy Communion, even to an infiltrating Baptist. Without making the first glance of eye contact, he'd blessed me quickly while I shot back the consecrated church wine and ate a wafer fashioned from the Catholic loaf of life. By the way he'd looked down and around when I'd done it, I thought I'd crossed a fine Catholic line. I knew the Vatican frowned on Protestant participation in its Eucharist, despite belief that Catholic and Protestant, Redemptorist and Baptist belong to the larger body of Christ. But I'd figured, what the heck? This was Father Joe.

As if to allay any concern, or perhaps just to greet me, as Father Joe had led the clerical processional down the long aisle to conclude the service—white cassock flowing, palms pressed prayerfully together—he'd waved to me, a hummingbird flutter of his right hand to say, *Hey, man, all's cool.*

That's the last I'd seen of him until the next day when I noticed those two waist-high first graders shaking him down outside his Mercy house. That's where he'd donated his last 20-baht bill. Penniless again, he patted his pockets flat, laughing and pouring me a mug of coffee. Then he collapsed on the couch, eyes closed.

It was at that moment that I realized I finally felt entirely at home. I dropped all pretense with the old guy. I asked where the milk might be, all the better if it were cream, and could I please get some of the sugar he'd offered the first day before I casually waved it away. I appreciated his slum blend and had been drinking it black and straight for two weeks, but I confessed to the manly man that I was more accustomed to sweetened coffee and a refined blend, something in line with Hawaii's kona bean. He snorted a chuckle and didn't bat an eye; in fact, he kept them shut. He pointed toward the kitchen and the fridge and mumbled "top shelf."

⚜

After his improvisational sermon at the Holy Redeemer, Father Joe and a couple of Mercy's students and staff had squeezed through downtown's Saturday night traffic to the sixteen-thousand-seat Impact Arena for a sold-out concert by Thai pop star Tata Young, the Eastern equivalent of the 2005 Britney Spears. Tata's *Dhoom Dhoom* tour was the hottest ticket in town, with the best seats selling for 2,000 baht ($50, a vast sum for most Thai). Mercy's free tickets had dropped like manna into Father Joe's lap two nights earlier when Oscar-winning *Lord of the Rings* producer Barrie Osborne gave up his seats. The offhand way in which Father Joe relayed this fact—name slid unqualified into the middle of an answer—suggested to me that brushes with celebrity weren't unusual for Bangkok's most celebrated priest.

Wait, wait, hold up. *Osborne? Barrie Osborne? Lord of the Rings? The Matrix? That* Osborne?

"Yeah, yeah. Phoned late the other night with tickets. Woke me up. But he's cool, way, way cool."

The kids picked to partake of the surprise were rising Mercy stars, girls set to leave Klong Toey in a few weeks for the greener pasture of schools abroad. They were members of the Travel Team, the big deal on Mercy's campus. Father Joe had graciously accepted

Osborne's gift and promptly invested it, sown it like seed. The tickets would be more than a reward for hard work. Ideally, the seats would deliver a jolt, put a real kick into the girls' ambitions. Father Joe wanted them exposed to the infectious promise of celebrity and then to be extra pumped up about the advantages that awaited them around the corner, opportunities they'd earned. Each member of Mercy's Travel Team must be at or near the top of his or her Bangkok class and fluent in English. But for Klong Toey girls there's more to their success than books and tests.

Tata Young was twenty-four, Bangkok-born, a Thai-American superstar whose concerts brimmed with female swagger and pyrotechnics. In a highly patriarchal culture like Thailand's, girls needed confident role models, women outgoing and comfortable in their success. Moved by the pop music and fireworks whose every upbeat and blast were dictated by the strutting Tata, an ambitious Mercy teenager might give herself permission to dream bigger. In the resonance of the bass and a stage's neon lights, she might even let her imagination soar beyond self-imposed limits—even if it meant shedding old boyfriends and the status quo.

At the Mercy turnaround or dead end, the universally accepted axiom that if you study hard, work hard, and stay out of trouble, you can achieve anything you set your mind to had not been self-evident or true. When you're from a squatter camp or a shantytown and your parents "are dead, in prison, or missing in action," Father Joe said, any dream that required a college tuition hasn't been very realistic, no matter how hard you worked.

But four years earlier, Mercy had begun sending students to elite international schools like those of the United World Colleges program, where tuition, room, and board can cost several thousand dollars per semester, and to other private high schools and universities abroad. In 2005–2006, eight females and one male would be living on rural campuses like Saint Lawrence University in Canton, New York, and urban ones, like John Cook's alma mater, Saint Louis University, and on three of the ten (twelve today) campuses of United World Colleges. The Travel Team was now strewn among Singapore, Norway, British Columbia, Ottawa, New York, and Missouri.

These were the harvests Mercy had been building toward since it first dubbed itself the Human Development Foundation in 1973 and opened a slum preschool.

With significant donor help, an assortment of international grants, and a serious dent put into Mercy's annual budget, the age-old axiom had become more than a game of bait and switch. The Klong Toey poor could be honestly encouraged to work hard and to set their sights high, higher, highest.

To prove it, most of the slum alums planned to return to Bangkok some day, to cross back over the vast economic divide as college graduates and professionals. Mercy girls returning home educated and with a swagger of confidence would be a big deal, Father Joe said, smiling at the thought of it. It would be living proof to the have-nots and ne'er-do-wells that they could aspire to have and to do well. Self-determination is a mighty motivator.

"If you can motivate a child," Father Joe said, enlivened by the discussion and leaning forward on the couch, though his eyes were still rimmed red from the Tata concert, "if you can open a door for them even a little bit, they *will* motivate themselves."

Father Joe hadn't returned home from Impact Arena until after midnight, and it was much later before the adrenaline of Tata and *Dhoom Dhoom* subsided and he'd fallen asleep. The day's first Mass was all the way across town at seven in the morning, so he'd not gotten much sleep.

It was a scorcher of a Sunday, even for summertime in Bangkok, and I wished I'd brought a change of shirts. Between my comings and goings from Lumpini to Mercy to my hotel room nearby (nothing like the five-star Banyan Tree suite in 2000, but nice, inexpensive, and across the street from the Klong Toey Starbucks), I'd been consuming a gallon of water each day and showering morning and night. Father Joe kept two clean shirts in his car, and by evening, he would often run out of fresh changes. I quoted him a line from English playwright Noël Coward's *Mad Dogs and Englishmen,* where Sir Coward writes of the Bangkok summers, "At twelve o'clock, they foam at the mouth and run. . . ." And as I yammered on about the day's furnace blast, Father Joe stood like he wasn't listening or didn't care to commiserate and padded silently past me. I was about to read another line from *Mad Dogs* when, without fanfare or warning, he pressed play on his stereo. Whatever CD was cued up was intended to shut me up. A burst of show tunes roared forth. So I did, of course, shut up.

This was our fourteenth consecutive day of interviews. That's to say, we were comfortable. It was OK for me to go rummaging into his groceries for sugar and cream and even OK for me to prop my feet up on his coffee table. He'd told me so. It was also OK for him to tell me to please, dear God, shut up, in whatever manner he chose.

I sat and watched and listened. The merrymaking ensemble of oboes, flutes, violins, and clarinets clashed noisily with the image I'd long ago filed away—of the highly educated Grateful Dead hippie I thought I knew. This was definitely not the stuff of Jerry Garcia. But Father Joe stood in its gust, in his stocking feet and directly in front of a speaker, and he wobbled side to side to the beat. Arms folded across that shelf of a belly, his back arched, neck limp, eyes closed, head tilted backward, he looked to be under its spell. I watched his forearms ride each undulation of deep, restful breathing.

Maybe I didn't "get it," as Father Joe says about things that should be intuitive after you've been steeped in his world, but the song didn't cast any magic on me. The lyrics seemed to state the obvious: there are dreams and dreamers and there is good fortune and bad fortune. In the same refrain there was a strain of the universally accepted axiom, which I thought Father Joe had exposed as a lie posited on the poor: "If you think it, want it, dream it, then it's real; you are what you feel."

It was the prologue to the children's pop musical by Andrew Lloyd Webber, *Joseph and the Amazing Technicolor Dreamcoat.* Lloyd Webber uses the story of Joseph (or Yusuf), a prophet in the Torah, Bible, and Koran, to encourage kids to dream, to *really* dream. "Any Dream Will Do," cowritten with Tim Rice, is the best song on the album, or so it would seem. Father Joe played it three times at full throttle, inhaling the lyrics, his arms riding waves of breathing.

Satiated, he turned the volume down and returned to the couch refreshed. It seemed to me, I told him, that Lloyd Webber's biblical Joe, like the Joe in front of me, helped kids interpret their dreams and then encouraged them to aim toward the moon. I nodded and smiled, thinking I was sounding clever. He frowned, like he'd expected more of me, and suggested that I'd made a shallow first cut. In Klong Toey, he explained, the struggle is less about *interpreting* dreams, the way a high school guidance counselor might, and more about trying, fighting, struggling just to plant a few.

At Mercy, it can be a battle just to keep some of the kids half-healthy and fully alive. The headcount for the AIDS brigade was fifty-three. The number fluctuates. Other children have other demons eating through their psyche, and everybody has something or they wouldn't be there—malnourished, bug-ridden, beaten, raped, sold, drug- or glue-addicted, or just worn out by the streets.

First things first, he told me, Mercy has to doctor the wound and its figurative bleeding. (Sometimes the bleeding is literal, but those wounds are visible and easily stanched.) Then it tries to apply hope, just a little at first, real basic stuff like safety and sanity. Only much later, and only if the damaged child begins to heal and buy into the program, is there the chance that a dream might begin to take root. In art class or music or dance or in the library-quiet study hall, a child's eyes will sometimes light up.

"But we're getting ahead of ourselves," Father Joe said. "One step, one moment, one *day* at a time."

⚜

As the afternoon burned on, it looked like Father Joe's eyes had, too. He pushed himself off the couch to reheat some pre–Tata concert vegetable stew, and on the way to the stove, he again pressed play on his stereo.

I took that as my cue.

On my way out the door, he hollered to me, "I want you to listen—really *listen*—to this guy. He'll speak to you."

All the way to the carport and beyond, I couldn't help but hear the lyrics. Lloyd Webber is telling us that someone was weeping but we're sleeping. So "any dream will do."

I got it, I thought.

But just in case I hadn't, a week later, Father Joe copied me on an e-mail, as if he were giving me the answers to the quiz. It was addressed to John Cook and dated Sunday, July 24, 2005:

> Sent our younger Miss Pueng off to Norway's—United World College—she is our 3rd one there. . . . On British Air to London then Oslo then small plane for 45 minutes to this small town in the middle of Norway. . . . Our three children there have been stars. . . . Our Klong Toey children have really made an impact.

As all of us have said for years, just give these kids a chance . . . and watch them fly.

On the other side of the bell curve . . . also last night, got a ten o'clock phone call from someone who knows us . . . could we come and get a 9 year old boy—on the street in the Girlie Bar—Boy Bar section of Bangkok—Pat Pong—so we sent our team down there . . . kid was hungry and beat up . . . so wanted to come with us—but still had make-up (powder and rouge) on his face . . . so gay he is perhaps . . . either really or economically . . . our house moms fed and watered him last night—ran him thru a "sheep dip" as he hadn't bathed or changed clothes in a week (some customers like the kids dirty like that—which makes these jerks even more "bent.")

His mom is from Cambodia—was caught and is in immigration jail on her way back to the border . . . said his dad was Thai . . . but the real issue is that he escaped the net of local mafia . . . for a while at least . . . who use these kids . . . so we will see—if he stays today and doesn't run away—we have an open house as you know . . . we will take him to the doctor tomorrow to check for AIDS and VD, etc., and once we sort out his health . . . then take it from there—a day at a time.

Must go—time for Masses—talk soon—prayers. joe

CHILDREN *are not the people of tomorrow,
but are people of today. They have a right to be
taken seriously, and to be treated with tenderness
and respect. They should be allowed to grow into
whoever they were meant to be. "The unknown
person" inside each of them is our hope for the
future.*

—Janusz Korczak, Holocaust-era Polish-Jewish
child advocate and namesake of Mercy Centre's
school for Bangkok's older street kids
lacking formal education

Graduation day at a Mercy preschool. Since opening its first preschool in 1973, Mercy's three-year program has taught reading, writing, basic hygiene, and diet to more than seventy thousand children living in poverty.

PART III
The Light

The Human Development Foundation/Mercy Centre in 2005, after $3 million in upgrades and expansions paid for by Atlanta's John M. Cook

FOURTEEN

Weapons of Mass Construction

The deeper we go inside ourselves discovering the inner kingdom of which Jesus spoke, the more we go outward in compassion to help humans in need.

—Father Joe's daily journal

T he first week arriving back in the United States in that summer of 2005, I bought the cast album of Andrew Lloyd Webber's *Joseph and the Amazing Technicolor Dreamcoat.* "Listen—really *listen*—to this guy," Father Joe had told me. "He'll speak to you."

So I wanted to hear—really *hear*—what the Brit had to say.

I played "Any Dream Will Do" at least a dozen times, sometimes loud, just like Father Joe. I read the lyrics and followed along with the music. Some stanzas exuded optimism: the dawn was breaking; the world was waking. Others seemed pessimistic, or maybe realistic: lights and dreams were dimming; the world was sleeping. It sounded to me like Lloyd Webber was describing the tension between yin and yang, wrong and right, selfishness and selflessness.

At its core, the perky music of "Any Dream Will Do" isn't about dreaming at all. It's a plea for the world to wake up.

It's the same plea the United Nations would make six weeks after my return.

That fall, as world leaders gathered for the UN World Summit in New York, the Bush administration was reeling from the public relations fallout of New Orleans's broken levees and the ongoing war in Iraq. In an obvious dig at U.S. weapons intelligence, the UN Human Development Report, released on September 7, 2005, featured a quote from Brazilian president Lula da Silva, a former shoeshine boy raised in peasant poverty: "Hunger is actually the worst of all weapons of mass destruction. . . . Fighting hunger and poverty and promoting development [is] the truly sustainable way to achieve world peace."

None of the eight Millennium Development Goals—including pledges to provide access to basic primary education for more than one hundred million children still not receiving it and to halve the proportion of poor living on less than $1 per day—were on pace to reach their 2015 promises. Not even close. There had been no significant progress in the five years since world leaders declared, with media fanfare, "to spare no effort to free our fellow men, women and children from the abject and dehumanizing conditions of extreme poverty."

The UN Human Development Report—the most definitive, quantifiable measure on how well the haves are sharing with the have-nots—gave the rich world a failing grade. And it sounded exasperated and pleading in its attempt to reason with political leaders:

> Extending opportunities for people in poor countries to lead long and healthy lives, to get their children a decent education and to escape poverty will not diminish the well-being of people in rich countries. On the contrary, it will help build shared prosperity and strengthen our collective security. In our interconnected world a future built on the foundations of mass poverty in the midst of plenty is economically inefficient, politically unsustainable and morally indefensible.

Weeks earlier, the United States' UN representative, John R. Bolton, had suggested an easy remedy: eliminate quantitative measures. In his 2007 book, *Surrender Is Not an Option*, Bush's nominee for U.S. ambassador to the United Nations (Bolton was never confirmed by the Senate) says that the United States may have signed the Millennium declaration in 2000 and understood its ambitious objectives, but the heads of state in the Bush administration had never agreed to definable measures. In his opinion, much of the data coming out of the developing world was unreliable and difficult to obtain; therefore, the specific targets should be deleted.

Criticized by "lazy reporters and leftists NGOs," as Bolton calls them in his book, the proposal was retracted.

But I didn't need to read Bolton's book or hear his excuses—or even listen to *Joseph and the Amazing Technicolor Dreamcoat* a dozen times—to understand why Lloyd Webber had a captive audience in Father Joe. In that album, he's preaching Father Joe's gospel: there are children weeping, and the world isn't listening. We *forget*, Father Joe says. Or as *Joseph* says, we hide our heads in the sand.

Lloyd Webber's songs describe the easy fit of complacency. Privilege lulls its beneficiaries to sleep. It's much easier to drink a cold Jamaican Red Stripe beer and listen to reggae than to confront the great divide. "Don't Worry, Be Happy," Bobby McFerrin tells us in his sunny a cappella, and he's rewarded with a Grammy.

But I don't know if that's Father Joe's interpretation of Lloyd Webber. I haven't asked, and he hasn't offered. I think he prefers to let people fish and see if they catch on through revelations of their own. If they do, it could strike a chord in a way a sermon never could. If they don't, perhaps they weren't ready to hear or to see or even to listen.

⚜

It's an easy thing to miss, after all. Distance paints poverty in abstractions that invite comfortable conclusions. From a Banyan Tree suite or the Chalerm Mahanakhon Expressway, the Slaughterhouse is just a crust of rusty tin over the lazy poor. Unless the effects begin to spread uptown, things like fetid canals, shuttered butcheries, and daily compounded interest rates can go ignored.

Father Joe interpreted bureaucratic indifference as permission. If no help was coming, then by God, the people would help themselves.

The first of Mercy's squatter preschools sprang up informally and unnoticed in 1971 in a crate wood and metal shack pieced together like other shacks—in strips, like papier-mâché. It was near the Buddhist temple down by the slum bridge, not far from the first slum preschool that had been run since the mid-1960s out of the one-room shanty home of Imam Selep Develah. It served a couple of dozen poor Muslim children for 1 baht per day, but the imam usually settled for one fistful of rice or the promise of it.

In 1973, Mercy moved its classes to its first official school, a two-room clapboard church house built from the salvaged walls of a vacant U.S. military barracks trucked south to Bangkok from northern Thailand. But with the Yom Kippur War that fall and the subsequent OPEC oil embargo of Israel's supporters, inflation increased worldwide, and the imam's school closed. Fistfuls of rice alone were not enough to sustain it.

Father Joe and a freelancing Sister Maria Chantavarodom— who'd completed a term as mother superior of her order and taken a sabbatical to work full time in the slums—searched Klong Toey's outback for a building large enough for Muslim, Buddhist, and Catholic kids to meet under one schoolhouse roof. About a fifteen-minute walk from the Slaughterhouse they found it: a dilapidated and abandoned eight-room government building in the mucky, bug-infested Lock Six squatter camp. It's the same spot where John M. Cook would later see scratchy red welts on the kids from "creepy, crawly things." The same spot where Mercy is built today high off the ground on concrete stilts. Father Joe and Sister Maria immediately staked their claim to the vacant building the way squatters do: they jimmied a door and waved everybody in.

Breaking into the city's industrial electric lines proved just as easy, and no one felt the need to offer up a Hail Mary, least of all the nun and the priest.

"No one had the authority to give us permission. Everyone only had the authority to say, 'No, you can't do that. You must not. You cannot,'" Father Joe says. "So it's just better not to ask. You never ask *permission* for something like that from somebody who can't give it to you."

That same forgiveness-not-permission philosophy would drive Mercy's building campaign for the decades that followed. Without building permits, property taxes, and all the uptown legalese that put names to faces and numbers to houses, bureaucrats had long ago turned a blind eye to the Klong Toey squatters. No help was needed where nothing was seen. It's why early education systems in squatter slums everywhere are frequently built like a shotgun shack—illegally and from scratch. Or are located in a clergyman's house with a seventeen-year-old girl as the teacher (the imam's daughter). It's the same reason why sewer lines and bus lines, garbage collection, paved roads, water, electricity, and basic security are slow to arrive. Given the infrastructure of normal society, Father Joe says, squatters will begin to see themselves as normal. There may be illusions of permanence. Illegitimate neighborhoods will begin to look legitimate, and those are the most difficult to evict, should the time ever come.

What the bureaucrats didn't see, Father Joe, Sister Maria, Imam Selep Develah, and anyone else who bothered to look did: at a critical age, when a child's brain neurons are popping on all cylinders to lay a foundation of synapses intended to support a lifetime of learning, the poorest of Bangkok were underfoot instead of in a book. Most still are, with only one seat for every five preschoolers in the impoverished areas of the port district.

Neuroscience tells us that physiology, like the slum, doesn't suffer fools. A use-it-or-lose-it policy is enforced. Neurons not used are pruned, beginning sometime in the second decade of life. Father Joe could see opportunities being lost, but he didn't need science to point that out. He could just look around.

In Klong Toey, the first tutorials in math come in games of dice and cards played on streets and catwalks where children have been shooed when they have no school or caregiver. It's in these same slums that a quick study of the metric system is compulsory for the drug deals ferried by the young, too young to throw in prison. And reading and writing aren't always considered mandatory, even for adults and even today, Father Joe says, so long as you can scribble a signature and understand the bold print of the daily compounded interest rate. And any squatter kid understands that. The loan shark gets paid before the grocer. No exceptions. That transaction is settled in a timely manner even if you have to borrow from another. Then, when push comes to shove comes to worse, which invariably it does, you roll more dice or sell more drugs or sell your body or someone else's—often a wife, son, or daughter.

Those are the sorts of lessons that are home-schooled and recycled when there are so few options, when the politicians and taxpayers aren't ready to see or listen or hear. From the highways, high-rises, and Washington's Capitol Hill, it's easy to miss.

⚜

To know what's in the slums and what's possible there, take the journey, Father Joe says. But it's not like he wanted to take it himself. "No one *plans* to live in a slum," he'd told me, standing outside his shack in 2000. "It's something that just happens."

His insides had been screaming when he was kicked to the Slaughterhouse curb, knees literally trembling. "Any success I've had is all by accident. . . . I've had to be dragged into [it] by the scruff of my neck, kicking and screaming," he'd told me in Washington.

But in Klong Toey's children, he would eventually see poets, artists, biologists, economists, and neuroscientists—though not in the brains already pruned of idle neurons or in those long ago pickled by neglect, abuse, and quart-sized bags of glue that offered an escape. In those whose synapses still crackled, he saw dreams and dreamers, children primed for motivation.

Even during the earliest harvests, the mid-1970s, anyone who had bothered could have seen for themselves. The walls of the abandoned schoolhouse with the just-jimmied lock were constructed of brick slurry and a gardener's cheap lattice. Looking through the slats of wood, anyone could've seen hundreds of kids hunched over their daily lessons, sitting on the dirt floor with legs crisscrossed beneath desks made from cinderblocks and old doors. The school, too, sat directly on the ground. The fact that it was built without stilts in a low-lying area near the tributaries of the Chao Phraya indicated that it wasn't intended to last. Any structure with its foundation flat to the ground in Bangkok's flood zone is not considered a permanent structure, by law or locals.

When Father Joe and Sister Maria "reopened" it, the building had been sitting empty for two years. But in one fell swoop and with that first roll call, two hundred Buddhist, Muslim, and Catholic children, ranging in age from three to six years, injected it with new life. The deal was reciprocal. In the first months, the school's rusty tin roof dripped like a faucet in need of repair, yet attendance remained solid, even when students had to sweep away puddles just to sit at their desks. Storytelling, drawing, books, the Thai alphabet recited in singsong—all are like candy to a child's mind. Brains crave stimulation, especially young, budding ones.

No sooner was the roof repaired and a concrete floor poured over a weave of bamboo rebar than Mercy went looking for another door to jimmy.

Thus it began. That first effort begat another, which begat another, which begat several more. The community pitched in—

Buddhists, Muslims, Catholics, everyone—and for three decades, the Klong Toey slums averaged about one new preschool per year. Whenever police were dispatched by the bureaucrats to shut construction down, Father Joe would shrug and say, "Go ahead, but you'll have to explain it to them," pointing to the children, "and to them," pointing to grandmothers and mothers.

What the bureaucrats never figured out, Father Joe says, was that the brothers, cousins, and uncles of the policemen were helping build the schools, and their children and nephews were often students.

By 2000, thirty-two schools had sprung up in converted shophouses, refurbished shacks, and several newly constructed flats. The children's cognitive skills were being tested, monitored, and retested. Special-needs children were given extra attention, and the malnourished (about one-fourth of the student population) were nursed with extra milk, rice, and chicken congee.

Families of the students are now asked to donate 10 baht per day (a little more than 25 U.S. cents), but it's primarily an attempt at partnership, Father Joe says, like two kids pricking fingers and pressing their wounds together. A pledge of kinship. No child has ever been turned away for a lack of 10 baht or fistfuls of rice.

Today, on the same Lock Six plot where the abandoned government school sat rusting and empty, stands the new four-hundred-seat preschool built with John M. Cook's donation.

Hanging on its walls are colorful banners with Mercy's slogan: "We are a partnership with the poor."

"We didn't begin this by saying, 'We're going to build thirty or thirty-two or thirty-three preschools,'" Father Joe says. "We *looked* and saw a need. We couldn't just sit back and do nothing. . . . *Nothing* wasn't an option."

Holy Redeemer Church in Bangkok
© Carlos Oñate

FIFTEEN
Fruit of the Spirit

The S. Dakota church where I was baptized. St. Rose grade school in Longview. Cookies at Grandmom's house. Picnics at the playground. Dreams—I was taught to dream! These are symbols of America. No one can take those from me.

—Father Joe's daily journal, sermon notes for 9/11 memorial service at Holy Redeemer Church

A s Korean Air flight 653 flew toward its landing in Bangkok at 12:20 A.M. on March 6, 2006, I sat in coach watching *Lord of War,* a fictional portrayal of the world's most renowned weapons trafficker, Viktor Bout. In the film's narration, a rogue arms dealer, Yuri Orlov (played by Nicolas Cage), quotes from the complementing philosophies of an eighteenth-century founder of modern conservatism and one of the twentieth century's smartest agnostics and then injects his own cynical perspective.

"They say, 'Evil prevails when good men fail to act,'" Orlov intones, echoing a famous quote attributed to the British statesman Edmund Burke and a similar one from Albert Einstein, who contended that the world is dangerous not because of evil but because of people too scared, too selfish, too comfortable, too apathetic, too something to act against it.

"What they ought to say is, 'Evil prevails,'" Orlov concludes.

The cynic in me must've survived Father Joe's initial onslaught of pep and optimism because I thought Cage's character was profound.

However, I arrived at Father Joe's house six and a half hours later relieved to discover that if evil does indeed prevail, its voice sounded angelic. In the carport were Father Joe and Sister Joan Evans, a scrappy nun from Perth, Australia, who runs her own slum charity and possesses a handshake as firm as any man's. Following quick nods of good-morning and howdy-do, they resumed a joint study of Monday's front pages with me now reading over their shoulders. The *Bangkok Post* and the *Nation* were spread out on the trunk of Father Joe's car with news of an ongoing protest that had begun the night before in the historical center of Bangkok. The painstakingly polite, gracious Buddhists of Thailand were demanding the resignation of Thai prime minister Thaksin Shinawatra, and tens of thousands of them had been bused by his political opposition to a field outside the Grand Palace. The rebellion had been building since at least January, when Thaksin's family sold its controlling stake in Thailand's largest telecom conglomerate to Singapore's government for a tax-free $1.9 billion. Although Thaksin, a former Thai police officer and graduate of criminal justice programs at Eastern Kentucky University (master's) and Sam Houston State University (doctorate), had survived previous allegations of corruption, tax evasion, and conflict of interest, any public outrage before had paled in comparison to the anger that was now growing. (On September 19, 2006, a bloodless military coup would replace Thaksin and install martial law while the prime minister was in New York attending a UN General Assembly meeting. Thaksin went into exile in London.)

But the sound greeting me that Monday at Mercy carried no strains of prevailing evil. The morning at the slum turnaround began like any other weekday. A chorus christened it at precisely 7:00 A.M., its crescendo rising softly, then quickening into a staccato of soprano that pinged like wind chimes as it floated across the small campus and through Father Joe's house. Nothing about it was orchestrated. You couldn't if you tried.

"Does a rock have life?" Father Joe asked me the next day, entirely out of the blue, after we'd resumed our predawn walks in Lumpini.

Silly question, I replied.

"Do rocks make noise?"

I stared at him like the Mercy kids had when he'd asked in the breezeway if God speaks Indonesian, Filipino, English, Thai—like he was a crazy old man. But whereas the kids had responded, "Yes, of course, of course," I was speechless.

We climbed into his car to thread our way out of Lumpini, and he waited for my answer. I shrugged and gave him an I-dunno stare from the passenger side seat, which was on the left. Like England, Thailand drives on the "wrong" side of the road.

This is a riddle, isn't it? I said.

He laughed. "No, no, nothing of the sort."

Outside Father Joe's house is a preschool playground with no swings or slides or ropes to climb, just beige sand and giant boulders, plenty of both. An elderly friend of a friend in Thailand had donated the rocks to Mercy a year or so earlier, just before she died. But she hadn't exactly given them away. She'd put them in Mercy's care.

"Please—*please*—take good care of these for me," she'd asked Father Joe, as though she were asking Mercy to adopt a beloved pet.

Father Joe promised—really *promised*—that the rocks would be given a good home.

He and the Mercy staff thought they'd sculpt a tropical Eden into Mercy's tidy landscape. So three dozen or so hefty boulders of various shapes, shades, and sizes were arranged around a sprawling, foot-deep bed of sand a few steps from Mercy's new four-hundred-seat preschool. A rock garden, they called it. They surrounded it with colorful ribbon tied to bamboo stakes. The first morning the kids saw it, they kicked off their shoes and dashed toward it as if they could hear waves crashing. They burrowed toes into the sand's cool depth and hopped boulder to boulder, as if a creek gurgled underfoot. They patted and petted the smooth granite, pampered the rocks like they were pets, and marched around singing and talking to each one. To *rocks*.

It turns out that those rocks were good for more than landscaping. The children were cut loose, told to go wild. The ribbon would be decoration, never a barrier.

And that's when the Mercy morning received its gleeful, soprano accompaniment.

A few days earlier, one of the kids had told Father Joe that if one boulder is touched or climbed on, every boulder must be touched or climbed on. All the kids know this rule. You don't leave even one rock out; feelings get hurt that way. Telling me this, Father Joe shook his head at the obvious wisdom. "Neither you nor I would ever think we could *offend* a rock, but actually it is a very spiritual concept, very cosmic—that all creation has life."

We were stalled in Bangkok's rush-hour traffic, so dense in the mornings that Father Joe often shifted his straight drive to neutral and applied the parking brake.

"So," he began again, confident that I would now have an answer, "does a rock have life?"

It can enrich it, I guess. Who knew? But left alone, it's still just a rock. And like the proverbial tree falling in the forest, if no one hears it, sees it, or gets crushed by it, no one cares.

That's where I figured he was headed: the philosophy of interdependence. Everything and everyone affects everything and everyone else. Life does not exist in isolation. We receive by giving, and vice versa. Unlike material possessions and the natural resources we treat like material possessions, our compassion, love, wisdom, or knowledge multiplies when given away. Nothing of the soul is depleted when shared. In these transactions, both giver and receiver are benefactor and beneficiary.

Before returning to Bangkok, I'd watched a video of a commencement address delivered by Father Joe to the 2005 graduates of Acadia University in Wolfville, Nova Scotia, Canada. He'd told the graduates that they'd been living as beneficiaries of the world and now had an obligation to be its benefactors. The roles were not dissimilar, he explained. When knowledge is shared, it breathes and lives and evolves. Sown back into humankind, education prunes ignorance and ideally expands to grow stronger with each generation. But when held and protected like a possession because of our fears, laziness, selfishness, whatever, knowledge goes with its owner to the grave or crematorium.

"You *can't* keep knowledge," he'd told the graduates. "The more you give it away, the more it comes back to you."

These matters of the mind and spirit are kinetic—when shared. It's why Father Joe calls the daily grind of serving in hospices and orphanages and wading with others through the consequences of living downstream an *"unbelievable* privilege." The sick, dying, orphaned, abandoned, abused, neglected, or otherwise broken kids of Klong Toey *allow* him into their lives. Their trust, he says frequently, is electrifying.

"Yes," he answered finally. "A rock *is* a form of life."

He thought about it for a second longer.

"Probably not one of the higher forms."

⚜

Not long after the Mercy Centre began jimmying locks and planting preschools in the 1970s, Father Joe realized that thirteen years of Catholic school training had not fully prepared him for the work of a Redemptorist, not for the building and rebuilding of squatter camps and shantytowns.

In otherworld slums, it isn't enough to preach a good homily, bandage scraped knees, take confession, and solicit donations of money and corkwood caskets. Squatter families could be evicted from their homesteads in a hurry and en masse by bureaucrats, floods, and most often fire. The shacks favored by shantytowns everywhere tend to catch fire easily, like the kindling they're constructed from, then ignite shacks on both sides and spread door to door both ways. Once or twice a year, a Klong Toey slum would burn and have to be quickly rebuilt—the quicker the better, before the government and its business interests could move in to claim the vacant land, Father Joe said.

As the parish priest of migrant slums, Father Joe was well schooled in Catholic rituals in various languages. He could baptize, preach, absolve, and say the Rosary in Thai, Lao, English, Spanish, Latin, and some broken Italian and Hmong. But when it came to rebuilding homes and community from scratch, he felt helpless.

So in 1979, at the age of thirty-eight, he had begged off ("literally *begged*," he says) from noon prayers at Bangkok's Holy Redeemer Church. He would recite prayers, of course, but could he please say them at the Asian Institute of Technology? It was an hour's drive north of town in normal traffic—which always meant bottleneck—but it offered a top-rate graduate program in human settlements and urban development.

Or, as Father Joe interpreted it, in "how to really, *really* make a difference."

As a Redemptorist, he told his bosses, he must return to school. It was a moral imperative. That's how he explained it in written requests, in face-to-face meetings, and eventually, in shouted expletives to church superiors in Thailand and at Bangkok's Holy Redeemer Hall, the apartment dorm where he'd lived when he was pushed into the Slaughterhouse.

He reminded them of their founding saint, Alphonsus Liguori, and his charge to Redemptorists to help the world's "desperately poor and most-abandoned people." These were those people, Father Joe told the church. Let him learn how to help, *really* help.

"I made a promise to the children of the Slaughterhouse, to the peoples of Klong Toey, to educate their children and to walk with them in honor. To uphold the dignity of a holy place called Klong Toey," Father Joe explained to me now, in 2006, pulling from the scene in the 1994 thriller *Clear and Present Danger*, where James Earl Jones's character explains to Harrison Ford's character, a CIA deputy director, that his *first* obligation is to the American people, not the

White House. "I've risked it all, my entire life's work, on two cards: the promise I made to the Catholic Church and, through the priesthood, the promise I made to the people of Klong Toey.

"My *first* promise, however, is to the people. When some folks hear me say that, they get upset. 'What about God? You're a priest, for Christ's sake—*He* comes first!'" he said, feigning hysteria. "But God *is* the people, and the people *is* God, don't ya *see*?"

Forty-four years after his death in 1787, Saint Alphonsus was honored for his "enormous tenacity of purpose" and canonized by Pope Gregory XVI.

But Father Joe was told no. Miss daily devotions? Never. Go to school if you *must,* but prayers and readings should be recited as always: inside the hallowed walls of the Holy Redeemer Church, an awesome alabaster sanctuary with a slanted and tiered roof designed to resemble a Buddhist temple. Only there, in a vaulted nave with a virgin white font at the door and a twenty-foot-tall gold-varnished statue of Jesus at the altar, should a Redemptorist priest offer up daily liturgies.

"I remember I really broke down in tears in front of these guys," Father Joe recalled, referring to some of the old-school priests who had wanted him out of Redeemer Hall. "I said, '*Jesus,* have mercy on me, will ya? I am, you know, *trying* to do something good here.' They said, 'But you can't do that. We've never done that here. What *is it* with you, Joe? Why do you want to go back to school? Isn't your seminary, your theology enough? What do you *want,* Joe?'" he said, sounding angry from the memory, or maybe just from the traffic that we were still idling in.

"The problem was as much my immaturity as their dysfunction. I can see that now. I've always been out of step, always the angry one, always confronting others, always making mole hills out of other people's mountains. I don't have any social skills when it comes to that stuff."

In the end, Father Joe would lose the argument. He'd drive to AIT, then back, nearly every school day for three consecutive semesters crowded with the extra classes of a souped-up schedule. For twenty weeks, he schlepped through the cursed traffic for the return trip and mandatory prayers whispered at the feet of a giant Jesus, always twenty-five miles and sixty minutes from where the desperately poor and most-abandoned most needed him to be. In class, learning how to build a better slum.

Father Joe said the Bangkok diocese never approved of Mercy's mass building of preschools, orphanages, and hospices and certainly not of the seventy-eight communities and some ten thousand slum homes that it claims today. The church couldn't, really, since the construction didn't follow the letter of the law. "We're outlaws," Father Joe said; then he began speaking in the Irish lilt of, presumably, an old Catholic superior. "'There goes that rotten Joey Maier again, breakin' all of our rules and their rules too. Just ignore him and maybe, *maybe,* he'll go away.'"

⚜

Graduating from AIT in 1981 with his master's degree in human settlements and urban development, Father Joe became more daring in his lawlessness. He'd studied the tactics of slum revolutionaries like Saul Alinsky, a brash social organizer from Chicago who, like Father Joe, had grown up poor to become a champion for slum dwellers. Father Joe's copy of Alinsky's 1971 book, *Rules for Radicals: A Practical Primer for Realistic Radicals,* was as worn as his Bible. In it, Alinsky, a fierce critic of social passivism, argues for the use of aggressive nonviolent tactics for the good of all mankind—damn the politics and rules.

Alinsky espoused the view of the eighteenth-century humanist Johann Wolfgang Goethe, who'd said, "Conscience is the virtue of observers and not of agents of action." Alinsky wrote that "in action one does not always enjoy the luxury of a decision that is consistent both with one's individual conscience and the good of mankind. [But] the choice must always be for the latter. Action is for mass salvation and not for the individual's personal salvation."

To Alinsky, "means-and-end moralists" and "practical revolutionaries," as he defined them, were opposing forces. The former maintained the status quo; the latter worked for change.

Father Joe likened it to sacramental priests who live in relative comfort, learning all the rituals and conducting Mass and "doing good, good work," compared to slum priests who learn all the rituals, conduct Mass, and get their hands dirty doing good, good work.

"When you talk about the rules of the Church, I figure, *we* are the rule," he said, referring to the imam, the abbot, and others like Sister Joan, Sister Maria, and himself. "We are the ones following the rules, really trying to follow the rules. *This* is how it should be."

In the earliest story I can find on Father Joe, he'd told a reporter from the Associated Press in 1985, "You can't live nice and then drop by the slum for a few hours a week. I couldn't pull it off. I dress like a slob, sleep under a mosquito net, don't have a radio or an air conditioner."

To serve the poor, you needed to love them; live with them in their struggle, and you will understand and love them, he told me as we approached Mercy.

The turnaround that day was dense with foot traffic, cars, and motorbikes. Government schools had started the summer break (vacation runs March to May), but Mercy's still had a few classes remaining. Children surged through the breezeway headed in both directions—students and residents, some in cleaned, pressed school uniforms, others in blue jeans and T-shirts. Directly across from the breezeway, near the statue of Our Lady of Klong Toey, was the spot where Mercy had brought all the children—Muslim, Buddhist, Catholic—together under one leaky roof in 1973. If not for a man of the cloth daring to break the law and jimmy a lock, then remodel in brick slurry and a gardener's cheap lattice, and hold on until a Catholic from Atlanta remodeled again, I wondered what sort of traffic, if any, we'd be witnessing thirty-three years later. The original just-jimmied abandoned building was now filled with donated computers, art supplies, and a graphics lab.

"We should all get our hands dirty, don't you think?" Father Joe continued, never alluding to any of the obvious changes that surrounded us.

A dog-eared page in Father Joe's copy of Alinsky's book lists the "rules pertaining to the ethics of means and ends." First among them is the belief that a person's concern with the ethics of a social action correspond to one's distance from the consequences of action or inaction. He quoted the seventeenth-century French philosopher La Rochefoucauld: "We all have strength enough to endure the misfortunes of others."

Alinsky's self-styled methods of organizing and rallying vast numbers of poor people into political voting blocs and activism are legendary for improving the living wages and conditions of Chicago's underclass. A favorite story of Father Joe's is one from 1964, when Alinsky planned to deploy twenty-five hundred activists at O'Hare International Airport to occupy all of its bathroom stalls and urinals, in effect shutting down the toilets of America's busiest airport. The strategy was in response to Alinsky's belief that Chicago's mayor, Richard J. Daley, who considered O'Hare a jewel of his administration, was reneging on pledges to help the desperate poor living in Chicago's overcrowded Woodlawn ghettos. Alinsky leaked word of the scheme beforehand, and Daley agreed to reaffirm his pledges, publicly and to the Woodlawn residents.

"*That's* liberation theology," Father Joe said. "The establishment has the money and the guns and the police and the influence and

the lawyers and the law all on their side. *All* of it. They can do anything they want. The people have no weapons, so we have to orga-
nize, and we give them *that* weapon. Not to kill with, but to
survive with. And for us in Klong Toey, that weapon is a house or
some semblance of one, on some piece of squatter land. Possession
may not be ninety percent of the law, but it's better than nothing.
It's something."

⚜

When a fire in the Tap Gaew slums in 1986 displaced 103
families from the thirty-one homes they were crammed into, railway officials offered to help them all rebuild on the same catwalks, but they warned that it could take a year or more to work
out the details. There would be lots of red tape and bureaucracy.
Feeling certain that the squatters would lose the land, Father Joe
hosted a community meeting in Mercy's Tap Gaew preschool. Village leaders decided that night to wait until the railroad officials
went home on Friday and then to rebuild over the weekend
while no one was watching. If anyone in the group of guerrilla car-
penters was arrested for building on the land without a permit, the
entire village planned to descend on the police station and confess
collective guilt—children, mothers, aunties, uncles, grandparents,
everyone.

"In that case, they all decided that just before they arrive at the
station, the moms would give their children plenty to drink and as
much sticky candy as they could eat, so that the smallest children
will end up peeing on the station floor and leaving messy hand-
prints on the police officers' trousers," Father Joe later wrote in his
Bangkok Post column. "Someone then suggested bringing along
puppies too, so they could pee on the floor as well. The room
exploded in laughter."

It sounded like something pulled straight from the pages of Alinsky's *Rules for Radicals*.

The entire community worked through the weekend, from sunrise to way past the sundown, and by the time the railroad bosses came to work on Monday, all of the burned homes of Tap Gaew had had at least their walls rebuilt—enough of a structure to lay partial claim to a pitch of land.

Many of the new wood-and-tin homes would eventually include windows cut knee-high, an idea Father Joe had picked up while at AIT. This allowed breezes to sweep over the children while they slept on the floors. Also, burned sections of the Tap Gaew catwalk were rebuilt with pillars anchored to platforms made from beer bottles tied together and turned upside down, the long neck of the bottle going mouth first into the mud. Buried four inches deep, the bottles filled up with air and remained level. In other Klong Toey slums, including the Slaughterhouse, catwalks had shifted when pillars sank gradually deeper into the soft ground. On the floor of Father Joe's old shack, you could drop a marble and watch it roll.

In 1989, several years after Mercy had begun using this technique of "floating piers," the model was adopted by the National Housing Authority of Thailand.

"The concept isn't new," Father Joe said. "The Netherlands is built on these kinds of pillars—Holland floats. But until I went back to school, I didn't have the confidence to try building them."

⚜

Twenty-four years after the Catholic Church refused Father Joe's request to skip daily prayers at the Holy Redeemer Church, Thammasat University saw something that the Redemptorists had perhaps missed. Like Pope Gregory's endorsement of Alphonsus,

Thammasat recognized in Father Joe an enormous tenacity of purpose.

Thailand's second-oldest university gave Father Joe an honorary doctorate in social administration in 2003. The honor came with three cotton stripes on a burgundy sash, one for each degree of university education.

Only a member of the royal family of Thailand presents a sash like that.

So Father Joe brushed up on the strictest of Thai protocols, and on Thammasat's graduation day, he bowed to His Royal Highness Crown Prince Maha Vajiralongkorn, careful to never make direct eye contact with royalty. He then approached in three small, well-rehearsed marching steps, arms at the sides, stiff and formal in the way Buckingham Palace changes its guards. He extended his right arm rod-straight, palm up. When His Royal Highness set the diploma onto his palm, the Rev. Dr. Joseph H. Maier crossed his right arm as if saying the Pledge of Allegiance and pressed the certificate reverently to his heart. He left the stage in small backward steps, never turning to show his backside to Thai royalty and never staring directly at His Royal Highness.

In a nation where well more than half of the "formal sector" workforce has no schooling beyond sixth grade and the "informal sector" is presumed to have far less than that, a three-stripe Thammasat sash means something important on both sides of the class divide.

In the Klong Toey slums, it meant something even more: the stubborn priest encouraging the slum kids to dream didn't just preach it.

Mercy Centre rock garden and playground

SIXTEEN

Elvis

Do <u>not</u> allow the children to sit and play at the computers. Children need to be outdoors.

—Father Joe's daily journal

The bare ground that housed Mercy's first classes of Buddhists, Muslims, and Catholics sitting cross-legged and together at desks made of old doors on cinderblocks could host a Lumpini Park picnic today. It grows in a shag of emerald during the rainy season and fades into a patchy olive in dry spells, but year round, the Mercy courtyard would not look out of place alongside the Klong Toey Starbucks or next to the uptown Sheraton, Westin, or Millennium Hilton.

Framed by a kempt jungle of teak, palm, bamboo, mango, and rain trees, and scented on breezy days by the come-hither honeysuckle spritz of the night flower, the campus acts as camouflage. You forget the grip of poverty it's in.

Towering over the Malaysian redwood deck of the director's house is a reminder no local could miss: a fifty-foot-tall jackfruit tree. The poorest of the poor of South Asia plant these trees outside their shanty homes for the excessively sweet, dense fruit that grows fat and oblong, some as large as a watermelon. One tree can produce thirty to forty jackfruits in a year. Unripe, the fruit is cooked and eaten like a vegetable. Ripened, the pulp is pulled off messy and fresh. "If you have a jackfruit, the thinking is, no matter how bad things get, no matter how poor you are, you will have at least something to eat, a little something to sustain you," Father Joe explained, standing in the shade of a tree he prays no child of Mercy will ever need.

At the peak of any day, you can look in either direction from that deck and see Mercy's children running, skipping, playing, always with abandon, always with a keen sense of ownership. On a hot afternoon, I've seen a trail of children swinging like a comet's tail from the backside of a Mercy groundskeeper as she meandered around watering the lawn. Each time she turned, a gaggle of children followed her, screaming and darting through the cool arc of her hose as if it were a theme park ride.

Watching the kids from under the jackfruit one afternoon in March 2006, Ian Patterson, an Irish writer from Laos in town to interview Father Joe about the Hmong hill tribes, said to me, "I didn't expect this."

Didn't expect what?

"Smiling. I didn't expect to see children smiling."

I hadn't either my first time at the hospice in 2000 when I'd regrettably handed a stack of Polaroids to Father Joe. But Patterson was right. These damaged kids of Klong Toey smile. They limp, laugh, and get along.

What were you expecting?

Patterson shrugged. "Not *this*."

⚜

If a guy named Father Joe was someone to *find* in 2000, as I'd been advised to do, this was no longer the case in 2006; he'd long been found. And if foot traffic was any gauge, he'd been found to be credible. That's one reason we met early each day in Lumpini Park: to escape the crush of visitors and phone calls from people who, like me, needed, wanted, demanded time with "a guy named Father Joe." We had to start early. The cantankerous Catholic who'd been pushed out of Redeemer Hall thirty-five years earlier couldn't walk across his village in the middle of the day without being pulled in different directions by volunteers, school groups, NGOs, politicians, celebrities, or "slum tourists," as the staff called visitors who popped in unannounced. Even in Lumpini, his Nokia phone left us alone only in the earliest hours.

Since my visit in 2000, Bangkok's slum protagonist had been featured in Jeanne Hallacy's *Mercy* documentary, PBS's *Father Joe: Slum Priest,* CNN's *Live This Morning,* Voice of America News, the Associated Press, London's *Sunday Mirror,* Hong Kong's *Far Eastern*

Economic Review, Oxford's *New Internationalist, Readers Digest Asia,* and other productions and publications. More news media than ever—print, TV, and Internet, secular and religious, from Dublin to Toronto to Los Angeles—were reporting on the everyman's holy man who'd somehow resurrected hope in a place where there had appeared to be none. "A straight-talking guardian angel watching over Klong Toey," the *Los Angeles Times* would say of him on its front page on October 2, 2006. "Each day, the Grateful Dead–loving priest makes his rounds at the complex through its grassy court-yard overlooked by palm trees."

But the "straight talk" that defined him as tough and down-to-earth, endearing him to readers, had not always been well received by reporters. A couple of decades earlier, in stories from two of Australia's largest newspapers, Father Joe's blunt handling of an Aussie heroin trafficker who had been sentenced to thirty-three years in Thailand's Bang-Kwang prison became fodder for tabloid headlines. It was reported that a prison chaplain named Father Joe Maier had told the trafficker's wife that it would be best for her if her husband, Warren Fellows, died in prison.

Fellows had been receiving the equivalent of $400 each month for several years from his wife, said Father Joe, who visited Bang-Kwang and gave a monthly Mass. He'd known Fellows ever since he was arrested in 1978 and said that Fellows used his family's money to buy heroin inside Bang-Kwang. Fellows was a notorious drug trafficker from Sydney who by his own admission in his 1997 book, *The Damage Done,* had reaped what he'd sown when he became addicted to heroin in prison. "I told his wife to save her money, use it to buy groceries, feed her babies," Father Joe told me two decades later, same as he'd told the Australian media in 1987. "I told her she was better off if the jerk died in prison. He was using her, and I knew when he got out that he'd keep using her. Was that harsh? Yeah, but somebody needed to tell her."

On October 18, 1987, a headline in Sydney's *Sun Herald* read, "'I Hope He Dies in Jail,' Prison Chaplain Tells Drug Smuggler's Wife."

The same story reported that when Fellows had asked Father Joe to bless him, Father Joe replied, "I'm not going to bless you, asshole." Father Joe explained to me, "He wanted that blessing to show off, to make people think he'd changed. But he hadn't. He was the same jerk. The same addict. I wasn't going to bless him. Not in front of everyone like he wanted. But I did bless him. Later, away from everyone," Father Joe said.

On October 24, 1987, a headline in the South Australian *Advertiser* read, "No Blessing for Traffickers from Father Joe."

That same day, the *Advertiser* published a profile of the "Pragmatic Priest of Slaughterhouse Slum." It began with a quote that would be damning for anyone, especially clergy. When asked how the Slaughterhouse residents handled heroin dealers and addicts, Father Joe allegedly responded, "We chop their heads off. . . . We put the heads to one side, the guts to the other and the body down the chute—just like dressing a pig."

The report continued, "U.S.-born Catholic priest Father Joe Maier, who ministers to the wretched slum dwellers . . . , said the executions are cold-blooded and matter-of-fact."

The profile added, as though it were scandalous, that Father Joe had been seen "womanizing" in the red-light bar areas of Patpong, not far from Klong Toey. To which Father Joe replied, Guilty as charged.

"Sure, I know half the whores in Patpong," he told the *Advertiser*. "These girls and the gangsters and drunks are the people who need to see the light. What is the point in hanging around the diplomatic circuit with the nice, well-brought-up bourgeoisie? On the rare occasion I go to a cocktail party, it's the servants, not the guests, I know."

Today, he adds, telling me, "Those are the Mercy people, our family, our neighbors. They are the mothers and the aunties—the families of our students."

Church officials had long been aware of the night ministry of the new breed of Redemptorist emerging from the liberal shift of Vatican II, as the Reverend Harry Thiel had told me in 2005, and some of Mercy's biggest donors today are Bangkok bar owners. But city and Church officials did question Father Joe and the Slaughterhouse parish about their methods for handling heroin dealers. After village leaders and social activists vouched for Father Joe's nonviolent nature—calling him a tough talker who fights his battles with pencil, paper, and textbooks—Father Joe says the authorities agreed that he felt no differently than they about Klong Toey's drug dealers and addicts: angry and frustrated, in that order, but not homicidal. "In the slums, though, you always talk tough," Father Joe told me. "You have to in order to cower the bad guys, keep them away. But I did *not* say we kill them, gut them, chop off their heads. I hate murder. Of course I don't condone it."

However, at around that same time, two heroin dealers had been killed in the Slaughterhouse—in "a hail of police bullets," Father Joe said. But not at the end of a butcher's knife. Two Mercy preschoolers had found a stash of heroin near the Mercy school, and they'd "done the right thing," Father Joe said: they turned it over to the teacher, who turned it over to Father Joe. He phoned a "good guy" police chief and asked him to make a big show of retrieving the drugs and to turn the two boys into heroes. So police showed up with sirens screaming and marched in full dress down the catwalks, causing all heads to turn. The boys were feted, held up as good examples and presented with medals. But at 1:00 A.M., Father Joe was awoken with news that the two boys, no older than eight or nine, had been beaten up badly by two of the drug dealers who'd lost the heroin.

"That breaks *all* the rules. All the rules of the slum. All the rules of society," Father Joe recalled. "These guys really stepped over the line. Up until that point, everybody had done the right thing. The boys, the teacher, the police, the neighbors, and the family and friends who had cheered and praised the kids. It had all gone perfectly. But then the dealers, they *really* stepped over the line."

Father Joe phoned the police chief, who was just as angry as Father Joe, and he promised to send his officers back to the catwalks. "By 2:30 A.M., the bad guys were dead. In a hail of police bullets," Father Joe said. "Lots of times people resist arrest, you know."

⚜

In the 1980s, the "Golden Triangle" of Southeast Asia, named for the vast fields of opium poppy grown where the borders of Thailand, Laos, and Burma (now Myanmar) converged, was a supplier of heroin worldwide. The same tabloids that would take Father Joe to task in October 1987 for wishing ill of a prolific heroin trafficker had reported three months earlier on "Thai white," an especially potent heroin sold at top baht, euro, and dollar (American and Australian). It was lethal and being smuggled into Sydney, the *Sun Herald* warned in a July 1987 report about a spate of overdoses: "The 90 percent pure heroin—almost five times the normal dosage—induces respiratory seizures in which the victim literally can't breathe."

The British documentary filmmaker Mick Csaky would follow this ghastly trail of addiction that same year, from Europe to Klong Toey to heroin's apparent antidote at the Wat Tham Krabok, a Buddhist monastery founded by a narcotics officer turned monk. The temple, fifty-five miles north of Mercy Centre, was treating hundreds of addicts each month with holistic detoxification (a secret herbal-caffeine concoction inducing intense vomiting and diarrhea, Father Joe said) and spiritual-personal responsibility. The course's goal was for a thorough physical and spiritual cleansing. The Mercy Centre ferried Klong Toey's addicts there regularly because methadone, Father Joe said, just wasn't working on the hard-core junkies. They often became addicted to methadone, then returned to heroin.

In Csaky's one-hour film, *Killing the Dragon,* Father Joe tells Csaky, "Methadone sucks. [We need to] stop talking about methadone and therapeutic bullshit!"

In ten days, sometimes less, crazed-eyed Slaughterhouse addicts were kicking their habits at the Wat Tham Krabok. Not all of them, Father Joe said, but far more than had been successful using methadone. At the conclusion of temple detoxification, recovered addicts were given a new name in a spiritual ceremony that was taken very seriously by all involved, Father Joe said. The day after detox, each member would begin a "new life" by helping the Wat Tham Krabok's new arrivals. That was key to the monastery's famous success—an element that Mercy later adapted to its hospices.

Fifteen years after *Killing the Dragon* featured the Wat Tham Krabok and its founder, Phra Charun Bhaanchan, Jeanne Hallacy's *Mercy* documentary showed tai-chi master and Mercy volunteer Tew Bunnag sitting on a bench in Mercy's courtyard. Beside him, looking frightened, was an attractive twenty-something woman, her face thinned by the angular carving of AIDS.

"Don't think back to the past," Tew advises her gently.

She stares into the distance, looking tearful.

"You *must* face reality. Do you understand?"

She nods tentatively.

"Look around and see if someone needs some help. Or come and play with the kids. You will see the change in *yourself*."

Father Joe says the late Phra Charun Bhaanchan, winner of the 1975 Magsaysay Award for public service (Asia's equivalent of a Nobel Prize), was spiritually wise: "He really *got it*. He understood what it's all about, didn't he?"

He was referring to the kinetic nature of selfless action, the magnanimous energy that expands as it connects to greater community. "And that's the essence of it, of it all, of everything we've been discussing," Father Joe told me, nearly two decades after Csaky's film about the Wat Tham Krabok won first prize for social documentary at the 1988 San Francisco Film Festival. "Community—the support and the sharing and the helping of one another. That's it. *That* is what it's all about."

In the decades since, maybe because time has smoothed the roughest edges or success makes them appear that way, media coverage of Father Joe and Mercy usually points where Father Joe directs it: toward the moon, not the dirt beneath fingernails. Foreign journalists such as Ian Patterson, the Irishman from Laos, go on pilgrimages to Mercy with notebooks filled with questions about the Hmong or "the wretched slum dwellers," as the Australian reporter had referred to them, or about childhood AIDS, yaba, and an oasis of damaged misfits blooming with smiling children darting through the arc of a gardener's hose.

"Incredible," Ian said softly, speaking almost to himself and taking it all in.

The most incriminating material on Father Joe today is most likely to come from his own laptop. In his *Bangkok Post* column, he appears to relish the role of outlaw priest ignoring the "funny little rules" that get in the way of helping the "desperately poor and most abandoned people." His book of newspaper columns, *Welcome to the Bangkok Slaughterhouse*, published as an English-language paperback in 2005, reads like wartime dispatches from poverty's front lines. It was intended to give Western readers an insider's account of the Eastern world's slums. But the author omitted one thing: himself. Only in the book's foreword, written by former *New York Times* best-selling author Jerry Hopkins, do readers get more than a glimpse of the revolutionary driving each story.

In July 2005, I'd met Hopkins, who's written biographies of Elvis Presley and Jim Morrison, among others. He occasionally volunteers at Mercy and had profiled Father Joe in a collection of short stories, titled *Bangkok Babylon,* about some of the city's extraordinary expatriates. Alluding to my standing predawn date in Lumpini Park with the city's most popular and most sought-after straight shooter, he told me pointedly, in a tone that suggested I wasn't worthy, "I hope you understand what you've got. To have that kind of time with Father Joe is like getting interviews with Elvis. Only better."

A poor man's Elvis. That's what Father Joe had become.

⚜

"I'm the flavor of the month." Father Joe smiled, then groaned, one day in the spring of 2006, just before being dispatched to a charity golf tournament where he had to make small talk and play a character that doesn't come naturally.

Since at least the 1990s, fundraising golf and snooker tournaments, banquets, campouts, and concerts for Mercy's children, have carried Father Joe's good name, and helped keep Mercy's budget afloat. "But you *work* for it. Oh, you work for your supper," he told me in Lumpini Park on March 10, 2006, two hours before the tee-off of the Eleventh Annual Father Joe Charity Golf Classic.

After leaving Lumpini around midmorning, Father Joe rushed home to shower and change, then drove forty-five minutes south to the Vintage Golf Club and the charity tournament hosted by Bangkok's Bourbon Street Restaurant, Bar & Boutique Hotel. For three or four hours, he rode the course in a golf cart making "jolly, jolly with everyone," as he put it, a smiling celebrity slum priest handing out free beer, soda, and bottled water to 160 golfers. Then that evening, after rushing back for the children's mandatory weekly Mass in Mercy's small upstairs chapel, crowded with a couple hundred kids, he returned to the golf club with a dozen children in tow. Mercy's modern Thai dance team performed that night at the event's dinner and auction. Nong Bla, the HIV-infected girl who'd wandered Mercy's hospice several years earlier delivering news of her mother's passing—"My mother just died, my mother just died . . ."—was out front in a sequined dress, her dimples lightly polished in rouge. Long after the kids had returned to Mercy that night, Father Joe lingered in his role, smiling and acting jolly, jolly. It was long after midnight before he crawled into bed and still dark outside when he crawled out a few hours later. He had a weekly Mass to give that Sunday morning at his alma mater, the Asian Institute of Technology.

The Eleventh Annual Father Joe Charity Golf Classic raised 1.2 million baht (roughly $32,000), funds sorely needed for the 2006 Human Development Foundation/Mercy Centre budget of 95 million baht (about $2.9 million). At the time, the ongoing expense of helping the tsunami-wrecked villages twelve hours away in southern Thailand was still heavy, but the tsunami donations had slowed. Mercy's budget during a normal year is about $1.3 million. But Mercy was continuing to pay for the schooling of 375 "sea gypsy and rubber plantation children," as Father Joe called them, from the coastal villages, eighty-eight of whom were set to graduate from the sixth grade. One-fourth of those graduates had dropped out of school before Mercy pulled them back in.

"Don't let them box me in and trot me out to dinner," Father Joe had written in his daily journal in 2001. "It will kill you."

But he did—and does. For the children.

In an August 2005 audit of Mercy's programs and budget, John Frederick, a consultant ("My guru," Father Joe calls him) with decades of experience working with the neglected and trafficked kids of Nepal, cautioned Mercy about relying too heavily on "Father Joe's charisma" and Mercy's "longstanding reputation." Although Frederick acknowledged the short-term effectiveness of the strategy, Mercy had no "excess of money," and Lord willing, the charity would outlive its media-friendly founder. Father Joe was a robust sixty-five at the time.

⚜

If Father Joe's name had carried overseas on the back of a bold reputation before 2000, it rushed abroad on waves of publicity generated by Mercy's postmillennium expansions, visits from Thai royalty and international celebrities, and excellent reviews of Father Joe's *Welcome to the Bangkok Slaughterhouse*. And, occasionally, at the savvy hand of Mercy staffers who strategically plant Father Joe's name in populations likely to be well heeled. An entry in the 2004 book *To Asia with Love: A Connoisseurs' Guide to Cambodia, Laos, Thailand, and Vietnam* invites visitors and volunteers to a charity led by the American Catholic Father Joe Maier, even though Father Joe has no real need for either. Mercy Centre has a full staff and a backlog of veteran volunteers. (New or short-term volunteers who aren't fluent in Thai are often more of a burden than a blessing.)

By the time I returned in March 2006, Mercy and Father Joe were on travel Web sites and discussed on the blogs and Web pages of foreigners from Asia to the Americas. "If wisdom means knowing what to do, then virtue is doing it," wrote Eddie Hoo beneath a photo of Father Joe's book on the Flickr photo-sharing Web site.

"With greater emphasis being placed on academic achievement, professional success, material gains and the pursuit of satisfying our senses, moral excellence is indeed a rare find." Hoo, an editor from Kuala Lumpur, added, "The author of this book is a virtuous man named Father Joe Maier—a Redemptorist priest from the United States who has lived and worked with the residents of Bangkok's Klong Toey slum for more than 30 years. . . . However, this book is not about him, it is about a mosquito-infested shanty town choked with garbage and broken dreams."

After a bottleneck of visitors formed late one morning in 2006, I went down the standard laundry list of journalist questions: who, what, where, when, why. How did Mercy get so crazy?

"I don't know," Father Joe said, looking genuinely perplexed. "People just find us."

Even a year earlier, his Nokia had tweeted and I'd listened as he arranged to have dinner with former U.S. Secretary of the Navy James Webb (the freshman senator from Virginia whose 2006 election would give control of the U.S. Senate to the Democrats). Webb, an ex–magazine writer and best-selling author, had met Father Joe when he'd written about him a decade earlier in *Parade*. They'd spoken occasionally since, and when they met for dinner a couple of nights later in July 2005, it was at the overcrowded O'Malley, O'Leary, O'Brian expatriate sort of place with live music, a haze of cigarette smoke, snooker tables, and attractive Thai waitresses dressed in kelly green. Father Joe walked in apologizing, one Irishman to another, telling Webb, "Sorry, sorry, sorry, I hate meeting in bars." A mutual friend had made the arrangements. Webb, a former Marine Corps officer and decorated Vietnam War combat veteran, had no doubt frequented bars far less refined than The Dubliner. He laughed it off, no offense taken. "No, no, no, this is great, Father Joe, just fine."

But later, reading Webb's 2001 novel *Lost Soldiers,* it sounded to me like the two had met at The Dubliner a few times before. In

Chapter Thirty, Webb introduces an uncommon everyman Catholic named Father Mike. He's a wily, balding Redemptorist priest fluent in the Thai language and the ways of the Bangkok street, highly respected among "the ramshackle slums of Klong Toey." Father Mike lives modestly alongside the poor and doesn't flaunt priestly credentials or show off his Roman collar. It's not an affectation; it's just who he is. Readers meet Father Mike as he walks into a smoke-filled Bangkok bar that plays loud music and caters to American expatriates who are served draught beer by attractive Thai waitresses. Father Mike is wearing a short-sleeved pullover that covers his white priestly collar.

"To smooth his way with the predominantly Buddhist Thais, he mixed his message with their own cultural symbols. He did not discourage his parishioners from setting up shrines similar to those in Buddhist homes, with a statue of Christ instead of Buddha at the center, on which they left fruit and flower offerings and burned their joss sticks," Webb writes. "And Father Mike matched the raucous American expatriate community drink for drink, curse for curse, so long as they allowed him his moment of ministry."

Webb makes little effort to throw readers off Father Joe's scent, except to describe the fictional Catholic as a "small, frail priest" (Father Joe is neither) who owns a Honda (Father Joe drives a Toyota). Also, unless Father Joe is presiding over Mass or attending an official function, I've rarely seen him wear clerical accessories, such as the Roman collar. The last time we'd walked parts of the Lock Six slum, he was dressed the usual way: khakis, black loafers with no socks, and a short-sleeved pullover. There was no priestly collar underneath, though the collar of his pullover was flipped coolly upward to protect his neck from the sun.

Novelists, singers, actors, and such were bound to find Father Joe. The man, the character, the material is Hollywood rich. So like journalists, volunteers, and NGOs, they brave the city's dark sanctum to help the orphans and to meet this guy "Father Joe."

Leaving, they usually write a few words and their signature on a wall, like names scrawled in a yearbook. "All is Love," the Tibetan Buddhist actor Steven Seagal wrote in the common area of the new orphanage upstairs.

"All happiness comes from cherishing others," the Zen Buddhist actor and activist Richard Gere penned on the wall near the Mercy courtyard, bestowing on the village the gentler half of the Tibetan proverb that begins, "All suffering comes from cherishing yourself."

Alongside colorful murals of Pooh, Tigger, and the Powerpuff Girls, the Irish musician Johnny Logan wrote simply, "Thanks for making me see how lucky I am."

Logan is a three-time Eurovision Song Contest winner who in the 1970s played the lead in Ireland's production of *Joseph and the Amazing Technicolor Dreamcoat*. At Mercy, he sang for about two hundred children in a large upstairs corridor, then took his guitar downstairs to a much smaller venue: the children's AIDS hospice. For two dozen of the sickest kids he said he'd ever seen, he performed a private concert, a repertoire of his deceased father's favorite ballads To liven things up, he mixed in several upbeat Irish songs. The children sat up in bed and clapped along, probably not understanding a word of the English but smiling and keeping rhythm nonetheless. "As I sang to the children on the bed in front of me, I found it near impossible to look them in the eye. I didn't want them to see the pity and pain I feel for them," Logan later told London's *Sunday Mirror*. "AIDS is so cruel. All of the children I saw were guilty of nothing. Yet it's as if they're on death row for crimes they didn't commit."

Three years after performing at Mercy in 2003, Logan phoned me at home almost immediately after I'd sent him an e-mail seeking an interview. He said that he was eager to discuss Father Joe and Mercy—that the effects of his visit there were still visceral. Celebrity scribbles with permanent markers on beige walls were *not* the indelible marks that mattered, he told me. "You have to understand, *I* was the one marked—Mercy is something you never forget. Performing for the children and Father Joe was far more beneficial for my soul than for their hearing. It made me feel like I was giving something back as a gift from God. . . . I left that day feeling God was pleased with me."

Logan hung out with the straight-talking priest long enough for Father Joe to size him up and tell the Australian-born Irishman that he thought Logan was a misfit, like himself, an ancient poet-warrior born out of place and time, someone who'd come back from perhaps four hundred years ago needing to complete a task. Logan would never be entirely comfortable in this life, like himself, Father Joe told him. And if he were to ever find himself too cozy and living easily, he should check himself, make sure that he hadn't lost his zeal, his integrity, and then gone soft and lazy. Logan recalls being awed by Father Joe and slightly intimidated: "He's a strange one to hang around with. When you're sitting and having a jar [of beer] with him, you know he could give you wise advice or he could thrash you in a heartbeat if he chose. I find that quite refreshing. Father Joe has to be so emotionally and physically tough to just survive every day in that environment. Me? I was heartbroken in just one day."

He thought about that for a half minute of international long distance, having phoned me from a home of his in Germany. He concluded, "I'd bet there are days when the only one he feels he can talk to who understands . . . is God."

The Irish folk legend Finbar Furey had visited Father Joe a year before Logan and would visit again a year after him. But before Logan was baptized into the wonders of Mercy, Furey warned his friend and countryman about the ache that would crawl up inside his heart and leave Klong Toey with him. Mercy isn't the sort of place you turn your back to when you leave, he told Logan. It remains with you.

Furey has a friendly, smiling face resembling that of Sean Connery, with deep character lines suggesting a life lived expressively well. He was the third of four musical brothers born in a poor area of Dublin in 1946, the same year the League of Nations officially transferred its mission of peace and a better standard of life for all people to the United Nations. Although the Furey boys were traveling minstrels at an early age and life was often a financial hardship, Finbar credits family for softening poverty's blow. "I like people who had a tough growing up," he tells reporters today. "They know about life." At Mercy in 2002 and again in 2004, he spun legendary stories of leprechauns for the AIDS brigade, pausing long enough for them to be translated into Thai, and sang his hit love ballad, "When You Were Sweet Sixteen." Later, in a December 2002 issue of the British tabloid *The People,* Finbar, a father of five children, said of the AIDS brigade, "It's just so sad looking at their beautiful little faces with great expectancy from life and knowing what lies ahead for them is very, very heartbreaking. I think every parent would feel the same."

Logan, too, left feeling heavy, but his mood was lifted by this single realization: "Some of these children have never known what care and love is; they've never lived in a protected environment. But the one thing . . . I will never forget is how much this place was their *home.* The only home many of them had ever had. As sad as everything else was, that's what I remember the most. . . . They were home."

After *Lord of the Rings* producer Barrie Osborne toured Mercy in 2005, seeing terminally sick kids smile and orphans laugh, hearing the gleeful chorus rise from, of all places, a rock garden, he gripped a dark marker and gave a succinct critique. Just beneath Mercy's mission statement—"We are a partnership with the poor"— he wrote, "Thank you for welcoming us in the Shire."

For any J.R.R. Tolkien junkie (and Father Joe is one), there's no better review. Middle-earth is the inhabitable area of Tolkien's fictional earth, called Arda, and the Shire is its promised land, the fertile ground where hobbits feel safe, cared for, and guarded over by Gandalf, the wise wizard of Middle-earth. In Tolkien's words, "There in that pleasant corner of the world they plied their well-ordered business of living, and they heeded less and less the world outside where dark things moved, until they came to think that peace and plenty were the rule in Middle-earth and the right of all sensible folk."

Mercy Centre chapel

SEVENTEEN

Devil in the Details

Looking out window from house . . . girl late . . . hurrying, hurrying to class . . . but she slowed to walk the circle of rocks . . . not a shortcut . . . only to make rocks feel good and loved.

—Father Joe's daily journal

S o you think I have angst. '*Angst*,' you say?" Father Joe
asked me.

Oh, boy, yes, off the charts.

In another 2006 sherbet-orange Lumpini Park sunrise, I felt
plenty comfortable with Father Joe. Too comfortable, maybe. I'd
mentioned the Polaroids from six years earlier—the way he had
seemed angered by my irreverent treatment of the old photos of
Mercy's deceased. I'd told him that whether he knew it or not, he
could intimidate people with just a grumble, growl, or stare. Even
Johnny Logan talking to him from across a pub table knew he was
looking into the eyes of a bear; cuddly and aggressive, but a bear
nevertheless. A member of Mercy's staff had told me once that he
would never visit Father Joe's house without first being invited. Yet
from an office window at Mercy, I'd watched with Father Joe as six
Mercy orphans crept through his carport one afternoon and into
his house's side door. Watching this trespass, Father Joe emitted a
belly laugh and seemed wildly amused by such boyish mischief.
"They just want to look around," he assured me, smiling. After a
Mercy staffer collected the gang, all six filed out of the director's
house with their heads appropriately downcast and their feet shuf-
fling. But they couldn't hide their sheepish grins. Children, at least,
had no reason to fear the bear.

"Yes, yes, maybe it is angst that I have," he said in the park,
repeating my description.

He looked insulted. Thai Buddhists preach *jai yen*, a "cool
heart." A cool heart is cool. It allows you to be open and accepting
and keeps the tension of yin and yang hanging loose. The most
accommodating monks and priests are *jai yen*. Of course, I didn't
mean to insult him. My remark was just an uninformed observation best kept to myself.

He stared at me and nodded as if he were chewing on the idea for the first time.

"I have *angst*."

He spat the word. Clearly, I was missing something. Any suburbanite flying coach from halfway around the world could miss something in the slums of Bangkok. Blink and you miss it. Stare and you miss it too. I'm pretty sure that's what he was thinking while he continued to nod and chew on a word that apparently sounded foreign to him.

Later that morning, as on most weekdays, visitors were due at Mercy. It was no different from my visit in 2005 when Father Joe and I had stopped to talk in the main breezeway for a couple of minutes, just long enough for Father Joe to be pulled into a series of conversations: with the nine members of the Indonesian Red Cross (which included his lecture on the medicinal value of food for HIV/AIDS kids), with a half dozen nuns and lay volunteers from Dublin and Belfast (they'd been treated at The Dubliner the night before and then given rooms and a month's worth of chores), and with an expatriate aristocrat from Germany, who'd flung her blonde hair to one side and explained in as sweet a voice as is possible with a German accent that her family had put her in charge of distributing 13 million euros (roughly $16 million at the time) to help rebuild southern Thailand after the Indian Ocean tsunami. She'd added, somewhat teasingly, that the relief organizations she'd checked with were already pretty well funded and she didn't know how best to spread the wealth.

Father Joe's response had been subdued, I thought, considering the amount of money mentioned. He'd made jolly, jolly—no more, no less than he had with the Red Cross or the Irish—and told her about the triplet girls who'd just that second skipped past us. Fon, Fa, Fai were their names—bossy, gentle, and fragile, in that order. They were seven years old, ranked at the top of their class, and slept in the orphanage upstairs in single beds shoved together as one. In a tone I'd use to describe a bargain at Costco, he explained to the German that a year or so earlier, the triplets' step-grandfather was about to bid the girls out to brothels. Father Joe knew the man, a junk cart pusher who was fond of his liquor, and made a preemptive offer for the girls, convinced that the old drunk would be too tempted to turn it down. He was correct. In exchange for two cases of Mekong whiskey, the man handed the skipping triplets over to Mercy. The woman had smiled approvingly through-out the story, gasping at all the appropriate spots. She'd then writ-ten Mercy a check for 20,000 baht (roughly 400 euros or $500.) Father Joe had thanked her kindly, looking no more or less impressed than when he'd met her.

The following day, in a voice just as subdued, he'd told me, "We appreciate every penny. But please, please, please do *not* come in flaunting the fact you have 13 million euros to give away, you don't know what to do with it, and then say our kids are worth a nickel."

⚜

We often left Lumpini after our morning sessions in a rush for him to meet this or that appointment or greet another round of guests. It didn't matter if he'd been out late the night before mak-ing jolly, jolly in order to collect alms for the poor at some dinner, conference, university, or pub or if he'd been up late visiting the sick and dying in Mercy hospices. His appointment book never shrank. Each day's itinerary seemed longer than the one before.

When the world hears of a bona fide holy man with an approach-able name like Joe, people want to go. By jet, taxi, motorbike, rickshaw, or tour bus, locals and foreigners—including me—had dared to find the street whose name had more syllables than my

Southern tongue could navigate. It was as though the turnaround on Dhamrongratthaphiphat Road was exactly as Barrie Osborne had described it. And in the Shire, we were safe to search for life's mysteries.

Despite our collective professed faith in Christ, Allah, or just the omnipotence of God or gods or goodness, many of us seek proof, something tangible to see, touch, hear, something convincing. Belief seems to carry us only so far. Humankind is programmed to rely on the five senses.

"Do you *know?*" a writer from the *Washington Post* had asked me years earlier, referring to God's existence.

Yes, I do.

"*How* do you know?"

Well, I've twice witnessed the miracle of childbirth. I feel the ineffable swell of parental love and *know* it originates from somewhere I want to be. Each night when I'm making my usual appeal for another round of pardons, I'm thankful for the omniscience that knew my life needed to be lived in brief sequences rather than one long unforgiving stretch. And all too rarely—but even once is enough to *know*—I write, but I do not feel as though I'm the one speaking.

That's what I should've said and wanted to say, but I was caught off guard. I shrugged, then mumbled something about feeling God's presence and seeing it whenever I stopped and *really* looked. The writer smiled politely, as if he felt bad for putting me on the spot, and I knew I'd fumbled the question. It was awkward.

Remember Nancy Fowler of Conyers, Georgia? Beginning in 1990 and continuing for many years afterward, she said the Virgin Mary appeared to her on the thirteenth of every month. That's all it took for the farmland twenty-five miles east of Atlanta to swell into a Catholic Woodstock. Hundreds of thousands of people from across the Americas began making pilgrimages, ascending her hillside needing to see, touch, hear. The soft-spoken Catholic mother offered the masses messages from the beyond and drinking water from the "Holy Well on the Holy Hill," as the news media called it. Pretty soon donation boxes on her property filled up like a Sunday collection plate.

In the winter of 2000, a few months before I met Bangkok's revolutionary Catholic, I'd traveled to Miami to interview an elderly Catholic mother who said the Virgin Mary visited her three or four times every week. For thirty years, Kaye O'Bara had been holding, feeding, brushing, and bathing her comatose daughter in their clapboard flat with burglar bars on the windows, in a neighborhood of burglar bars on windows. Five months after Edwarda O'Bara slipped into a diabetic coma in 1970, Kaye had begun caring for her around the clock, turning her every few hours to avoid bedsores and rarely sleeping more than a few hours at a stretch. She didn't drink coffee or soda but had all the energy she needed, even at age seventy-two and with a back slightly bent. "Oh, honey, I don't need caffeine. Old-fashioned love keeps me going," she'd told me, referring to the love of a parent and of the Virgin Mary. "The Blessed Mother visits me three or four times a week. I talk to her as I would a friend," she said.

Four years earlier, the author and speaker Wayne Dyer had written a small book about Kaye and Edwarda, *A Promise Is a Promise*, titled for the commitment Kaye had made to her daughter to remain by her side. In motivational speeches, Dyer described Kaye as a "modern-day Mother Teresa" and her house as a place of "high spiritual energy," on par with the Saint Francis of Assisi chapel. Sitting on Kaye's couch, he told me that the first time he'd entered Edwarda's bedroom—heavily decorated with crucifixes and ceramic angels with two single beds abutting, mother's and daughter's—he'd been so overwhelmed with its spiritual energy that he'd wept. Prayer requests poured into Kaye's house, some with donations. More than forty letters arrived the January day I was there. In every batch, Kaye said, some people asked to have their letters touched by Edwarda or rubbed against her skin, and Kaye always complied. Other requests came more directly, she said, with strangers knocking on her door to ask if they could see, touch, hear Kaye's graying middle-aged daughter. For just a few minutes, they'd ask, just long enough to feel the energy of something divine.

I, too, was impressed by Kaye's buoyant spirit and the joy that seemed to emanate from her house, and I remained so even after the angry phone call she'd made to me after my story ran in *USA Today*. Why hadn't I included an address where readers could send her donations? she demanded to know. She had bills to pay. (Last I read about Kaye, she was holding an open house in March 2007 to celebrate Edwarda's fifty-fourth birthday.)

So how do you *know?*

Maybe we don't.

"I don't answer those people," Father Joe said when I told him of my fumble of the agnostic's question and asked how he would've handled it. "They're on such a different plane. Nothing will satisfy them."

We were in Lumpini and still in the grip of my "angst" faux pas. I figured he was irritated by my suggestion that he lacked *jai yen*. I waited for him to add something more, but he walked on in silence for probably fifty yards.

So that's it? I finally asked.

"That's it."

Father Joe's office is not a stationary place, and on that same morning, not halfway into the first mug of Klong Toey blend, he said he was going on his early rounds. Seen in the morning's soft light, before visitors and all manner of distraction encroach, the Mercy village takes on a different character than the one viewed from under the jackfruit tree.

So at precisely 8:07 A.M. on Wednesday, March 7, 2006, he put the newspapers down and stood to go, as if something was weighing on his mind. "C'mon," he said, "let's walk."

It was more of an order than an invitation, and I knew not to question it, just follow. In my notebook that morning, I would scribble synopses of the following report while rushing to stay on the heels of Mercy's village don:

8:10 A.M. Immediately outside Father Joe's door is Dominick, a twenty-something Canadian sweeping a Mercy sidewalk. It's an odd sight. A six-foot-tall, slightly slouched, unshaven white guy with a broom. In Bangkok's largest slum. A migrant worker from Quebec, he picks fruit in North America until he has enough money to travel to Bangkok. Here he parties hard with the locals—drugs, sex, and more sex, Father Joe suggests. During one of those parties, he had impregnated a local woman, the older sister of one of Mercy's leaders, a girl at school abroad as a member of the Travel Team. Dominick's baby boy is three months old. Father Joe is trying to keep Dominick close until he secures a passport for the boy from the Canadian embassy near Lumpini. Such documents are priceless in the developing world, Father Joe says. A passport from North America could someday be the boy's gateway to better opportunities. But obtaining it is difficult. Embassies require lots of paperwork, blood work, and proof of birth date, residence, mother, father, et cetera. It requires the unflagging focus of coherent parents, neither of whom appear suited to the task. Father Joe worries that any day now, Dominick could disappear again into the apple orchards of a faraway land and the opportunity will be lost. So he's plying him with daily encouragement and part-time employment. The broom is a leash.

You're keeping him close because you want to make sure he gets the passport while his son is still young? I ask.

"No, no, no. I want him to get that passport before he *dies*. He's as unsteady as the wind."

8:14 A.M. An older Thai woman, weathered and bent over like Kaye O'Bara, is spraying the Mercy sidewalk with a garden hose. She's a slum grandmother and the primary supporter for four mentally handicapped grandchildren. Mercy helps her with odd jobs and handouts, but she feels better if she works for the money given to her. Village matriarchs have their pride.

"Great lady," Father Joe says, nodding good morning to her. "She waters the sidewalk. Waters the sand. Waters the rocks. Then she sweeps the grass until it dies. . . . But really, a wonderful, wonderful lady."

8:16 A.M. A member of the Mercy staff approaches in tears. I recognize her. When I was here eight months earlier, she had interviewed for a job at Mercy. She was all smiles that day. Father Joe had told me that she was a recovering drug addict who had rehabbed on her own and had been clean for several years. A gritty local, he called her, the type he prefers to hire. The day Mercy offered her a job, I'd been a fly on the wall. She had looked like she would float out of the room. Now she looks so shaken I hardly recognize her. Her voice trembles when she explains to Father Joe (who later translates for me) that she had discovered the previous night that her twenty-eight-year-old brother has been raping her fourteen-year-old daughter. Four times he's assaulted her. After an urgent huddle with the woman, some of her family, and a couple of Mercy's staff, Father Joe tells me that the brother's wife left him a few weeks or months ago, not sure which, and so the brother is shrugging off the assaults as a logical consequence. "My wife was gone," the brother told the sister, pleading sexual frustration.

The brother's grandmother, mother, and two sisters are reluctant to have him arrested. Just the thought of Bangkok's stark, overcrowded, tuberculosis-infected Bang-Kwang prison gives them the shudders. And as the grandmother of the twenty-eight-year-old brother keeps repeating, "the boy promised" he would never rape again. That's good enough for us, she says.

Hearing this, Father Joe loses his *jai yen*. If the brother remains free, the girl must move into Mercy. Immediately and indefinitely, Father Joe demands loudly. These things do *not* heal themselves, he tells the girl's mother, who is torn between the demands of her own mother and grandmother and now those of Father Joe. The brother *will* try to rape her daughter again if you let him off. That's just a fact, Father Joe tells her.

When the grandmother resists Father Joe's demands to move the girl and insists that the family will work things out without interference from him, Father Joe waves her off and tells her that she is dead to him. He says he will not even attend her funeral. By now his cheeks are fireball red, and I wouldn't cross him if he spat in my face.

That day, the fourteen-year-old girl moved to Mercy. Indefinitely.

8:41 A.M. Father Joe explains to me, "The brother has raped not only his niece [but] his whole family. His older sister, his younger sister, his mother, his niece, even his grandmother. No, he didn't put his pee-pee in them all, but he raped them. This shit tears the whole family apart. It is the *ultimate* act of violence. That girl can never, ever go back to her village as long as he is on the streets. She will *never* feel safe."

We walk on in silence, out of the offices, into the breezeway and on into the courtyard.

8:44 A.M. A blind woman infected with AIDS and a nine-year-old girl relearning how to walk are holding on to one another, linked together with a volunteer and taking baby steps on the sidewalk around the courtyard. We stop in our tracks.

"Look at that; just *look* at that," Father Joe says triumphantly, and his mood shifts from red hot to *jai yen.*

The girl, Fon, is a newcomer. After receiving a tip about a case of child neglect, Mercy's social workers had found her locked in a room in her slum flat. She is mentally retarded with the IQ of a two-year-old. Her mother works days, sometimes from morning until evening—sometimes even later when she needs extra money. She could never afford a caregiver, so she locked her daughter in a small room, day and night. Like a pet cat, Father Joe says later. You put a bowl of milk down when you leave, make sure all the windows are closed, and when you return the cat is waiting for you.

"Slum budgeting," a staff member says to me later.

"Cruelty for the sake of economics," another says.

No one at Mercy knows yet exactly how long that room served as Fon's day care. Perhaps years. By the time the staff found her, she was a spill on the floor. Now she must learn how to walk again. She toddles slow laps around Mercy and brakes for every scent, like it's all new. Every sound turns her head, every touch is explored like it's telling her something in braille. And every climb of every step is a success celebrated. She smiles and lifts her arms slowly, just a little over her head in victory. When she arrived a month ago, she hit her funny bone on a desk, and her reflexes were so eroded that she grabbed her elbow in slow motion. Her cry sounded like a yawn. The other day in Mercy's small and crowded chapel, the children had waved small paper fans to cool off, and one of them accidentally struck Fon in an eye. She reached up quickly and yelped loudly. Everyone smiled.

Circling the courtyard, she has her right hand in Tatasanee's left. She's a blind, middle-aged woman in the late stages of AIDS. The last time I'd seen Tatasanee was in the summer of 2005, and she'd been wearing only diapers and a white T-shirt. She would sit up late every night in Mercy's adult hospice, rocking back and forth in her hospital bed saying, I want to die, I want to die. When the volunteer nuns and nurses from Belfast and Dublin had tried to befriend her, she'd responded sternly, "Go away," speaking perfect English learned from years of working in the touristy strip bar area of Patpong. One of the Irish ladies had returned with a wheelchair and persistently but cheerfully prodded her to get out of bed and go for a stroll. "Go away!" Tatasanee had repeated, louder and firmer.

The following day, I'd watched as Father Joe sat on the bed directly in front of her. He'd spoken to her gently at first. "Go away," I'd heard her say. Then, "Leave me alone; let me die!" She blamed bad karma for her AIDS, and she just wanted to skip ahead to the next life, a healthy body, anything but this life of diapers and hospital beds. "Let me die," she'd repeated. At that, the patience in Father Joe's voice evaporated. "I'm tired of this crap," he'd snapped, speaking Thai. "Who do you think you are? You have no right to die. You don't have that kind of control over life. I took you into my house, and *this* is how you act? . . . If I have to *drag* you, you're getting out of bed!"

Tough love, he'd told me later, looking upset either by the fact that he'd had to speak harshly to her or perhaps that it hadn't appeared to help.

Now, eight months later, she's found her strength by helping a child. It was just as Mercy adviser Tew Bunnag had told the younger AIDS woman in Jeanne Hallacy's film several years earlier. "Look around and see if someone needs some help," Tew had said. "Or come and play with the kids. You will see the change in *yourself*."

Tatasanee is dressed in a festive sarong skirt and a lime-green soccer jersey with the name of an Irish team emblazoned on it. During the meandering lap, she grins softly, taking each step like a baby step, hand in hand with Fon.

"Wow," I say.

"Yes. Wow," Father Joe says.

8:50 A.M. A couple of Mercy staffers approach Father Joe in the courtyard to give him an update on another child rape. The case has consumed the senior staff for a month, Father Joe says. He sighs and appears to brace for bad news. Months earlier, a ten-year-old slum girl (not one of Mercy's) was assaulted by a neighbor. In order to pry open her legs, the man had punched the girl in the chest until she began bleeding internally. Then he raped her. She had ended up in the government hospital and, as in many of these cases, she was the crime's only witness. Fearing that she might be killed by the rapist, who would want to silence her before he was arrested, Father Joe had paid a police officer who was visiting his wife at the same hospital to keep a close watch. Then, to expedite the arrest, he bribed a police clerk with a bottle of whiskey—not the cheap stuff. An arrest warrant was issued two days after the assault rather than the usual two weeks or two months or longer, depending on who you knew, Father Joe says. When the bail was set low enough for the man to get out of jail, a Mercy staffer had made an appeal in the judge's chambers. The bail was quadrupled. Father Joe isn't sure, but he suspects that a bottle of whiskey was used in those negotiations as well. "It's something you do *after* the judge has agreed to help, not before. It would be in bad taste to pull it out before," he explains.

Today the girl is recovering safely in the hospital, studying for her school finals, the staff report. It wasn't bad news after all, and I can see Father Joe relax. Mercy had bought her a new school uniform for Bangkok's government schools because her old one was torn and bloody from the assault. Mercy paid for a new pair of dress shoes also. The left one of her old pair had been lost in her scramble to get away. Meanwhile, the neighbor is still in jail, a universally torturous place for child rapists.

That is the update that concludes our walk at 9:06 A.M.. Father Joe smiles.

At 9:07 A.M., he says to me, "It works, doesn't it?"

I looked at him like he'd gone mad. But he was referring to life's precarious system of checks and balances, the way good damps down bad, and yin is kept in check by yang and vice versa. It's how Tolkien's Middle-earth is able to carve out a pleasant corner of the world where little people ply their well-ordered business of living. It works, Father Joe says. The spiritual tug of war in all of us and the balance that's somehow achieved—it's not always the best we can do, rarely is, but light overcomes the darkness," he says.

The day after London was bombed, he'd said the same thing a little differently. "We are really just fighting against *ourselves*, aren't we?"

To varying degrees, he explains, the tension visible in the soft light of a Mercy morning is present everywhere. Selfless and self-ish. Love and hate. Knowledge and ignorance. In words and actions, yin and yang are set into motion, triggering cascades of consequences good and bad.

How do you *know*?

Without light, we'd know only darkness. Without goodness, we'd know only evil. And without God in the balance, a village of the broken would only be a broken village. Mercy is the Shire.

Father Joe had brushed the question off. "I don't answer those people," he'd said.

But at precisely 9:15 A.M., he answered definitively for me, although he didn't realize it. In his mind, he replayed the brutal rape of that ten-year-old girl, and as he imagined a grown man climbing on top of a frightened child weighing less than eighty pounds, then striking down again and again until her guts bled and her legs parted, he lost his *jai yen*.

"*That*," he barked, "is evil!"

Fern, semiquarantined in the Mercy cafeteria in July 2005, eating rice congee

EIGHTEEN
Mercy's Mercy

Abiding Sin of Our Culture: Acedia—a weariness which comes when we are not amused or happy and are depressed or dissatisfied with life in general and our own life in particular—leads to desire for distraction. . . .

—Father Joe's daily journal,
paraphrased from *Sacred Readings*

Fern had died five months before I returned in the spring of 2006, but death had seemed like a blessing in the way such things are blessed. In her final weeks, tuberculosis had spread to her spine and confined her to a hospice bed, and at the end, there were no belly laughs, smiles, giggles, or huddles of little-girl gossip.

The October day that Father Joe pulled music teacher Mary McLean aside and said, "C'mon, there's someone who needs a song," Fern had needed painkillers more than music. Mary was a 2005 Acadia University graduate who had heeded Father Joe's charge to live as a world benefactor instead of its beneficiary. By the time Father Joe and Mary arrived in the AIDS ward, Fern was in a numb haze. She stared at Father Joe and Mary with eyes that looked like mud puddles. "Actually," Father Joe whispered to Mary, "I don't think she wants a song right now."

Instead, he comforted Fern the usual way. He caressed the soft hair at the top of her forehead. For longer than Mary remembers, he leaned over her bed and silently combed two fingers—middle finger laid loosely over the index—through the wispy strands. The light touch was Fern's last luxury.

Days later, Mercy's children placed trinkets into Fern's small fiberboard casket, inside the unzipped body bag and next to a small bowl of rice (nourishment for the journey ahead, Father Joe said), and then tucked her burgundy change purse in one hand. They had checked to make sure it was weighted with heavy coins. "They wanted her to have a little something to buy candy with, you know, for when she got to heaven," Father Joe said.

There had been the three customary days of monks chanting the Buddhist sutras, and at the funeral, the children heard the same refrains about there being no escape and no waking up. *Nee mai pon*—to go and not return. *Lap mai dhern*—to sleep and not wake up. Just before the cremation, Father Joe sprinkled Fern's tiny corpse with holy water and whispered a few rosaries, none of which seemed to fit the death of a child because, he said, "children aren't supposed to die." Helping push Fern's casket across the rollers and into the crematorium furnace, he probably bit his lower lip but he did not weep. All of it seemed pretty routine.

The dorm mother later scattered Fern's ashes where all of the ashes of the slum's Buddhists go: into the canal alongside the slum bridge, five crumbling concrete steps down a craggy Slaughterhouse slope littered with cigarette butts, potato chip bags, empty cans, and crumpled newspapers. An English-language billboard towered overhead, staring down on the Slaughterhouse slum from above an overpass to uptown. It advertised a Bathroom Design I-Spa bathtub made from imported dark granite with six adjustable whirlpool jets. The billboard's huge photo sparkled with a rectangular tub filled with Caribbean blue bathwater. Contrasted with the dung-brown water below, fed by a city sewage pump, it looked bluer still.

Mercy's children and staff, the temple monks and Fern's chain-smoking father had attended the funeral, and afterward, Father Joe approached the father off to the side. He squared up to the young and handsome AIDS-infected man who'd confessed months earlier to Father Joe, "I've killed my family; I've killed my family." Father Joe stared him gently in the eyes and said, "You know I think you're a real asshole."

Fern's father looked toward the ground.

"But," Father Joe continued, "when the time comes and you can't take care of yourself, you can come live with us. We'll take you in and care for you. You're family."

Fern's father had begun crying and kneeled in the dirt in front of Father Joe, who reached down and lifted him up. Telling me the story now, several months later, Father Joe's voice sounded like he was in a complete state of *jai yen*. "It's about forgiveness, isn't it?" he asked. Anger, resentment, judgment, arrogance hurt the accuser and the accused, he explained, and to forgive is a gift we give ourselves. "The burden becomes too heavy otherwise," Father Joe said. "And you know, he probably didn't *want* to get AIDS. He probably didn't *want* to kill his wife. He probably didn't *want* to kill his daughter. And he probably didn't *want* to be there watching his daughter be cremated."

We were on the second floor of Mercy's main building just outside the cafeteria, near the beige wall where Richard Gere had scribbled a dharma two years earlier: "All happiness comes from cherishing others."

"I don't need to kill him again, do I?" Father Joe said of Fern's father. "It's not my job to kill him, is it? It's my job to tell him he did an asshole thing. It's also my job to tell him, no matter what, in spite of all of this, there is a place for you. When it gets bad, we *will* take you in. We're here for you, too."

He thought about that for a second.

"And that's what mercy is about, isn't it?"

I wasn't sure if he was referring to the highest attribute of Christ or to the charity, but I figured the difference didn't matter.

We walked down the hall and into the common area of the upstairs orphanage, a large, well-lit, colorful room where children can watch TV from leather couches or from among piles of friends spread out on a wood floor surrounded by poster-sized paintings of Pooh, Tigger, and Eeyore. In a quiet study hall off from the orphanage, several students were working with tutors, and as we walked through, Father Joe nodded toward a teenager. Her head was buried in a book. "She has final exams coming up. Look at her, just look at that spirit," he said, as though I should have known who she was. "She's going to die one day soon, but that doesn't stop her. That life force, it's something else."

It was Joop Jang. She looked thinner than before but had survived and even thrived academically during the eight months I'd been away. She would occasionally go to the government hospital, but she would catch her breath and return to Mercy eager to complete her studies. Her health, though, remained in a slow, steady decline, Father Joe said. The antiretrovirals were only delaying the inevitable. "But we've got *now,* you see," Father Joe whispered, staring at her with admiration. She never looked up and appeared unaware that we were even there. "We all have now; we all have the very moment that we're in. So we should make the most of the moment. Joop *wants* to study. She *wants* to learn. She's not going to stop just because she knows she's going to die. We're *all* going to die. Just some die sooner, some later."

⚜

By the spring of 2006, the World Bank was calling Thailand "one of the most successful developing countries" in the world, and although it questioned its economic resilience, it said Thailand had quickly recovered from the 1997–1998 Asian financial crisis and was "set to continue its expansion into the future." In that spring's report on Thailand, it stated, as though its conclusion were definitive, that "finding work in Thailand is not a problem." At the time, 21 million of Thailand's 36 million–person labor pool (58 percent) were working in the "informal job sector," according to Thailand Development Research Institute, a leading economic policy think tank. This included millions of uninsured hawkers, prostitutes, motorbike taxi drivers, pushcart flower and food sellers—the gamut of the Slaughterhouse's homegrown economy.

The World Bank euphemistically titled its 2006 analysis *Thailand's Growth Path: From Recovery to Prosperity.*

And the prosperity was visible for all to see. It crawled into Lumpini Park at dawn each weekday and was stuck in the city's knotted traffic morning and night: the ubiquitous Mercedes wedged in with the ubiquitous motorized rickshaw. Or just as likely, a BMW idling alongside motorbike taxis (often scooters), of which there were 150,000 registered in the city in 2006 and far more, it seemed, unregistered. They sounded like swarms of bees as they threaded through traffic in perpetual search of the next 20-baht fare. But as economic recoveries go, Thailand's sounded pretty typical. Both the World Bank and the Thailand Research Development Research Institute agreed that the gap between rich and poor remained unchanged and substantial.

In the immediate aftermath of the Asian financial crisis, there had been "high levels of leakage" in government programs intended to help the poor, including half of the school loans for primary education and two-thirds of the government scholarships for secondary grades and higher, the World Bank reported in 2001 in a working paper titled *Thailand Social Monitor: Poverty and Public Policy*. One-third of the "free" low-income health insurance cards—intended for homes where family income did not exceed 2,800 baht per month (about $80)—had gone to the middle and upper classes. In its report, written for Thai policymakers, the World Bank warned that this "implies that a large number of the poor [remain] vulnerable to the adverse economic effects of a catastrophic illness." Yet in the same 123-page report, the World Bank said that Bangkok had "virtually no poverty." Four years later, the United Nations Development Programme, the manager of development assistance worldwide, had praised Thai policymakers for how well their country was evolving economically: "Thailand is determined to leap-frog in development status. The ultimate goal is its transformation into a developed, first-world nation."

At the same time that Thai policymakers were being applauded for the nation's progress, Father Joe was leaving the business of Mercy more often and returning to the Slaughterhouse ("I must be in Rong Mu," he'd written in his daily journal, referring to his old slum by its Thai name. "I must get back to what I'm good at."). And on the catwalks, his former parishioners had directed him to a shack where an elderly lady and her mentally handicapped adult daughter lived. They had not been healthy for a long time. Looking in on them, Father Joe saw the forty-one-year-old daughter, Arun Pohn, lying listless and incoherent on a plywood bed with no mattress or mat. She looked like the nine-year-old girl Fon—a puddle on the floor—but worse. Her arms, face, and entire body appeared to be eaten away by disease. AIDS, late stages, Father Joe thought to himself. He had her moved on that summer 2005 day to the AIDS ward at Mercy, where she was immediately diagnosed as free of HIV. Turns out it was poverty that gnawed at her. She was starving, and her body had been feeding on its own fat and muscle. For two years—soon after the death of her taxi-driver father—she and her mother had survived on small daily rations of watered-down rice gruel, with no chicken, vegetables, or anything else added. Arun's neck was so weak, she couldn't lift her head. The mother was also weak, though not as bad off as her disabled daughter.

A year after the World Bank said Bangkok had virtually no poverty, researchers from the Institute for Population and Social Research at Thailand's Mahidol University had conducted a cross-sectional study on the nutritional status of more than two hundred Klong Toey slum kids aged one to five. The study estimated that the prevalence of malnutrition (25.4 percent) for children in Klong Toey's slums was nearly five times that for children of the same age in the Bangkok metropolitan area (5.25 percent) and nearly three times higher than in Thailand overall (8.7 percent). "Although malnutrition is no longer considered to be a major health problem in Thailand, it remains a threat to the health of the urban poor in Bangkok," the report concluded.

Klong Toey's poor were far better off than the poor of war-torn Darfur in western Sudan, where more than one million children were living in refugee camps in 2006. They were better off than kids in the Horn of Africa, where a two-year drought had killed half the livestock and threatened forty thousand children with starvation. "But if poverty means not having enough to eat, then yes, we have poverty," Father Joe said. "The food of the poor throughout Southeast Asia is instant noodles. Noodles are cheap and they taste good. And *of course* they taste good—the entire nutritional content is salt and fat."

When I saw Arun in 2006, her face, arms, and legs were filling out and looking close to normal, but she was still not walking. Father Joe wasn't sure that she ever would. But a 13,000-baht ($325) wheelchair with a portable toilet inside it allowed her to get around and take herself to the bathroom. I'd been there when Mercy gave it to her on July 8, 2005—the day after London was bombed. Father Joe had dressed in his priestly garb and turned it into a ceremony. He sent a taxi driver to retrieve Arun's mother while two girls from the AIDS brigade applied makeup and lipstick to Arun, and an AIDS woman in the bed next to her brushed Arun's hair, and Arun, with her head propped up by pillows, watched the fuss being made over her and smiled, giggled, and purred like a kitten. Father Joe had been going on and on in Thai and English about her "absolutely beautiful—*beautiful!*" name (Arun Pohn means "blessings of the dawn") when the mother walked in, bent over and supported by a cane and one arm from the taxi driver. From across the hospice ward, a crippled woman in the late stages of AIDS had then climbed down from her bed and onto her wheelchair and pushed herself over to the party. Two volunteers from Ireland—a mother and daughter from Dublin—had been watching this when one of them, a twenty-six-year-old journalist for the BBC, said of Mercy, "We thought they were desperate for help. Then we get here and see it's a well-oiled machine. . . . We're surplus."

About the time a Mercy paramedic, a local and regular volunteer, readied his camera and pointed it, the AIDS woman from across the room wheeled into the frame. Father Joe stood back, squinted his eyes like they were teary, and announced to no one in particular, "Now isn't this *neat?* This is neat, neat, neat. This woman now knows that she is important. She is somebody. That is positive stuff. *That's* how you fight terrorism, and that's how you fight your wars. With one good deed at a time, you just *try* to get some positive energy going."

Billboard at the temple down by the slum bridge at the Slaughterhouse

NINETEEN

Slaves of the Economy

Budgets *are* moral *documents.*

—Father Joe's daily journal

On the day I first heard the United States Congress declare its intent to go to war against sex trafficking—April 4, 2000—I also heard an American Baptist missionary testify. Dressed business professional and standing almost six feet tall with blonde hair perfectly coiffed, the Reverend Lauran Bethell didn't look like a Third World informant. More Terri Garr than Mother Teresa. But she'd traveled from Thailand to Washington, D.C., armed with thirteen years of experience in the trenches of Chiang Mai, an urban hub of northern Thailand. Her New Life Center charity helped young women and girls escape Thailand's sex industry by offering them literacy training and vocational skills.

Capitol Hill was well into a presidential election year, and the Republican governor of Texas and the Christian Right were charging toward the White House. A topic such as "sex slavery"—the visceral label used by politicians and media—was nonpartisan and gave Democrats and Republicans a righteous platform for campaigning. Five weeks earlier, the Evangelical pollster George Barna had released a study titled *The Faith Factor* that estimated that 45 percent of the votes in the November election would come from people identifying themselves as born-again Christians. Other polls said that more than nine of every ten Americans believed in God, 30 to 40 percent attended a religious service weekly, and according to a CNN/Gallup poll conducted four months before the April hearings, 51 percent of registered voters were more likely to support a presidential candidate in 2000 who openly discussed his religion. Such polls never go ignored on God-fearing Capitol Hill.

Senator Sam Brownback, a churchgoing Methodist who would convert to Catholicism in 2002, proved the ideal torchbearer on "sex slavery." The caucus room had just filled with TV news cameras and print reporters when the folksy Kansan Republican known for his laid-back, soft-spoken manner slammed the gavel and began in a grave tone. "I hope these proceedings will help pry open a door of freedom just a little further for those who are presently trapped and in despair," he said sternly. "We must continue to speak out about this insidious practice called trafficking. Every time we expose its tactics through hearings, conferences, and other gatherings, another ray of light invades the darkness."

Three months earlier, Brownback had traveled through Asia, where he'd seen close-up the consequences of sex trafficking. "I met with young girls from Nepal [who] were trafficked to India," he said, "most of them eleven, twelve, thirteen years old when they were tricked out of their Nepalese villages and then [moved] into Bombay, into the brothel district. When I met with them, they were returning to Nepal, and they were in Kathmandu at . . . [an] aftercare facility."

Brownback is a father of five (two of them adopted, from Guatemala and China), and his eldest daughter was thirteen, about the same age as the trafficked girls he'd visited in Kathmandu. He had met a "great, great lady of kindness" there, he said, who was ill herself but ran the hospice. Walking through the ward, she had pointed to the sickest girls and told Brownback the prognosis for each: "She's dying, she's dying, she's dying."

Recalling this, Brownback's voice quivered with anger or heartache, maybe both, and the only sound other than the break in his Midwestern monotone were photographers' cameras, which whirred when he grimaced in recollection. Two-thirds of the trafficked girls were returning to Nepal with HIV/AIDS or tuberculosis or both, he continued. "Coming home to *die*. It was just one of the most awful things I've seen anywhere in the world. . . . These girls were taken from their childhood and tricked into just a hell most of us couldn't even imagine."

Following Brownback's testimony, trafficked women from Russia, Ukraine, and Mexico told similarly grim stories, and the caucus room was still pin-drop quiet as Reverend Bethell scooted close to the mike. Bethell had worked with prostitutes in Bangkok and Chiang Mai and was considered an expert on that region's sex trafficking. Seated and facing the rostrum of senators as if it were a confirmation hearing, she began with a story about an eleven-year-old girl from the hills of northern Thailand who had been sold into prostitution by her opium-addicted father. The girl was then resold to a brothel near Bangkok, Bethell said, and forced to "sexually service men" for four months before Thai police raided the brothel and rescued her.

Bethell explained that the goal of the New Life Center, which she had helped found in 1987, is to use education and vocational training as tools to keep former sex industry workers from returning to prostitution and to give girls likely to enter the sex industry other options for income. Headquartered in Chiang Mai, about 400 miles north of Bangkok, the New Life Center had a satellite branch 125 miles east in the Chiang Rai region, a remote area near the Thailand-Laos border.

Pressed by senators for statistics and the defining characteristics of trafficked victims, Bethell said the sex trade was too fluid to guess numbers. But, she continued, the majority she saw crossed into Thailand from the rural poverty of Myanmar (Burma) and Laos. Typically, she said, they were girls between the ages of fourteen and seventeen, but some had been as young as eleven or twelve.

The senators nodded knowingly before Bethell added a detail that countered the hearing's assumptions and much of its lurid testimony (including her own). What she said next should have informed every subsequent discussion on sex slavery, but in reviewing my notes, reading the hearing's transcripts, and poring over media archives, I don't see that anyone, including myself, initially caught its significance. Only Minnesota senator Paul Wellstone, a Democrat who would die in a plane crash two years later, followed up on it with questions that day. In as emphatic a manner as Bethell could politely muster, she said that the vast majority of trafficked victims that she knew were *willing* recruits of the sex industry—not duped, drugged, kidnapped, or sold by opium-addicted fathers. They were not victims of slavery per se. They were captives only of a desperate economy.

In response to Wellstone's inquiry about similarities between trafficking victims from Europe and Asia ("Is it that they're low-income, poor, unemployed, without work? Who do they tend to be . . . ?" he'd asked), Bethell jumped in before he could finish the question.

"Right," she said. "Uneducated. Education is *absolutely* key. I mean, these young women mostly are not literate or have a very, very low level of education, from very poor communities and communities where they are socialized and raised to believe that they are economically responsible for their families."

She had stressed that point in order to make another. "They will, in fact, *sacrifice* themselves," she said emphatically, "and work as prostitutes if that's what they feel that they can do to support their families."

She paused for a beat, as if she wanted Congress to digest what she had just said, then finished: "In our situations—and many other situations in Asia—that is *absolute* core."

⚜

One Sunday in the winter of 2005, three of Mercy's teenagers had approached Father Joe near the courtyard. They looked nervous, especially the girl in the middle. A shy sixteen-year-old, Pim (not her real name) stared at Father Joe's loafers and handed him a note penned in a schoolgirl's neat handwriting on paper ripped from a notebook and folded twice. It got directly to the point:

"Thanks for raising me and being both my mom and my dad, but I have to leave. I'm going to work in a bar in Pattaya."

A "bar" in Pattaya. It was a thin disguise for prostitution. As in Bangkok, in Pattaya you could (and can today) purchase a beer and a teenager from sidewalk vendors selling both from kiosks no fancier than a New York newsstand. It's the same in go-go bars, karaoke bars, barbershops, and golf courses that offer extras and at the massage parlor "fishbowls" where you are served drinks while you window-shop. Women smile or stare at the unseen clientele from behind one-way glass partitions, and customers order, menu-like, using the numbers pinned to bikinis, dresses, and blue jeans or scrawled in marker on thighs and shoulders.

Father Joe stared at Pim's note for far longer than it took him to read it. If he looked up, he feared, he'd start sobbing.

Mercy operates an "open house," which means that if you don't want to stay, you may go. Younger residents run away occasionally but always return. Older ones, however, don't always come back. Pim was relatively old for an orphanage, where teenagers are expected to move on when they grow up. Nepal's John Frederick had advised Mercy in 2005 to begin reintroducing children to their home villages and extended families immediately after they arrived at Mercy, even if it was just to an auntie or a distant cousin or the village elders. Mercy might be the Shire, but it was also a mirage. The peace and structure of life there wouldn't last forever. At some point, children become teenagers and then adults and move out. Even some of the AIDS kids with the new and free antiretroviral medicines would outlive the free daily servings of congee and come-hither scents of night-flowering jasmines.

Pim was old enough and mature enough to make it on her own. But not like this, not her, Father Joe said.

"Why?" he growled, swallowing hard. "What is so *effing* impor-tant that you're willing to throw everything away?"

She had lived at Mercy since age seven, when "one of the good guys," as Father Joe calls police he trusts, showed up with her bruised and beaten after a slugfest with her stepfather. Her mother worked nights outside and often inside low-rent hotels dealing cards, telling fortunes, selling massages, and more, Father Joe said. And like her second husband—a street beggar with one leg and no job prospects—she was HIV-positive. Often when Pim's stepfather drank, which was most nights, he'd pick a fight that he was sure to win. That usually meant beating up Pim or Pim's mom, often both. So with Mom's blessing and a cop's good sense, Pim had shown up at Mercy with a pillowcase stuffed hurriedly with dirty laundry. She moved immediately into a two-thousand-square-foot bedroom intended for orphans. But in Father Joe's way of thinking, Pim had been orphaned. She qualified. In the room he fondly calls a "big barn" and in the house dubbed Soi Forty, Pim would live for the next nine years, lying side by side every night with girlfriends who whispered long past the housemother's call for lights out. Some of her best friends were on Mercy's Travel Team chasing dreams that had fueled many late-night whispers and fantasies.

But breaks from dysfunctional homes are rarely clean for Mercy's children, especially if the source of the problem resides in a nearby slum and your older sister has moved to Klong Toey from upcountry. Pim's sister Noi (not her real name) had been sent to Bangkok by Pim's paternal grandparents, who had no idea about the stepfather's poor character or the mother's advancing illness, Father Joe said.

As the years and the HIV had progressed, Pim's mother couldn't or wouldn't sleep with her drunk husband. That chore had fallen to Noi, who gritted her teeth and endured it, unbeknown to her mother. About eighteen months earlier, Noi had turned up at Soi Forty's front door too, beaten, bruised, pregnant, and testing positive for HIV.

By then Pim had matured into a serious student, was studying English, and ranked near the top of her high school class. No one in her family had continued past fourth grade, but Pim was on track for the Travel Team. Reading the note, Father Joe knew the decision to work as a "bar hostess" in a coastal red-light town like Pattaya ("Its biggest businesses: water sports and street sex"— *Lonely Planet Thailand*) couldn't be hers. And he was correct. Indirectly, it had been her mom's. As Father Joe put it, "Mom owed a few big notes from a handful of unlucky card games" but was in the charity ward of a government hospital, saddled with a debt she couldn't pay and a virulent strain of TB that wasn't going away. Doctors had said they could not save her, but they prescribed some expensive painkillers to make death easier. That's when a debt collector whispered threats during visiting hours and Pim's mom offered up the only collateral she had left. Her beautiful and loyal teenage daughter would find a way to pay. Mom promised the collector that Pim was good for it. Feeling pressured to find quick cash for the sake of her mother, Pim had let a friend of a friend secure the job for her at the bar in Pattaya. Easy money was promised, especially in the first few weeks when customers would regard Pim as fresh to the industry and naive. The friend of the friend of the friend promised to take good care of her and set her up in "the business," as Father Joe said.

Pim had begun crying halfway into her explanation. Father Joe had even sooner. They stood in the shadows of the courtyard, sobbing like they were at a funeral, Pim's two girlfriends trying to console them. "I'm a blubbering idiot when it comes to this stuff," Father Joe told me. "I never get used to it."

If it's not the lure of Pattaya's fast cash or of its beach bar rival, Phuket, it's one of Bangkok's pockets of Mardi Gras, like Klong Toey's Patpong, where beer bars are next to strip clubs that are next to massage parlors that are next to seedy hotels renting rooms by the hour. It's the same basic business model applied to seedy districts everywhere dating back at least to Wild West saloons with the cathouse upstairs. Las Vegas improved on the model by making profits circular: liquor stores next to casinos next to pawn shops. In *Lost Soldiers*, James Webb describes Patpong's business model in seven apt words: "Nothing but bars, strip clubs, and prostitutes."

"This is very noble of you," Father Joe told Pim; then he demanded that she not let go of her dreams. "Tomorrow you *will* put on your school uniform and you *will* go to school. Go to school!"

It sounded like his preschool graduation commencement speech. *Dhong bai rong rien hai dai!* Go to school!

"I'll go see your mother," he said, hugging her. "This will work itself out."

It was eight months later now, March 2006, when Father Joe told me the story, and in the light of a Lumpini morning, we could see women working "in the business." We had made the final turn of the day's last lap, and on the sidewalks of Rama IV Road, women of the night were lingering into the morning. All looked to be older than sixteen, perhaps more desperate and definitely more daring than Pattaya's bar hostesses, dancers, and masseuses. On the streets there's no protection, Father Joe said. Each trick becomes Russian roulette.

"Let's stop and watch," Father Joe said, so we stood next to a broad tree to spy on prostitutes and johns. "Now you could look at them and think to yourself, 'Oh, you blasted whores, what a scourge on society.' But you need to look again, take a *second* look. And when you look again—*really* look—things don't always look like they did when you glanced. My whole life has been about taking second looks."

I counted five women ranging in age from probably their early twenties to mid-thirties. They stood along a busy quarter-mile stretch of Rama IV Road and were dressed pretty conservatively for prostitutes, I thought: blue jeans or blue jean shorts and T-shirts or halter tops. A medium-priced sedan, Toyota or Honda probably, stopped a few feet in front of one of the women, and she approached the driver's window. We watched the two talk for several minutes until the car pulled slowly away, as if the driver were giving her a chance to rethink the price. She retreated to her spot on the sidewalk, always close to the curb, never in the shade.

"Now when you look again—*really* look—you have to think to yourself, 'Wow, what an *awful* predicament, what a terrible job that must be. To put yourself out there every night, every morning, sometimes seven days a week. To have to climb into cars with absolute strangers. You don't know what they're going to do to you, do you? Not really. That has to be a very frightening thing. That has to be a miserable, *miserable* thing. So now you ask yourself, 'What could force someone to subject themselves to this?'"

Addicted to yaba or heroin? I suggested. Maybe medical bills or loans with daily compounded interest rates? Maybe gambling debts?

"Yes, yes," Father Joe piped in. "*Or* maybe they're paying off poor Mom's gambling debt."

I guess we don't know.

"*Exactly.* We. Don't. Know. And maybe those girls right there"— he pointed toward Rama IV Road—"were like (Pim) just five, ten years ago. Maybe they started in the business but couldn't find their way out of it. It's hard to go back to 80 baht per day selling garlands curbside when you're used to making 400, 500, 600 baht overnight. And maybe they're out here risking their lives out of compassion for their moms or a son or a daughter. Maybe it's selflessness and self-sacrifice that brought them out here. Maybe they're far more compassionate than you or me."

He pointed again and nodded. "Always look twice. Always."

✼

As the congressional hearing on April 4, 2000, in D.C. stretched into its third hour, it became obvious why Bethell had chosen to use a provocative anecdote. Her tale of an eleven-year-old girl sold into prostitution did not characterize the sex workers she knew. Bethell had used the girl's story to explain how best to defeat sex trafficking. With the help of the New Life Center in Chiang Mai, the girl who had been rescued from a brothel had returned to school and eventually earned a high school diploma. In 2000, she was newly married, and she and her husband worked in northern Thailand as drug counselors.

Bethell had traveled across twelve time zones to tell Congress this and, even more important, to share a laundry list of weapons they would need to fight their war on sex trafficking. She'd gathered the list from her thirteen years of working with prostitutes from Patpong to Chiang Mai. Primary on the list was literacy training, basic education, vocational training, and alternative opportunities for earning an income while attending classes. In other words, if the senators really wanted to defeat "sex slavery," they would need to dig to its root and work it from the ground up. Anything less would be a shallow cut at it. This was one of those wars that could be won with pencil and paper.

Reading from her list, Bethell told the powerful bipartisan panel of senators, which included Brownback, Wellstone, John McCain, Christopher J. Dodd, and Paul Sarbanes, "Opportunity for education toward literacy in the major language of the home country needs to be a priority. Participation in school programs leading toward a diploma should be pursued whenever possible. Literacy is *essential* for having choices in one's life."

The senators, some of whom ducked in and out of the hearing, took notes, asked questions, and appeared to listen, *really* listen. In a report that had recently been given to them, an analyst from the State Department Bureau of Intelligence and Research had cited Southeast Asia as a primary thoroughfare for women and children illegally trafficked into the United States. Seven months earlier, a Department of Justice investigation had wagged an even more pointed finger with a report titled *Operation Lost Thai*. Both had alleged that more than 250 brothels, massage parlors, peep shows, and strip clubs stretched across the United States, from D.C. to the Bible Belt and the West Coast, were being staffed in part with trafficking victims. In the State Department's eighty-page report *International Trafficking in Women to the United States: A Contemporary Manifestation of Slavery and Organized Crime,* analyst Amy O'Neill Richard wrote, "The average age of the trafficking victim in the United States is roughly 20 years old. Some of the Asian women may have been initially trafficked overseas at a much younger age, but then worked in cities such as Bangkok before being trafficked to the US."

Following the spring 2000 hearing—and nine days before the November elections—President Bill Clinton signed into law the Trafficking Victims Protection Act, which led to a new bureaucracy called the Office to Monitor and Combat Trafficking in Persons. Assigned to the State Department, it was charged with evaluating how other countries were faring in the newly declared U.S.-led war on sex trafficking. Any nation that graded too low would be subject to economic sanctions at the sole discretion of the American president. The new State Department agency has been given more than $150 million in federal funds that have gone primarily toward the sticks of police enforcement and prosecution rather than the carrots of education and job training.

☙

Three months after the legislation passed, in January 2001, Brownback dropped in to Mercy Centre as it prepared for a child's funeral. There were so many deaths after the opening of the expanded hospice a few months earlier that Father Joe cannot today recall which child had died. But he remembers that Brownback appeared to be in a hurry on a day that he, Father Joe, felt nothing of the *jai yen*.

Before arriving at Mercy, Brownback had traveled with a delegation of Congress to the Vatican to present Pope John Paul II with the Congressional Gold Medal (for using his "moral authority to hasten the fall of godless totalitarian regimes"), and on the way back to D.C., he'd stopped in Thailand. Brownback and a small entourage of Thais and Americans hadn't known what they were walking into when they arrived in a hurry and unannounced at Mercy. Given the weight of the day, any quick tour of Mercy felt glib, irreverent. "Walk through," Father Joe told me years later, making the words sound vulgar. "That's all they wanted—a *walk through*."

Smile, shake hands, give your condolences, and back out gracefully. Father Joe would have none of it. *"Hell*, no," he said to me.

Brownback presented Father Joe and Mercy with holy medals blessed by Pope John Paul II, but with a child's funeral beckoning him, Father Joe couldn't have cared if they were congressional medals of honor. Brownback had begun inching toward the exit when Father Joe barked, "Don't go; there's more you *need* to see."

Father Joe said the senator politely declined and continued in retreat, saying he was pressed by another appointment. "You're the senator," Father Joe recalled telling him. "They will wait for a senator. This is *the* most important thing you can do right now. All else can wait."

Four years later, Brownback recalled for me that Father Joe had been "very upset" that day about the death of a child: "He talked about how much of a reality this was for his children in this very difficult place."

Father Joe said he wanted to point out to the senator something that was missing from legislation and the U.S. war on sex trafficking: the children. After traffickers are busted and jailed and brothels raided and shuttered, what about the children? "Nobody follows up on the children," Father Joe said. "Police arrest the bad guys who sold the kid, but then what? What about the kid? What about the other kids and the kids after them who will do the same thing because they or their parents don't have any money or a pot to piss in? Nobody wants to talk about *this* stuff. It's too hard, too difficult of a thing to solve."

Brownback had relented and stayed at Mercy long enough to witness what Father Joe had demanded he see. In an e-mail dated May 12, 2006, Brownback recalled for me the scene: "I remember vividly seeing this horribly emaciated little girl of 10 years of age being laid in a small wooden coffin. Other children of the orphanage were gathered around and placed trinkets in her coffin that reminded them of her. . . . I kept wondering to myself why this tiny girl had it so hard. She was AIDS infected from birth—by no action of her own—and then suffered a painful life and death as a young child. Father Joe has difficult work and needs much, much prayer."

✤

On December 9, 2003, one day after President Bush had announced that $50 million would be added to the trafficking war, the State Department held a press conference to assess its progress.

In the National Press Building in downtown D.C., John Miller, a former Republican congressman chosen to lead the State Department's antitrafficking office, placed the blame for "sex slavery" on lax police enforcement and corrupt foreign officials. He had just returned from visiting the New Life Center in Chiang Mai but made no specific mention of the need for literacy education, vocational training, or of the one hundred million children worldwide that had no access to a basic primary education. "In the case of sex slavery, . . . you often find countries where the officials are either tolerating it or they are on the take," he said. "If you look around the world, complicity of government officials is a major problem."

In that morning's *Washington Post,* like every other weekday, more than a dozen ads for so-called Asian massage parlors (AMPs) were stacked like a wall of bricks in the sports section. Most were a short walk from the National Press Building at addresses clustered around K Street, famous for the offices of lobbyists and federal bureaucrats. And if you believe the glut of Web sites that rate the AMPs from D.C. to L.A. and swap reviews no differently than members of a book club, the State Department was correct in its April 2000 analysis: the women arriving in the United States from Southeast Asia to stock the massage parlors are young veterans of the business, coming to these shores after working in red-light areas such as Patpong, Pattaya, and Phuket. In graphic detail, the AMP reviewers—"hobbyists," they call themselves—make it clear that a "body shampoo" in downtown D.C. is a prelude to prostitution.

In 2006, as President George W. Bush prepared to announce another injection of millions of dollars into the war on sex trafficking, Capitol Hill updated the progress it had made. In reports and press releases, the number of "sex slaves" trafficked every year was estimated to be "600,000 to 800,000"—which to me sounded suspiciously similar to State Department estimates six years earlier of "700,000 victims," before the so-called war had ever begun.

Nonetheless, on January 10, 2006, President Bush signed the updated Trafficking Victims Reauthorization Protections Act, which gave another $120 million to the war. Bush assured a gathering of news media and lawmakers that goodness was on the march. "America has a particular duty to fight this horror because human trafficking is an affront to the defining promise of our country," he said.

The ceremonial signing was held in the hallowed Eisenhower Executive Office Building, next door to the White House. Flanked by Secretary of State Condoleezza Rice and U.S. Attorney General Alberto Gonzalez, Bush praised Brownback, who was in attendance, and other members of Congress. Americans are "called by conscience and compassion to bring this cruel practice to an end," Bush said, adopting the identical tone that he'd used when he said after 9/11, "You're either with us or against us."

Meanwhile, exactly two blocks north, the "Grand Opening!" of the "Oriental Spa," as advertised in the sports section of that day's *Washington Post,* proceeded on schedule. "We have table showers and young girls. . . . We open to four in the morning," said the Asian-accented man who had answered when I phoned.

How young are the girls? I asked.

"Young, young. You come in, you see."

In the Eisenhower Building, Bush finished his speech with another flourish of patriotism: "America is a compassionate and decent nation, and we'll *not* tolerate an industry that preys on the young and vulnerable."

The short speech had been interrupted five times by cheers and applause.

Pim turned down the fast cash of Pattaya. Father Joe and some local men who accompany him on such matters had marched down to a four-table slum noodle shop owned by the debt collector's mother. They ordered the day's special, and upon leaving, Father Joe discreetly paid an extra 1,000 baht. He leaned across the noodle shop counter and whisper-barked, "Now leave the girl alone! Enough is enough!"

Mercy had moved Pim's mother into its AIDS hospice, where she was eased toward her death on Mercy's free painkillers. A month or so later, Noi delivered a beautiful baby daughter, then ran away. At this writing, she was in a government mental hospital.

In the retelling of all of this, more than one year after Pim's life had begun to fall apart, she was still living at Soi Forty in a bedroom that seems to stretch a full acre. She was studying English harder than ever because she'd made the cut for the Travel Team and would be leaving in five months for a United World Colleges program in Canada. With twelve campuses from Singapore to Swaziland to Venezuela and with a rigorous high school curriculum attracting a diverse pool of top students from all over the world, the UWC is an ideal springboard for college. Founded in Wales during the Cold War, a primary goal is to foster better understanding between nations and cultures by bringing together the generations that will dictate the world's future. Six of Mercy's nine Travel Team members would be headed to UWC campuses in the autumn of 2006.

Noi's daughter was about a year old the first time I saw her. The Mercy staff had nicknamed her Miss Grasshopper—for her lively, hopping spirit—and she lived on the main campus in the upstairs orphanage where Tigger, Pooh, and Eeyore seem to spring in 3-D from the walls.

"So now you could glance at this baby and think about how her stepfather was raping her mother and they both had AIDS, and then you'd say, 'What a *mess*, what a terrible mess. What can we— *we*—possibly do for her?'" Father Joe said.

He looked at me like he expected an answer. I didn't have one.

"That's when you have to look *again*. You take a second look."

We were looking at her now. She was in a downstairs day care room surrounded by other toddlers with similarly harsh stories. She padded across the polished teak floor and bellied up to the baby gate in front of us. A knot of friends followed, eager for a better view of the big guy they always see patrolling the place and the stranger who had tagged along. Father Joe and Miss Grasshopper stared at each other for a few seconds, she looking up, as at the foot of a mountain, and he looking down and smiling.

"Now, when you take that second look at her . . ."

He paused and babbled playfully in Thai.

". . . you say to yourself, 'OK, this baby is going to be so *special* and so *neat,* and we *will* raise this child to be a nurse or a doctor or a teacher, something that will end up helping us all, helping society.' What a wonderful blessing she is."

Miss Grasshopper was wearing a clean white primrose blouse and a beaded bracelet, and her chubby cheeks and arms made her appear like she was still swaddled in baby fat. Each time Father Joe leaned forward and said, "*Jah-aye, jah-aye*" (the Thai equivalent of *peekaboo*), she smiled and babbled back, blowing spit bubbles.

"Ahh, she's a *great* kid," Father Joe said, leaning back to survey the blessing, folding his arms contentedly across his belly. "She's a happy kid, a smart kid. She's going to do real well."

If all goes as expected, she will grow up in the same house that Aunt Pim had and revel in spaghetti night and movie night and sleep in a big barn curled up in a nightly slumber party whispering long past the housemother's call for lights out. Someday she might even apply to a United World Colleges program. She had already been blessed with a head start, Father Joe said, nodding, smiling, and still staring down at her.

"She does *not* have AIDS," he announced triumphantly. "She checked out clean!"

That alone was a miracle, he said, considering the circumstances. With that, he began walking me to a motorcycle taxi that would return me to my hotel and then to another midnight flight home to D.C.

Looking back as we walked out, he spotted Miss Grasshopper and rejoiced again in the good news: "Can ya believe it? No AIDS! See, *this* story had a happy ending."

He quickly corrected himself.

"No, no, a *beginning*. A wonderful journey awaits her."

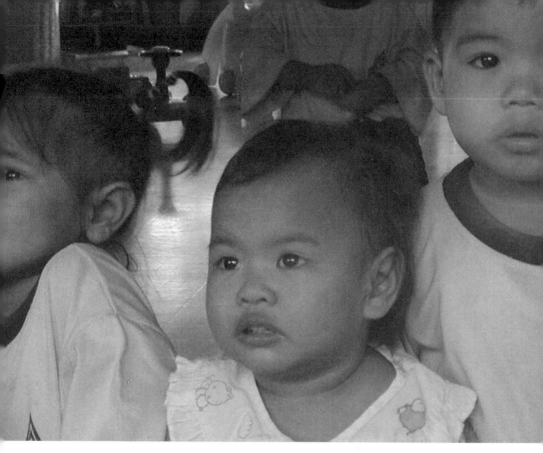

Miss Grasshopper (middle)

TWENTY

Of Mothers, Sons, and Holy Spirit

*Accept the present moment. God is now.
. . . Don't look to the future for salvation
cuz future does not exist. Only present
moment can make us free. God with us now
= Awake-en-ing.*

—Father Joe's daily journal

"My mother is sick until death. Pray for her. . . . Fr. Joe."

The automated reply to Father Joe's e-mail on Tuesday, September 5, 2006, didn't come as a surprise to anyone remotely close to the Maier family. The matriarch had been ceding ground to time and dementia for several years when Kathy Maier Roshak phoned from Portland, Oregon, to tell her big brother the latest bad news.

"She's had a stroke, Joe."

"*Ahh jeez.* When? Where was she? . . . Is she going to make it?"

Kathy was a sobbing mess by the time they'd hung up, and Father Joe was on the next Northwest Airlines flight to Portland, leaving Bangkok at six o'clock the following morning. By the time he'd landed sixteen hours later and made his way one hour north to Longview, Washington, Helen Mary Childs Maier had died. She was ninety-four.

I'd been aware of her failing health since the second interview with Father Joe in Lumpini Park in July 2005. He wasn't entirely comfortable with me yet and had been deflecting questions about his family. Each time I'd probe beyond the basic biography, he'd switch subjects to, say, the "corrupt" bicycle cop he'd just glared at aggressively ("Just letting him *know* that I *know* he shakes down the park's old ladies") or the fast-walking Chinese national polluting our predawn quiet with a transistor radio strapped full-volume to his shoulder ("But we shouldn't get mad at the guy because it's like what the storybooks say, 'His mommy must not have loved him very much or she'd have raised him better'"). He wasn't ready to discuss his family in any depth. But he did express concern about the visit he'd made two months earlier to see his "dear old mum" at her Longview nursing home. Kathy, a hospice nurse ten years younger than Father Joe, had walked in with the family's statesman ("The goal in any good Catholic family is to have a priest in it," she later told me) on her arm. She asked their mother excitedly, "Do you know who this is?"

Helen stared at her firstborn like he was a new orderly.

"Mother, don't you recognize me?" Father Joe asked.

She searched his face for a clue.

"Do you remember *Steve*?" Kathy asked, desperate to jog any memory.

Of course she remembered Steve. The handsome white-and-black-spotted horse behaved for no one but her. She had tamed him when she was a South Dakota farm girl, luring him close, closer, day after day, long after her extraordinarily patient father, Harry Childs, couldn't retrieve him from the pasture. She fed him sugar cubes, cooing and stroking and brushing him until one day he didn't realize he was wearing a bridle.

"*Steve*," Father Joe recalled in Lumpini. "She remembered Steve. *Jeez*. Steve is a damn horse she had when she was twelve."

He'd laughed at that, surprised, I think, by his own hurt feelings. "But mother's life is big. She's Scooby-Doo. She's in no pain, she eats whatever she likes, she's happy and still says the Rosary."

⚜

Flying home from Bangkok two weeks after the July 2005 visit, I had rerouted to Portland and taken the same fifty-mile drive that Father Joe follows to his Aunt Betty's house, where he stays whenever he's in Longview. Interstate 5 North along the Columbia River to Exit 36, where a billboard of Psalm 23 ("The Lord is my Shepherd . . .") greets you. Crossing the Cowlitz River and then going a few miles to Lake Sacajawea, you intersect with Father Joe's former 20th Avenue neighborhood and continue for five tree-shaded blocks to Saint Rose Catholic School, where the 1953 Rosarian yearbook staff predicted that Father Joe would grow up to be a dogcatcher. From there it's straight for a few more blocks to Aunt Betty's small, tidy house painted the color of emeralds. Most of the year it's trimmed in flowers: yellow, purple, orange, pink, blue, red—any perennial or annual that blossoms vibrantly. Begonias, marigolds, zinnias, snapdragons, geraniums, impatiens are all fussed over as if family. Aunt Betty and Father Joe's mother, Helen, were two of the four daughters of Harry and Anne Childs, raised on a 320-acre cattle and grain farm in South Dakota. And like their father, they were all prodigious flower gardeners. His gardens would burst with color because, I'm guessing, on the frozen tundra of a South Dakota winter, the only thing flourishing is an affection for spring.

The temperature in Spink County, South Dakota, was forty below zero on New Years Day 1912, the day Anne Bradley Childs gave birth to her first daughter. Harry set Helen's bassinet on the oven door in their large, drafty Spink County farmhouse to keep her warm, and according to Helen's recollections, she never overcame that first chill. "The family tells me, 'It was cold then and [you've] been cold ever since,'" she wrote in 1979 in a fifty-two-page loose-leaf recording of her family history and genealogy. "The [local] news editor wrote of my birth—'May this woman live to see the year 2000.' I WONDER."

Father Joe's mother would extend life six years into the millennium, but in the summer of 2005, and starting long before, she had not been herself. "You have to wonder why the good Lord keeps her. I mean, it's just not the sister I knew," said Betty McIntee. Of the four Childs girls, two were still alive in 2005: Helen and Aunt Betty, the youngest, who had just turned eighty-two.

The inside of Aunt Betty's house was as fussed-over as the outside, with more flowers, a small portrait of Pope John Paul II framed and hung on a foyer wall, and in the living room, paintings or drawings of ceramic statues of Christ and the Virgin Mary.

Aunt Betty smiled when I noticed. "Someone once asked me, 'When people walk into your house, can they immediately convict you of being a Christian?' Well, I think there is more here than in the church."

Like her mother, Anne Bradley Childs, and sister Helen, Aunt Betty is petite and wiry strong, the best of both bloodlines. Even in her eighties, there was plenty of grip to her handshake and spring in her step, and when we left her house for a tour of Longview, it was her fifteen-year-old Nissan we took, not my midsized Enterprise rental. "No, no, *I'm* the one who knows this town; *I'll* drive," she insisted, and as with Father Joe, I knew when to shut up.

❀

Longview is a blue-collar creation of the American industrial expansion during the prosperous 1920s, conceived and birthed entirely with private investments. In 1919, Robert A. Long, president of Kansas City's Long-Bell Lumber, came to Washington in search of good stock. Riding horseback through the virgin forests of northern Cowlitz County, some of them dense with centuries-old Douglas fir, he emerged convinced that "here indeed was the finest timber in the world," writes John M. McClelland Jr. in *R. A. Long's Planned City,* a historical tome published by the *Daily News.* Founded in 1923 at the confluence of the Cowlitz and Columbia Rivers, ninety miles from the Pacific Ocean, Longview would become the home of the world's largest sawmill. Protestant churches (Catholics worshiped across the river in Kelso until 1927), public schools, public library, a lake and its park fashioned after Washington, D.C.'s National Mall, and a checkerboard grid of working-class homes in neighborhoods with names such as the Highlands and Saint Helens, would all be built with help from Long, a multimillionaire businessman and philanthropist. With mortgages and rents fixed to fit company wages, Long-Bell Lumber expected less employee turnover. From its inception, Longview was the quintessential company town.

Although Long had promised to build the city and then turn it over to its own peculiarities, he was a hands-on tycoon accustomed to managing his interests. But with the Great Depression and Long's death, the company began to focus more on its business affairs than on Long's civic project and filed for bankruptcy protection the year Long died. It would eventually be absorbed by Connecticut-based International Paper Company and sell off the four-room bungalow homes that had been the backbone of the new city. With no mooring to the city benefactor and founder, streets that had once teemed with working families and reflected Long's civic-mindedness began a slow decline. By the time George Morris Maier moved his bride, Helen Mary Childs, to Longview in 1937 and later to a two-bedroom, one-bath bungalow in the Highlands, the neighborhood was attractive only for its low housing costs and rents.

By 2005, when I rode with Aunt Betty down Beech Street and turned onto 20th Avenue, the decline had hit decay. Lawns were overgrown; trash was strewn; a house had been vacated and boarded up. Pulling to the curb five blocks from Industrial Way, where eighteen-wheelers groan carrying timber to the Weyerhaeuser pulp and paper mill, Aunt Betty sighed. She pointed toward a house, stared silently, and shook her head.

Father Joe's former home was a wreck. A fitting metaphor, it seemed, for the broken marriage that had resulted in the fire that burned within him. "Any success I've had with damaged children is only because I was such a damaged child myself," he'd told me a week earlier in Bangkok.

The home's grayish paint peeled; its small lawn was cluttered with two empty liter-sized Pepsi bottles, two chairs—one a tan vinyl kitchen chair, the other fireball red and plastic—various fast-food wrappers, and a Big Wheel. Its grass and weeds had grown to calf height. Aunt Betty circled the block slowly, craning her neck to see into the backyard. It was more of the same: garbage, tall grass, daisies calf-high.

"Ohhh," she groaned, "if Joe saw that . . ."

That same week, the *Daily News* published a four-part series by a reporter who had been sent to live for one month in a Highlands home, as though dispatched on a dangerous Third World assignment. It began the series with the Highlands' vitals: Nearly 60 percent of its 4,500 residents had no high school diploma, triple the city's overall 18.7 percent. Thirty percent of its families lived below the poverty line, more than double the city's 12.3 percent. Its fifteen blocks accounted for 3 percent of the city's residents but nearly one-third of its crime. The house boarded up on Father Joe's street? It was very likely one of the six in the neighborhood condemned in recent years because of methamphetamine labs—crudely assembled firetraps cooking speed in porcelain bathtubs. Thailand had its home-cooked yaba; Washington State had meth.

Had Aunt Betty turned the other way at 20th Avenue, we would've driven less than a mile before reaching the lakeside homes of Kessler Boulevard. Two miles farther, and we'd have entered Longview Country Club.

"Beech Street is the great divide. Here ends the lush greenery that stretches from Lake Sacajawea, the prim houses with neat yards, the promise of the city's founders," wrote *Daily News* reporter Tony Lystra. "If you live north of Beech Street, you probably believe [the Highlands] belched forth the methamphetamine-addicted kid who smashed your Camry window and stole your stereo. If you live south of Beech, goes the conventional wisdom, you probably wish you had a Camry."

By the series's final day, however, Lystra had unwittingly evoked the voice of a Longview native living in far graver conditions in a cordoned-off corner twelve thousand miles away: "It's hard to dismiss this place as a slum after you've sat with its residents, laughed with them, listened to their worries and their struggles. Yet some of whom I talked with seem to have forgotten that there's a larger world beyond the Highlands. They have forgotten how to dream."

⚜

Born on Halloween morning 1939 in Cowlitz General Hospital three miles from the Highlands, Joseph Harry Maier slept peacefully as a baby—and in a dresser drawer when he outgrew the bassinet. But he'd entered life at a tumultuous point in history. The effects of the Great Depression, the Dust Bowl, and World War II, in that order, would forever shape the course of George and Helen Maier's firstborn child.

In the early 1930s, severe drought and dust storms were compounding the economic recession for farmers throughout the prairie lands, including Harry Childs, who eventually lost cattle and family savings. During this time, his eldest daughter, Helen, was at a business college more than one hundred miles away in Mitchell, South Dakota, but she completed the eighteen months of classes by working part time and, as she later wrote, "Mom would send me her last dollar from egg money, etc." With crops and jobs beginning to dry up in both Dakotas, she graduated in 1933 at age twenty-one and soon struck out for greener pastures in Chicago, where the 1933 World's Fair was hoped to be a relative boon for the city. Helen lived with a maternal aunt in Chicago and worked forty hours a week in a department store at the famous Merchandise Mart, the world's largest building at the time.

But she was homesick—and maybe lovesick. The summer before she left Spink County, she'd met a charming German-Norwegian with a long, angular face and a handsome smile. He was slim, which added two inches in appearance to his five-foot-ten frame, and carried himself with the right amount of swagger and with a Camel cigarette dangling from his lips. The fact that he yodeled beautifully while threshing Harry's grain encouraged Helen to forgive his Lutheran heritage and state in life. At age twenty-two, he was a traveling farmhand who had never completed high school.

In Chicago, Helen read in letters from her sisters and her father that some of the family's cattle were dying from drought and eating dust and weeds, and she'd break down crying. She said she was homesick and lonely, and sometime around 1934, she wrote or phoned George and encouraged him to join her. Apparently he did.

In quick fashion, befitting the speed in which Father Joe recounted the story for me in Lumpini and Helen described it in a single page of her loose-leaf history, a Lutheran farmhand and Catholic farm girl joined in a "mixed marriage" that seems to have only been blessed by a Father Goldrick at Chicago's Saint Sylvester Parish. George's parents didn't like the whole Catholic thing, and Helen's mother, Anne, didn't like or trust George. He "didn't appear very stable," Helen wrote. But Father Joe suspects it wasn't just about trust. Anne never thought George was good enough.

"So then," Father Joe had told me as we walked in Lumpini, "my mother and father stayed in Chicago and ran a short-time hotel before going west to Washington. And you know, that's where I was born. In Longview. But I grew up on the farm too."

Wait. . . . Wait, wait, I said. Back up.

"Well, you know, I was *born* in Longview. But I spent a lot of time in Spink County on the farm. I lived there too."

No, no, no. Your mom and dad ran a *brothel?*

"Well . . ."

❧

This was our third interview in Lumpini, following those two days of his parrying my questions and telling me very little about his family history. Now this. I smiled. It was going to be a nice walk in the park.

"Let's use a kinder, gentler word. After all, this is my dear Catholic mother. Let's just say she helped with a hotel where rooms were rented by the hour and the maids were always busy cleaning up after the noisy affairs. Think about it, though. You've this young Catholic woman just married to this Lutheran George Maier. You have the recession, depression, whatever, and they end up running a short-time hotel. Or rather, they manage an *establishment*. That's even better. A ten-room *establishment*."

He did the "bunny ear" air quotation marks.

"I think that's the word polite society used," he said. "*Establishment*. Here we just call them short-time hotels."

He hurried on to tell me about his first-grade classes in Spink County and a teacher named Harry Rhoades. An old classmate of his saint of a grandfather, who was also named Harry, "Mister Rhoades" would teach all first-, second-, third-, and fourth-grade classes at the same time. There were eighteen students total in the four classes. "Mister Rhoades" would teach on a loop, going through first to fourth grades with fifteen-minute lessons, then circle through to each class again and again to correct and guide assignments until the final bell.

How do you *know* it was a brothel? I asked, circling like Mister Rhoades.

"My sister asked Mother one day what kind of rooming house it was they'd managed in Chicago, and Mother said, 'People would come and go. They didn't stay long. The women had visitors.' So we surmised," he said, and by "we," he meant the three Maier children. Himself, Kathy, and one year behind her, Mike, the baby brother who had been Helen's second attempt at squeezing a Catholic priest from Lutheran-Catholic blood—as if it took two to make merit. Mike had lasted eighteen months in seminary, but he was more interested in football (he was offered a football scholarship at Olympia College), making wine, and stealing the seminary's station wagon for weekend joy rides." Father Joe said, "Mom being Mom and being Catholic, her conscience got the best of her and they quit the *establishment*"—bunny ears again—"returned to South Dakota for a while, and then moved to Washington."

I broached the "establishment" story delicately with Kathy when I met her in Longview two weeks later, and she confirmed Father Joe's suspicion and was as nonplussed about it as he was. Same for Mike, much later. Aunt Betty, however, was neither nonplussed nor amused.

"No!" she'd responded when I screwed up the courage to ask— the last day of my visit in Longview in 2005. I'd waited until I was saying goodbye on her stoop. "Absolutely not! I don't know where Joe gets these crazy ideas."

In the fifty-three-page double-spaced typed history of her life, later mailed to me by Kathy, Helen writes of that time in Chicago— the "idealistic" honeymoon year of her otherwise bad marriage: George had found a place in Chicago for them to live that provided living expenses "by staying in the apartment hotel. Think I was shocked at times by the people who cheated on their wives and husbands. I couldn't imagine people being so crude and/or unfaithful."

It sounded as if she'd been surprised. The very next sentence: "We decided to go west as soon as we saved enough money."

❦

By the time little Joey was five, the marriage seemed as though it was over. It took Helen only a half page of her memoirs to jump from describing her first response to her new baby, Joey ("I loved him, he was *mine!*"), to her separating from George five years later. She records nothing from the intervening years. She writes that World War II was in full force when Joe turned five years old, and she and George were having problems because he had a "thing" for "a gal."

George joined the United States Merchant Marines, becoming a ship's captain and ferrying supplies and soldiers from Seattle to Amaknak Island (Dutch Harbor) in the Aleutian Islands off the mainland of Alaska. At the same time, in the mid-1940s, Helen and little Joey moved to the farm in South Dakota for the remainder of the war. It was the best time of Father Joe's childhood, and certainly the most influential. On a huge family farm that sounds like the home of TV's John-Boy Walton, Joey, and eventually all of the Maier children, had free run of a broad five-bedroom farmhouse with a two-bedroom cottage out back and hundreds of acres that stretched to the Jim River. But most significant, they all say, the biggest blessing of the farm was the unfettered access it provided to the guiding gentle hand of Grandpa Harry. Harry Y. Childs— "Just a Y, no more, no less"—he'd smile and tell the kids.

A Scotch-Welsh Protestant who'd converted to Catholicism because it's what his bride requested, he rarely attended church but knelt nightly in prayer. The easy way he carried himself, the encouragement and patience and his selfless nature, along with the prayer every night in a long nightshirt, these examples of a holy man were more of an influence on Father Joe's early spiritual life than Rosaries or priests or sermons. "He was a wonderful and saintly man, always kind to us and gentle," Father Joe says, describing it as the fruit of the spirit. "I knew I'd had a good day, had been a really good boy, and was being rewarded when Grandpa Harry hollered down for me to kneel with him at his bed. That was a big, big deal for me."

Decades later, when the farm never fully rebounded from recession and drought and slipped deeper into debt, Harry and Anne sold it and moved to Longview. Aunt Betty says at age eighty-four, Harry, a college-educated bookkeeper, helped Mike and Kathy with their homework and often helped with dinner while Helen worked long shifts at various jobs and Father Joe was away in seminary school. "He was such a successful man, maybe not in the eyes of the world [of business], but in his care and his love," Aunt Betty said. "I remember I thought that the whole world was made up of fathers like him." None of the Maier children or Aunt Betty can recall Harry raising his voice or a hand in anger. Kathy would listen to Paul Harvey on the radio or watch boxing on TV just to be around him. "I have probably not met anyone so kind," she says.

George returned to Spink County a few years after the war, presumably to be with his clan: the Childses and the Maiers. This was around the time Kathy was born during a blizzard in 1948. George still patronized the bars of nearby Ashton and Redfield and didn't always return home, but he offered to try and change. Aunt Betty said that George asked Harry to give him a chance to run the farm. "He could be a hard worker, a real farmer, when he wanted," Father Joe said. "He was unstable, but he'd work hard on the threshing crews."

Harry liked George, if not his philandering ways, and was well acquainted with his work ethic. If he'd not hired him for the threshing crew, Helen would never have met and fallen for the charming and yodeling German-Norwegian. "I don't think Dad had a problem with George taking over the farm," Aunt Betty recalled. "Mom was the one. She felt he was trying to take it from the family. George was disillusioned after that, I think. Who knows how things might've been different if he'd taken over the farm? . . . But he was still a womanizer. From day one." Finally, in 1950, soon after Mike was born, George said he wanted out and left the family for the final time. Helen had finally had enough; she filed for divorce.

George drifted between jobs, remarried twice, and settled into a life of painting houses, collecting Sioux Indian relics, and polishing stones into arrowheads and occasionally turning them into belt buckles. He still chain-smoked, lived across the road from his favorite country and western bar, and drank wine he made in the basement of his home in rural Hemet, California, ninety miles southeast of Los Angeles. He had one orange tree in his yard, Father Joe said, and the fruit was always bitter.

Through the years, whenever Father Joe visited the West Coast, he insisted that Kathy and Mike go with him to Hemet to see their father. It was important for them to know their heritage—the good, the bad, the ugly. He traveled there whenever he could, and George remained convinced that Father Joe was something other than a priest. No one moves to Thailand just to live with the poor. "He always thought I worked for the CIA," Father Joe said. After George's third wife died in the late 1980s, leaving George alone with just his drinking buddies, Mike and Kathy attempted to get their dad to move close to one or the other. He politely declined.

Four years later, on December 9, 1992, George Morris Maier died of emphysema. He was eighty-two.

Father Joe told Mike that he was coming home from Thailand to bury his father.

"Too late," Mike said.

George had given orders to the hospital to turn off the ventilator and immediately cremate his body.

"You *have* to bury your father," Father Joe said. "He denied us even that. Children are supposed to bury their parents. . . . He was afraid no one would show up at his funeral. He wouldn't have wanted that; that would have embarrassed him."

Mike drove six hundred miles round-trip from Sun City, Arizona, to retrieve his father's ashes; then he took his dad to his favorite hangout. He set the metal box of ashes down on the counter and ordered a round of drinks at the country and western bar across from George's home.

⚜

Father Joe phoned the day before he buried his mother to tell me he was at Aunt Betty's house. I had not seen his automated e-mail asking us to pray for his mother.

My flight into Portland the next day, September 8, 2006, arrived late, and by the time I'd driven the fifty miles and taken the Psalm 23 exit, the funeral at Saint Rose Catholic Church had begun. I opened the first door I came to, and there was Father Joe, the bell sleeves of his white cassock fluttering as he led the sanctuary in an a cappella rendition of Ezekiel 37.

"Dem bones, dem bones goooonna rise again, dem bones, dem bones goooonna rise again, dem bones, dem bones goooonna rise again, oooh heeeear the word of the Lord. . . ."

By the time I'd retreated from the front of the sanctuary, gone back outside, and found the proper door, Father Joe had moved from the stage to the floor. He'd rapped his knuckles on his mother's white casket, which sat covered in the middle of two sets of pews.

Knock, knock.

"Mother, I'm here!"

Knock, knock.

"Mother, I'm here!"

It's an old Buddhist tradition to let the soul of the deceased know that family is there. No one is alone. (One month later, he did the same thing at the Reverend Harry Thiel's funeral in Seattle, and Father Joe said a priest phoned the diocese in Bangkok to accuse Father Joe of pagan practices. His superiors in Bangkok ignored it.) He waved incense over the casket, splashed drops of holy water on it from the church to the hearse, and then followed in a line of ten cars leading to Longview Memorial Park, two miles on Industrial Way past lumber mills and chemical plants to Helen Mary Childs Maier's plot. The Maier children kept her headstone simple and engraved with a rose. The Childs girls love their flowers.

There were about thirty of us at the gravesite, and Father Joe thought we were standing too far away, as if death and its rituals frightened us. He motioned us to move closer, closer. He read from Thomas Merton's comment on Psalm 23, the same psalm I kept passing on the Exit 36 billboard. "My Lord God I have no idea where I am going, I do not see the road ahead of me, I cannot know for certain where it will end, nor do I really know who I am myself, and the fact that I think I am following your will does not mean that I am actually doing so. But I believe Lord that the desire to please you does in fact please you. And I have that desire to please you in all that I am doing. . . ."

He told us to throw dirt on the casket. Kathy Maier Roshak slung a fistful, and a rock was hidden inside the dirt. It caused a loud clunk and provoked laughter. "Yes, yes, that's it!" Father Joe boomed, delighted that we were lightening up. "*That* is proper. Everyone, please, if you wish, please, get some dirt! That is what one does. You get your hands dirty."

And we did. We got dirty throwing dirt on Helen Mary Maier's casket, and then we beat a hasty retreat to Aunt Betty's flower-framed patio for beer, soda, chips, and one of Helen's favorites—

Kentucky Fried Chicken. It was a beautiful summer day, a little windy, and we sat in a circle to share stories the way "Mister Rhoades" used to teach rural farm kids reading, writing, and arithmetic.

Mike Maier, a project director for construction and reconstruction in Iraq and other conflict areas, told of how badly his mother wanted that second priest in the family. After his merrymaking had finally resulted in his expulsion in the mid-1960s from Oakland's Holy Redeemer School, the priests there sent him on the full day's train ride home. Helen turned Mike around and put him directly back on the train. "Umm, Mom sent me back," Mike told the Redeemer priests. "She says I *have* to be a priest." They spun him around too. The back-and-forth lasted four arduous days before Helen relented and sent Mike to Saint Martin's Prep School in Olympia, Washington. Harriet, a younger sister of Helen's who was married to a successful lumberman, paid the tuition.

The stories continued, like a baton passed from person to person. Aunt Betty recalled how her big sister so loved the tenderness of a certain restaurant's chicken that she asked the manager what the secret was. He said the restaurant only purchased certain-sized chickens. She thanked him, then turned to Betty, looking befuddled. "I didn't know they circumcised chickens," she said. She was serious.

Father Joe said his "dear old mum" never slept very well, and every night the kids could hear her praying with a taped recording of the "joyful mysteries" Rosary, over and over, until well past midnight: "Hail Mary, full of Grace. The Lord is with Thee. Blessed art Thou amongst all Women." Her children all recalled the long hours she worked and yet she still had to accept welfare and subsist on government cheese and powdered eggs, two-day-old bread, boiled hamburger, and butter sandwiches. But Helen never complained to them about George. The stories went nonstop around a broad circle underneath the hanging planters of Aunt Betty's patio, with Helen's cousins, aunts, uncles, children, and grandchildren recalling favorite memories, until it was my turn. Everyone smiled and waited.

What? I shrugged. I'd never met her.

But in a way, I told them, I guessed that I had. I'd been a thorn in Father Joe's side for long enough to see how her spirit lives on in his selflessness and respect for education. I see Helen in Kathy's empathy and caretaking. I see Helen in Mike's crazy dare to go to Iraq, willing to step up and rebuild what's been broken. So yes, I said, I guess I have met her.

When Father Joe returned to Mercy, Klong Toey had its own funeral party for Helen. Children drew pictures, the Thai modern dance team performed, and the choir from the Asian Institute of Technology sang. The AIDS brigade, the imam, the abbot, slum community leaders, the local good-guy police chief—several hundred locals in all—turned out to celebrate Father Joe's mom. The old imam was impressed with the show of respect.

He took Father Joe by the elbow and led him away from the din, then gripped both of Father Joe's hands, holding them tightly in front of him.

"You've been willing to accept the endowment and blessing your mother gave you," he said, smiling and nodding his approval, similar to how Grandpa Harry would read a good report card. "The greatness of men comes from their mothers, yet so few are willing to accept this greatness that's offered. You are a blessed man."

Mercy preschool graduations are family affairs.

TWENTY-ONE
Home

*I used to cry a lot in the confessional . . .
usually with people . . . literally . . . who are
almost Saints and just need a tiny little leap
. . . jump . . . to totally throw themselves
into the arms of Our Lord and Our Lady. . . .
I would beg them . . . please. . . . some did
and some weren't there yet.*

—Father Joe, e-mail to Father Denis Ryan,
December 7, 2007

F or my last ten days in the slums of Bangkok in March 2007, I moved from the nearby hotel—across the street from the Klong Toey Starbucks—onto the Mercy campus. There was a vacant room upstairs near the orphanage on the main campus, but Father Joe didn't exactly invite me to stay there.

"Pack your bags and get over here. Now." he barked, phoning me at the hotel.

I canceled my reservation and moved immediately into the Shire.

Having made three visits since 2000, I thought I'd seen about all there was to see at Mercy: children studying, children skipping, children laughing, children crying, children emaciated and dying. But no sooner had the sun set on my first day in 2007 than I began to hear a strain of voices that sounded slightly different, coming from a corridor near my door. I poked my head out and saw no one. It was a pleasantly warm evening fanned by a breeze. I inhaled the night air, retreated inside, and resumed reading. Immediately, I heard it again, fainter, as if it were on the move. I closed the book and took off exploring, more curious than anything.

In the dark as in the dawn, the half-block-long Mercy campus is mostly quiet and feels larger but more intimate. I strolled through webs of shadows cast by fluorescent light, around darkened corners, down flights of stairs, and around the tropical courtyard anchored by the five-hundred-pound bronze statue of the Virgin Mary. Then I heard it again: a piercing shriek from upstairs. I walked up the concrete ramp leading from the ground floor to the mezzanine cafeteria, not in a rush, just needing to see. And as I reached the top, they got me.

"Jah-aye! Jah-aye!"

A quartet of kids from the AIDS brigade jumped out and startled me. In the darkness of a Mercy night, they were playing hide and seek, shouting boo and gotcha, or the Thai equivalent, then

darting down corridors with the same kind of zeal that had characterized the spring evenings of my own privileged childhood. As
warm weather blossomed and summer vacation beckoned, we kids
could catch lightning in a jar. Barefoot on the cool blades of our
freshly cut lawn, my sister and I and others would play in night's sky
with Mason jars long emptied of canned okra and pickled beets,
catching, releasing, and catching again the year's first lightning bugs.

Now, as my shadow beat me to the end of a lighted corridor, I
was reminded of that magic and the spell nightfall could cast.
Mercy's children jumped from the corners in choruses of gleeful
gotchas and then convulsed in laughter. Just as quickly, they disappeared.

⚜

On the Sunday before the first of seven Mercy graduation ceremonies scheduled for the following four days of March 2007, students, siblings, parents, teachers, community leaders, and their
neighbors swarmed onto Mercy's campus. At noon, the campus
had been so quiet you could hear doves. An hour later, it crawled
with dozens of locals carrying hammers and nails, streamers, ribbons, and balloons; orange, red, green, purple, pink, blue—more
color than Aunt Betty's garden. By dusk, Mercy was dressed in garlands that hung from trees, doors, pillars, and lampposts. There
were kid-sized photo booths with word jumbles in English and
Thai and a large sign that read "Congratulations!" The beaten path
leading to the verbal high-five passed underneath an iron archway
strung with more flowers and balloons. It's where Klong Toey's children played in the dusk of that Sunday. Holding shoulders and
backs straight, a line of them walked like models balancing books
on their heads. Over and over, taking turns, a line of them moved
through the gateway. I stopped counting at fifteen rotations.

The next day, the weight of the occasion could be felt in the way the children carried themselves. Playful only minutes earlier, they walked into the graduation ceremony with the bearing of royalty. They didn't stir or fuss or fight as Father Joe gave his two-minute speech. *Go to school! Go to school! Go to school!* The starch in their postures held right up until he presented each with a laminated certificate of achievement. As they bowed the *wai*, Father Joe tried to lock onto their eyes, for just a split second, and to bless them in a wordless appeal (O dear Lord, please watch over the fragile future of this child). Trying to lock them into his own eyes, he'd nod or grin, anything to get their attention. At that point, faces would relax and smiles release.

Four days, seven graduations, thirty-two schools, seven hundred blessings, and not even one child was left unblessed.

"If you can motivate a child, open a door for them even a little bit, they *will* motivate themselves," Father Joe had told me many times since we'd first met, and he continued to say it like a mantra during the graduations of 2007. "They just need a little help to get started."

⚛

Joop Jang wasn't there in 2007. She had died in Mercy's broad second-floor orphanage fifteen days before Christmas 2006. She'd cried and tried to scream, pleading to go to the hospital, pleading for one more day, one more chance to live. But AIDS and heart failure had stolen her ability to breathe. There was nothing the hospital could do, Tom Crowley told me. She died wearing the Saint Christopher medal. Joop was sixteen.

"She didn't die well," Tom said sadly. "To die well—I think that's asking a lot of a sixteen-year-old."

Imam Selep Develah died two months later. He was seventy-six. When Father Joe heard the news, he put on his most sacred and most official white robes and went to the mosque to pray with the abbot at the open casket. It was six minutes before the evening prayer time for Muslims, and for the first time, Father Joe was invited inside the mosque's prayer room, where non-Muslims aren't generally allowed. He was asked to speak about the imam in front of sixty Muslim men. The imam and Father Joe went back more than thirty-five years, and they'd watched from a distance as religion worldwide was used to pry things apart rather than bind them together. They'd been talking about that just days before the imam died—the senselessness of it all, and in the name of God, no less. Father Joe looked out onto the roomful of Muslim men and cleared his throat. "My dearest friend and comrade the imam," he began, "was a reflection of the one true God. Allah, God, Christ, call Him what you want." By starting the first slum preschool near a sacred grove of trees in Klong Toey, he told them, the imam's legacy would live forever. "We had the same friends—love, patience, joy—and we had the same enemies—greed, ignorance, hatred."

Later, at the Muslim cemetery, Father Joe was invited to sit up front with the family at the graveside of a friend and mentor. "It's not about being a Muslim or being a Catholic," Father Joe told me later. "That's not what God is about."

Pim had completed her first semester at a United World Colleges campus in Canada, receiving good marks in all of her studies despite her continuing struggles with the English language. The route abroad, however, had been complicated. Before she could receive a passport, she needed to be certified by the Thai courts as an orphan, but court records revealed a lie her mother had told. The father she never knew wasn't dead, as her mom had claimed. He was a fifty-seven-year-old cowherd living seven hours away. After a few fourteen-hour round-trips and lots of red tape, Pim's gentle and illiterate father rode to Bangkok in a Mercy van one last time and scrawled an X on documents that would allow Pim to fly away.

Meanwhile, upstairs in the orphanage near my room was the niece to whom Pim pledged her good influence. Miss Grasshopper was so grown up that she was sleeping in a big-kid bed now. "Everybody's favorite girl," Father Joe boasted. "Always happy, always smiling. You just watch—she's going to be something *big*."

Before Pim left, Father Joe said, she promised Miss Grasshopper that she would return for her. "For family," Father Joe said. "That's what family does."

God is not something *out there,* Father Joe had admonished me many times, and all the way to the end of this book, he continued to gesture toward the sky or downtown's crazed congestion, repeating it long after I no longer needed convincing. God is in our selfless action, in the acts of doing and giving and caring, in our smiles and laughter and kneeling, eye-level comfort. God is in our friendships, in our families, and in our friendships that feel like family. "In our mercy," Father Joe said. "It's the highest attribute."

⚜

An hour before I took a taxi from Mercy to Thailand's new $3 billion airport, Suvarnabhumi (which means "Land of Gold"), Father Joe and I sat in his living room eating tiny tangerines that tasted as sweet as hard candy. A *Lord of the Rings* movie dubbed in Thai played on the TV, and just as the Hobbit protagonist Frodo Baggins prepared to leave the Shire, Father Joe said, "Kawalee died one hour ago. Just got the call."

I wasn't sure how to respond. He didn't appear upset. Kawalee was an easygoing thirteen-year-old girl he'd met while walking a few months earlier in a particularly bad area of Lock Six. Her mother was halfway into a nine-year prison sentence for selling drugs, and her father had run off with another woman, leaving Kawalee living with relatives in a plywood-and-blanket lean-to. I had visited her "neighborhood" the day before. The only way to reach her lean-to was to walk on soggy two-by-six boards softened by mud and raw waste. One misstep, and you were in crap up to your ankles. Those shoes I'd thrown away.

"You wanna go to school?" Father Joe asked Kawalee the first time he saw her living in a fetid bog under a bodhi tree.

She had never been. She smiled and said it sounded like fun. If there's a Disney park for a slum kid, this was it.

Yes, yes, she told him. (*Ka, ka,* sounding like a dove.)

"We'll come back for you at sunrise," he told her, not bothering to specify an hour because he suspected she didn't have a clock or watch, and even if she did, she wouldn't be able to tell time.

Two weeks later, Kawalee moved into Mercy, where she ate three square meals daily and slept in a bed fitted with clean sheets and covered in a pale blue Little Mermaid comforter. It didn't seem to bother her that she was the oldest preschooler or that she stood a good foot or two taller than her schoolmates. But five months later, the fun ended abruptly. Doctors treating her for a strain of flu discovered she had leukemia. It was so advanced, it was deemed terminal. Her first visit to a hospital was also her last.

When a member of the Mercy staff told Kawalee's mother about the leukemia, she refused to believe it. "No, it's not true. I will not accept this. I *cannot* accept this," she said from a women's prison outside Bangkok. She asked that no one from Mercy phone or visit again. She wanted to be left alone with the knowledge that Kawalee was alive, happy, and living at Mercy. But if Kawalee died, the mother asked that someone at Mercy send her a letter. She wouldn't open it, but just seeing the envelope, she would know that her daughter had died in Mercy's care and had been prayed over, blessed, and given over to God.

Father Joe wrote the letter the night I left. He suspected it would never be read.

"Kawalee got to have her day in the sun," he told me. "She smiled and skipped and laughed and whistled. She went to school. That's all good stuff."

I sat quietly, still not sure what to say. "I'm really sorry," I offered.

"Hey, man, she died with a smile on her face," he said, and I heard his voice crack. "That's the way you have to look at it. She died with a smile."

⚜

I flew out of Suvarnabhumi four hours later, arriving home the next day at Dulles International Airport. I cleared customs extraordinarily fast, collected my bag from the carousel, and hustled toward the exit. Turning the corner, I saw that a new level of security had been added just since my last trip. So I waited in a line with my fellow passengers while CNN News entertained us: a deranged gunman had shot up a Manhattan pizzeria, and a new study by a Columbia University nonprofit reported that 49 percent of full-time college students in the United States binge-drink or abuse drugs. Also, Khalid Sheik Mohammed had allegedly confessed to being a prolific terrorist at war with the United States and the proud mastermind of 9/11. CNN's Pentagon correspondent grimly read the confession that Khalid had reportedly signed: "I decapitated with my blessed right hand the head of the American Jew, Daniel Pearl, in the city of Karachi, Pakistan. For those who would like to confirm, there are pictures of me on the Internet holding his head."

Welcome home, I thought. My turn at the next layer of customs arrived. It was one of those chummy interrogations intended to help filter out the bad guys. I always give brief answers and keep the line moving. The customs agent stared at my passport.

"Thailand, huh. Vacationing over there?"

"No."

"Business?"

"Yes."

"What do you do?"

"I'm a journalist, a writer."

"What are you working on?"

"A book."

"Really. What's it about?"

I paused. The question deserved more than an abbreviation. Should I describe tens of millions of children not being educated and the net sum of the economic divide? Or do I focus on the positive, as everyone advises me? Describe seeds of dreams flourishing in slum rubbish and tell of the American who invaded a sovereign land using paper and pencils, tell of how he is advancing his cause with smart children, not smart bombs? I could say how the social revolution there reverberates today and through generations and neighborhoods and how the legacy is impossible to track. There are so many kids and so many lives touched, so many dominoes falling one into the other, that we'll never know the full effect.

In line behind me were fifty people from my flight. Some of us had been traveling together for twenty-three hours. We were ornery, tired, dirty, hungry. An older gentleman with luggage parked on his heels and a jacket draped on his arm cleared his throat.

"The book?" the agent asked again, staring at me now. "What's it about?"

I smiled.

"How much time you got?"

ACKNOWLEDGMENTS

I never expected Father Joe Maier to agree to this book. From my first visit to the Mercy Centre in 2000, I was familiar with the insane demands on his time, and when I contacted him in 2005 about cooperating with research, his Human Development Foundation and Mercy Centre had just expanded to three tsunami-ravaged communities in southern Thailand. He was busier than ever. By the end of 2006, his charity's budget would be in the red because of these new commitments—which, I believe, he foresaw. If there is one thing Father Joe will prostitute himself for, it's his children. So I think he helped me with the hope this book might—*inshallah*—shed some light on our shared and cordoned-off corners. But regardless of the why, I thank him because, as the author Jerry Hopkins so eloquently put it, the access he patiently and continually provided is better than exclusives with Elvis.

Also, at the Mercy Centre and in Klong Toey, I am thankful for the selfless assistance of Ratana Chanto, Tom Crowley, Tew Bunnag, John Padorr, Sister Joan Evans, Mary McLean, John Cook, and many others I am shamefully forgetting. In Longview, Kathy Maier Roshak and her husband, David; Mike Maier; Betty McIntee; and all the cousins, nephews, and friends who shared beer, chicken, and stories with me after the burial of Helen Mary Childs Maier. In Seattle, the late great Reverend Harry Thiel, may he rest in peace.

I'm eternally grateful for the spiritual influences in the life of Jossey-Bass executive editor Sheryl Fullerton. Although I've never heard Siddhārtha Gautama's voice, I suspect that it possessed the same calmness, even on deadline and past it. From the first time we spoke about the book, I sensed that Sheryl "got it," as Father Joe would say. Also a big thanks goes to the people I know only through their e-mails and dynamic competence, aka Team Jossey-Bass: Joanne Clapp Fullagar, Bruce Emmer, Jeff Puda, Alison Knowles, and I suspect many others.

The Most Reverend Desmond M. Tutu lent his stellar name and summation to a book that is far better for his involvement.

My mother, sister, and father were all fed some early and uncooked versions of this book and lived to tell about it. God bless them. My big brother was my initial guiding influence on things of the East-West hybrid spirit, as well as the first indigenous Baptist to suggest to me that there was more to life than that old-time religion was telling me.

Of course, heartfelt gratitude goes to the name on my tattoo, who happens to be my wife and at the center of my life, and to my precious sons, who endured well without me—maybe fared better, I fear—during the final months of ceaseless work.

Thanks also to Laurie Liss and the fine name Sterling Lord Literistic, respected industrywide. I suspect that many doors and most e-mails would not have been opened if not for the two.

Finally, I must acknowledge my debt to Father Joe's Grandpa Harry Y. Childs—"just a Y, no more, no less"—who from his grave is living proof that the fruit of the spirit is infectious and alive in all of us. We just have to let it breathe. He didn't preach it, nor did he wish to hear it preached. He lived it and continues to do so.

G. B.

❧

Additional information on the Human Development Foundation and Mercy Centre can be found at the U.S.-based Web site, http://www.hdcf.org, and the main Web site, http://www.mercycentre.org.

THE AUTHOR

GREG BARRETT is a twenty-year veteran of local, national, and foreign reporting for wire and newspapers in Georgia, the Carolinas, Hawaii, and Maryland. He was a roving correspondent based in the Washington, D.C., bureau for Gannett News Service/*USA Today* when he met Father Joe Maier, and most recently, he worked as a state correspondent for the *Baltimore Sun*. He lives in northern Virginia with his wife and two sons.